100 Literacy Hours

YEAR 4

Published by Scholastic Ltd,
Villiers House,
Clarendon Avenue,
Leamington Spa,
Warwickshire CV32 5PR

6 7 8 9 1 2 3 4 5 6 7

AUTHOR
Chris Webster

EDITORS
Kate Element
and Clare Gallaher

ASSISTANT EDITOR
Clare Miller

SERIES DESIGNER
Joy White

DESIGNER
Mark Udall

COVER ARTWORK
Peter Stevenson

ILLUSTRATIONS
Beverly Curl

British Library Cataloguing-in-Publication Data
A catalogue record for this book is available from the British Library.

ISBN 0-590-53916-7

ACKNOWLEDGEMENTS

The publishers gratefully acknowledge permission to reproduce the following copyright material:
Andersen Press Ltd for *The Snow Queen* by Hans Christian Andersen © Andersen Press (1993, Andersen Press).
Doubleday for 'Piggy Bank' from *Mistakes That Worked* © 1991, Charlotte Foltz Jones (1991, Doubleday, a division of Bantam Doubleday Dell Publishing Group Inc).
Folens Ltd for 'School Cards' from *Press for Action: Oracy* by Neil MacRae and Chris Webster © Neil MacRae and Chris Webster.
Shirley Hughes for *It's Too Frightening For Me!* by Shirley Hughes © 1977, Shirley Hughes (1977, Hodder and Stoughton).
Wes Magee for 'Candle' and 'Robin' from *A Third Poetry Book* compiled by John Foster © 1982, Wes Magee (1982, OUP).
Janet Perry for the following units: 'Using a Rhyming Dictionary', 'Playing with Adverbs', 'Figurative Language' and 'Skipping and Action Rhymes' © 1998, Janet Perry.
John Rice for 'Big Fears' by John Rice from *Rockets and Quasars* © 1984, John Rice (1984, Aten Press).
Usborne Publishing Ltd for 'Body Framework' from *The Usborne Book of Body Facts* by Anita Ganeri, Text © 1992, Anita Ganeri, Illustration © 1992, Allan Robinson and Guy Smith (1992, Usborne Publishing Ltd).
Harris Morgan & Son for photographs used in 'The School Times' unit.
Every effort has been made to trace copyright holders for the works reproduced in this book, and the publishers apologize for any inadvertent omissions.

ISBN 0 590 53916 7

Contents

INTRODUCTION

ABOUT THE SERIES

100 Literacy Hours is a series of year-specific teachers' resource books that provide a core of material for the teaching of the English curriculum within the context of the National Literacy Strategy *Framework for Teaching* and within the structure of the Literacy Hour. Each book offers term-by-term lesson plans, complete with objectives and organization grids and accompanied, where relevant, with photocopiable texts and activity sheets. The materials are ready-to-use, and their adaptable format enables them to be used as flexibly as possible. The 100 hours provided offer a balance of both reading and writing, and of range: fiction and poetry and non-fiction. However, it is expected that you will wish to personalize the material – altering the order, interleaving lesson plans with complementary materials from your school's existing schemes, consolidating work by using the structure of a lesson plan as a model for a lesson with different content, and so on. The loose-leaf format of each book, with hole-punched, perforated, tear-out pages, makes the integration of other tried-and-tested and favourite material into the core very easy.

USING THIS BOOK

The materials

This book provides 100 literacy hours for Year 4, presented as 'units' of between 1 and 5 hours. There is a balance of reading and writing units, most of which are linked in order to demonstrate and reinforce the close relationship. The bulk of the 100 hours is fully supported with detailed lesson plans and integrated photocopiable resources. The remainder of the hours are plans for suitable follow-on or follow-up hours linked to some of the units. These can be found at the back of the book in the section called 'Follow-up' (see page 203) and are presented as grids outlining objectives and organization. Together, these materials should be regarded as a core, as a starting point for developing your own personalized folder for the year.

Adapting and personalizing the materials

During the trialling of these resources, wide differences in ability were found in classes of the same year group in different schools. This means that the *precise* content of the plans and resources will almost certainly need modification to suit the children in a particular school. One way to do this is as follows:

- Separate the pages of the book and place them in an A4 ring-binder.
- Adjust the level of the photocopiable resource sheets to match the needs of the children in your year group.
- 'Trade' materials with higher or lower year groups so that the average level matches that of the target year group.
- Add your own favourite teaching materials in the appropriate places.
- Substitute materials for others if necessary (for example, if you have a set of books which you wish to use instead of one of the ones recommended).

You have now created a tailor-made folder of plans and resources for your year group!

Preparing a scheme of work

All schools are required to write detailed schemes of work, and these materials have been designed to facilitate this process. The termly Overview grids provided on pages 12–17 have been compiled by extracting the 'Objectives' grids from each teaching unit and putting them together to provide you with what are, essentially, medium-term plans. These grids are photocopiable so, should you wish to alter the order of units and/ or add your own, they can be copied, cut and pasted to make your own plans. On page 18 there is also a photocopiable set of blank objectives grids for you to use when inserting your own material.

ORGANIZATION OF TEACHING UNITS

Each term is divided into teaching units comprising between 1 and 5 hours. Each of the main units has either a reading or a writing focus (although there is, of course, overlap) and a fiction, poetry or non-fiction content. The units are organized as follows:

Objectives grid
Outlines the word-, sentence- and text-level objectives of the unit.

Organization grid
Outlines the key activities for each part of each hour.

UNIT LESSON PLANS
Each unit of lesson plans is written to the following headings:

Resources
Provides a list of what you need for teaching the whole unit.

Preparation
Outlines any advance preparation needed before the hour(s) begins.

Synopsis
Gives a synopsis of the story where whole published fiction texts are used as the basis of units.

Each hour is then set out as follows:

Introduction
Sets out what to do in the whole-class shared reading/writing session.

Whole-class skills work
Sets out what to do in the whole-class word- and sentence-level skills session. (See page 8 for further information about whole-class skills work.)

Differentiated group work
Sets out what each group does in the guided group and independent work session. (See page 8 for further information about differentiated group work.)

Conclusion
Sets out what to do in the whole-class plenary session.

Follow-up
Some units lend themselves particularly to follow-up hours and these are indicated in the lesson plans and cross-referenced to the section at the back of the book.

Further ideas
Provides ideas for extending what is done within the hours of the unit.

Photocopiable sheets
Photocopiable resource and activity sheets that support each unit. These can be found at the end of each relevant unit and are marked with the photocopiable symbol .

Many of the sheets have more than one application and are therefore used in several units.

READING UNITS

These teaching units have three aims:
- to develop basic reading skills across a wide range of texts – fiction, poetry and non-fiction
- to develop skills of comprehension, inference, deduction and literary appreciation
- to encourage enjoyment of reading.

Using the texts

All shorter texts are provided on the photocopiable resource sheets. The following longer texts will be needed (half-class sets are recommended for fiction and group sets for non-fiction):
It's Too Frightening For Me! by Shirley Hughes, Young Puffin, ISBN 0-14-032008-3
The Usborne Book of Body Facts by Anita Ganeri, Usborne, ISBN 0-7460-0948-8
The Snow Queen by Hans Christian Andersen, illustrated by PJ Lynch, Red Fox, ISBN 0-09-94-8641-5
Cric Crac: A Collection of West Indian Stories by Grace Hallworth, Mammoth, ISBN 0-7497-1717-3
Hans Christian Andersen 'What's their story?' series by Andrew Langley, OUP, ISBN 0-19-910-443-3.

All the texts are intended for use as *shared texts*; that is to say, texts for whole-class and/or guided group reading. Use of appropriate teaching methods enables children to read and understand texts beyond their *independent* reading level. These methods include:

- preparation, for example giving the background to a story, prior study of difficult words
- an initial reading to the whole class with children following the text
- re-reading in groups with less able groups supported by the teacher
- differentiated follow-up activities which allow more able children to respond independently to the text while further support is given to less able readers
- guided reading, in which the teacher takes children through the text helping them with phonic or contextual clues (less able readers), or higher-level reading skills (more able readers).

Additional suggestions are given, where relevant, in the detailed lesson plans, for example use of different versions of the same story.

It is assumed that children will be following a programme of guided reading alongside their reading of these shared texts.

Managing the reading of longer texts

In those units where the whole of longer texts is read, it is assumed that sometimes the chunks of reading allocated to the Introduction session (whole-class shared reading) may need to be undertaken outside the session or lesson time. It could be included in guided group reading, or in other shared reading time or as homework. Recording and making copies of an audio tape of the text will enable those children who cannot read the text independently to have access to the story.

Responding to texts

Since the mid-1980s, a complete methodology for teaching children how to respond to texts has developed, and is becoming well established from KS1 to KS4. The materials in this book try to exemplify as many types of responses as possible, so that, as well as providing specific lessons, they also offer models which can be adapted for use with other texts. Some examples of responses to texts are:

- cloze – fill in gaps in a text
- sequencing – place a cut-up text in order
- design a storyboard – such as plan a film version of the text
- use drama techniques to explore a text – for example role-play, hot-seating
- design a newspaper front page about an aspect of the text
- comprehension questions answered orally or in writing.

Written comprehension

The majority of written tasks set in these materials encourage a creative response to reading. These often reveal children's comprehension of the text as clearly as any formal comprehension, and, like the oral and dramatic activities, they are just as effective in developing comprehension skills. However, children do need to practise formal written comprehension of different kinds, and activities for this have been provided in many of the units.

Note that the main purpose of the comprehension material is to develop understanding of the texts, not to provide detailed numerical assessments. Marking should therefore be kept simple. On most occasions the marking can be done orally in a concluding session. You might take each question in turn, asking for responses from the children and discussing them. The correct answer (or answers) can then be identified and the children can mark their own answers, simply placing a tick if they have got it right. Queries can be dealt with immediately. You can look at the comprehensions later to see at a glance which children are doing well at basic recall, which are doing well at inference and deduction, and most important of all, which children are struggling with basic understanding. These children should then be given further support during the next guided reading session.

WRITING UNITS

These units provide a series of structured writing experiences throughout the year leading to a more integrated, creative and open-ended approach in Term 3 which draws together and puts into practice previous skills taught and developed. The idea is to provide 'props' for learning and then to remove them gradually in the hope that children will be able to write with increasing independence and creativity. Examples of props are the many 'templates' to support writing. These include sentence and paragraph prompts for fiction, and page-layout templates for certain types of non-fiction (see 'Words in Windows' unit, Term 2). Other kinds of props are the Story Planner (see 'School Cards' unit, Term 2) and the Redrafting Checklist (see 'Redrafting Simulation' unit, Term 2). Regular use of these will help children to internalize the prompts they contain, and so help them build independence as writers. Towards the end of Term 3 the Writing Simulation unit ('Ninevah') provides a context for children to write in a range of forms for a range of purposes and audiences, so bringing together in a creative way, the wide range of skills covered throughout the year.

Cross-curricular writing

The best opportunities for most non-narrative writing occur in other curriculum areas. Therefore, when the necessary skills have been introduced through one of the non-fiction units, they should be applied to another curriculum area soon afterwards. It would be well worth holding year-group meetings specifically to 'map' opportunities for non-narrative writing across the curriculum.

REFERENCE AND RESEARCH SKILLS UNITS

Within each term there are two 1-hour Reference and Research Skills units. The purpose of these units is to focus attention on important skills that may otherwise not get appropriate time within the context of other lesson plans. In this book for Year 4, the Reference and Research Skills units deal with the following skills:
Term 1:
Dictionary work.
Using a rhyming dictionary.
Term 2:
Appraising non-fiction texts.
Preparing for research.
Term 3:
Using a dictionary: guide words.
Summarizing.

WORD PLAY UNITS

At the end of each term there is a Word Play unit. The purpose of these units is to demonstrate that playing with words is not only 'OK' and fun, but also a powerful learning tool. The Word Play units for Year 4 are:
Term 1:
Playing with Adverbs.
Term 2:
Figurative Language.
Term 3:
Skipping and Action Rhymes.

SPEAKING AND LISTENING

Speaking and Listening is also an essential part of literacy, and development of skills in this important area has been integrated into the units for both reading and writing. Speaking and Listening is *the* most important way of developing higher-order reading skills. Children must be able to explore texts through discussion, role-play and other forms of oral 'comprehension' before they can do justice to more formal written comprehension. 'Brainstorming' sharing ideas, helping each other to check work and so on, will all help children to write more effectively. The challenge for the teacher is to ensure that this discussion is clearly focused on the task and not merely idle chatter.

TIMING OF THE LITERACY HOUR

A brisk pace is an important feature of an effective Literacy Hour. The following suggestions, based on experience in trialling these materials, will help to keep things moving:

- Train pupils in efficient classroom routines (see below under 'Differentiated group activities').
- Don't talk too much! Keep explanations brief. Get children on task as soon as possible, and give further clarification and help in the context of the activity.
- Don't let skills sessions overrun, unless there is a good reason which has been previously planned for. Skills will be revised and practised several times throughout the year within the context of other slots in the Literacy Hour and outside it.
- When starting group activities sessions, give a clear message about what you want children to have achieved in the time allocated, and encourage them to work efficiently, such as not wasting time decorating a border before starting writing and so on.

Introductory session

Most often, these sessions involve the reading aloud of a shared text. Where possible, children should follow the reading in their own copy of the text. Using an overhead projector is the best way of doing this (see below). It allows a shared text to be used as a focal point for the whole class in the same way as a Big Book. Find ways to make them interactive by involving children in reading, asking questions and so on. Give appropriate background information and briefly discuss vocabulary and ideas. However, in all this, do not lose sight of the need to keep the pace of the lesson moving!

Whole-class skills work

It is during these sessions that the majority of grammar, punctuation, spelling and phonic skills are taught. The main principle is that the skills arise from the shared text and will also be used in the related writing unit. Over the year, key skills should be revisited many times so that children's mastery of them will grow incrementally. A word of warning: many grammatical concepts are difficult and abstract, so do not expect children to grasp them all at once. Expect it to be a slow process in which their understanding develops over several years. For example, many children may not master writing in paragraphs until they reach their teens – but they will not master it at all if a start is not made when they are much younger.

Although the materials in this book include spelling activities based on spelling rules and patterns arising from the texts, they cannot take the place of a programme of individualized spelling for children. Children could collect a list of words they need to learn in a spelling book. This could be supplemented at least once a week with words from a standard list to make a list of, say, ten (or more for more able/older children). Children then learn their lists using the LOOK/SAY/COVER/WRITE/CHECK method. Pairs of children can test each other on their own lists. Any words not learned can be carried over into the next list.

The same book, used backwards, can be used to collect new items of vocabulary. Again, these should be a mixture of words which children have come across themselves, and words introduced during teaching (for example character adjectives, synonyms of 'said').

Differentiated group activities

For most group activities, three levels of differentiation are suggested, usually shown as four groups to reflect a normal distribution of ability:

Group 1: above average pupils.
Groups 2 & 3: average pupils.
Group 4: below average pupils.

In the average KS2 class, group sizes would be between 7 and 9 (with some trade-off between groups according to the spread of ability in the class). This is fine for organizational purposes, and working with the teacher, but too large for most collaborative activities. These groups will therefore need to be subdivided into smaller groups of fours or pairs for many activities. There will also be occasions when mixed-ability groups are most appropriate for the activities (for example the drama units).

Children need to know which main group they are in and be able to subdivide into fours or pairs quickly and efficiently. To help this process, teachers could name the groups, for example 'Home Group', 'Small Groups', 'Pairs', and train children to get into the appropriate group immediately the group is named.

When this routine is firmly established, children should then be given the experience of working with children from other groups, for example opposite sex pairs, fours made up of pairs from different 'Home Groups' and so on. It is also important to give them the experience of working in mixed-ability groups for appropriate activities.

The teacher should try to divide teaching time equally between all groups over the course of the week – the more able need help just as much as the less able if they are given suitably demanding tasks. **[NB An asterisk (*) after the group number is used on the grids and in the lesson plans to show which groups the teacher should be working with during the group activities session.]**

Finally, it is important to stress that even when a teacher is working intensively with one group, the first priority is always the overall work rate of the whole class. The following tips will help:

- Train children to work independently. Tell them that you cannot help them while you are working with a group – their turn will come. In the meantime, they must find out for themselves, or ask a friend or a classroom assistant.
- When working with a group, sit in a position so that the rest of the class can be seen.
- Break off group work immediately to deal with lazy or disruptive children. They will soon learn that they are under supervision even when you are working with a group.

Concluding sessions

The key objective in most of these sessions is to review the teaching points of the lesson and ensure that the work of *selected* children, pairs or groups is shared with the class for discussion and evaluation. Enough should be heard to exemplify the variety of work produced, but not so much that it becomes boring, or takes too much time. Keep a record of who has presented what to ensure that all children have the opportunity to present their work in due course.

Finishing off

When the time arrives for the concluding session, children will be at different stages of their work. Some will have finished, but many will still have work to do. The following strategies are recommended for dealing with this situation:

- Expect children to be *on task* during the time allocated for writing.
- Encourage them to work at a reasonable pace.
- Make expectations of each group clear: 'I expect you to write at least a side during the next 20 minutes' (Groups 2 & 3). 'I want one paragraph of four or five lines written very carefully and checked over by the end of this session' (Group 4).
- Give frequent time warnings such as 'We will have to stop writing in ten minutes'.
- For key pieces of writing plan either a) homework to finish them off, or b) another hour of careful redrafting and presenting.
- Discourage time-wasting activities such as decorating margins. Pictures should only be encouraged when they have a specific part to play (as in many non-fiction writing activities).

PHOTOCOPYING

Please note:

- Where there is instruction to copy material from copyright texts, *you need to ensure that this is done within the limits of the copying licence your school has.*

■ If pupils are using their own exercise books or paper for answers, then all photocopiable resources are reusable.

USE OF OVERHEAD PROJECTOR

Having the use of an overhead projector (OHP) is ideal for whole-class work. Photocopiable texts and skills activities can then be copied onto acetate to make overhead transparencies (OHTs) which can be projected onto a screen or a bare, white or light-coloured wall. For best effect, try to clear a whole section of wall from floor to ceiling and have it painted white. A partial black out would be an advantage. You will then be able to project a huge impressive text or picture. It can also be used to project backgrounds for drama improvisations. Where an OHP is not available, photocopiable sheets should be enlarged to at least A3 size.

INFORMATION AND COMPUTER TECHNOLOGY

Word processors have revolutionized the way we write, making redrafting less of a chore, and allowing documents to be well presented. However, the benefits of word processing only begin to be felt when the user has acquired a reasonable typing speed. It is therefore recommended that all children should use both hands on the keyboard and spend enough time practising so that they do not have to search for letters. To achieve this, word processing should be 'on the go' at all times. In most classrooms this will mean that a rota will have to be set up. When children have mastered the basics of word processing, they should be encouraged to make judgements about choice of fonts and page layout. The 'Words in Windows' and Writing Simulation ('Ninevah') units provide good opportunities for this.

ASSESSMENT

Regular and ongoing assessment of children's achievements and progress is, of course, essential. These materials assume that you and your school have satisfactory methods and systems of assessing and recording already in place and therefore don't attempt to suggest an alternative. However, what these materials also assume is that your current procedures are based on clearly stated teaching objectives. Therefore the objectives grids at the beginning of each unit should be invaluable in providing you with a framework for ongoing assessment.

In addition, to facilitate individual children conferencing at the end of each half-term, a photocopiable record sheet has been provided on page 11. Specific targets for reading and writing can be set for each pupil at the end of the previous half-term and recorded on the sheet in the left-hand column. Interim progress towards these targets can be assessed when appropriate and noted in the middle column. Then, at the end of each half-term, during the conference, pupil and teacher together can record achievement and agree further targets for the next half-term.

HOMEWORK

The amount of homework should be increased throughout the Key Stage. In Year 4, it should be restricted to two types:

■ Finishing off work that could not be finished in class. *Note:* be careful how you manage this. Less able pupils are often the slowest workers, and could end up with the most homework. If there seems to be a lot of finishing off needed in children's own time, consider revising lesson plans to allow more time in school.

■ Preparation – for example finding texts, such as cereal packets, newspapers and so on, to be used in the next day's lesson.

PUPIL ASSESSMENT GRID

Pupil's name:				Class	Year group
Term	1	2	3	1st half	2nd half

	TARGET(S)	INTERIM PROGRESS (inc dates)	ACHIEVEMENT AT END OF HALF TERM
Reading			
Writing			

OVERVIEW: YEAR 4

TERM 1

HOURS	UNIT	SPELLING/ VOCABULARY	GRAMMAR/ PUNCTUATION	COMPREHENSION/ COMPOSITION
HOUR 5 (+2)	READING FICTION Short novel: *It's Too Frightening For Me!* by Shirley Hughes.	Revise spelling of common verb endings. Extend knowledge of homophones. Extend vocabulary.	Revise and consolidate work on nouns and adjectives. Investigate verb tenses and use of descriptive verbs. Identify paragraphs. Identify key words to convey meaning for headlines.	Develop basic reading skills. Investigate how setting and characters are built up. Identify and describe key characters. Explore narrative order. Respond imaginatively.
HOUR 5	WRITING FICTION Guided writing: 'Animal Adventure'.	Identify synonyms of 'said'. Spell two-syllable words with double consonants. Revise *y-ies* plurals, *f-ves* plurals. Learn other plural forms.	Start a new paragraph for a new topic. Indent paragraphs. Identify paragraphs. Use paired adjectives and items separated by commas. Punctuate speech.	Write a story with a simple structure. Use paragraphs to structure and order narrative. Build paragraphs with simple sentence patterns using adjectives and items in lists separated by commas.
HOUR 2	READING NON-FICTION Procedural genre (instructions): 'Greetings, I am a Zillon'.	Understand technical language in text.	Recognize the imperative form of the verb. Identify common adverbs with *-ly* suffix.	Identify different purposes for and features of instructions text. Skim and scan for information.
HOUR 2	WRITING NON-FICTION Procedural genre (instructions): Writing an Instructions Leaflet.	Review the use of apostrophe when spelling contractions. Use and spell appropriate technical language.	Use the imperative form of the verb.	Write clear instructions. Use style of procedural genre.
HOUR 1	REFERENCE AND RESEARCH SKILLS Dictionary Work: alphabetical order.	Use third and fourth place letters to locate and sequence words in alphabetical order.	Use knowledge of sentence construction to check for grammatical sense and accuracy.	Understand purpose of alphabetical order. Practise alphabetical order.
HOUR 2	READING POETRY Classic historical poem: 'Highwayman's Hollow' by Gilbert V Yonge.	Investigate new vocabulary in poem. Identify syllables.	Explore grammar of poetry. Practise use of possessive apostrophe.	Read a poem with a historical theme. Study the verse form and rhyme pattern. Respond through drama. Explore figurative language.
HOUR 1 (+1)	WRITING POETRY Haiku.	Practise tapping out syllables. Use a thesaurus to find synonyms with required number of syllables.	Learn how to bend the rules of grammar for poetic purpose. Use punctuation to clarify meaning.	Read and write haiku to develop understanding of verse format and economy of expression.

NB  = Number of hours in unit (plus number of follow-up hours)

OVERVIEW: YEAR 4
TERM 1 (CONTINUED)

HOURS	UNIT	SPELLING/ VOCABULARY	GRAMMAR/ PUNCTUATION	COMPREHENSION/ COMPOSITION
HOUR 3 (+2)	READING PLAYS 'Zarg Enters'.	Understand and use vocabulary related to drama conventions.	Mark up text to support reading aloud. Identify statements, questions, orders and exclamations.	Read a playscript with expression. Respond imaginatively to character and plot. Compare organization of a playscript with stories – how are settings indicated, storylines made clear?
HOUR 2	WRITING PLAYS 'Wolf in the Woods'.	Develop vocabulary related to television scripts.	Write a television script using layout conventions correctly. Identify and classify adverbs.	Write a television script with convincing dialogue. Compare features of playscript and television script.
HOUR 2	READING NON-FICTION Report genre: 'The School Times'.	Revise work from Year 3 on common homophones.	Recognize layout features: headline, subheading, columns, illustrations, captions. Investigate the grammar of headlines.	Identify different types of text. Identify main features of newspapers.
HOUR 3	WRITING NON-FICTION Recount genre: Newspaper Construction Kit.	Identify and use 'news' words.	Use layout features: headline, subheading, columns, illustrations, captions.	Develop note-taking skills. Write newspaper-style reports about school events.
HOUR 1	REFERENCE AND RESEARCH SKILLS Using a Rhyming Dictionary.	Use a rhyming dictionary to compose jingles.	Investigate rhymes and jingles.	Write rhymes and jingles.
HOUR 1	WORD PLAY Playing with Adverbs: 'Thumping, stumping, bumping, jumping'.	Recognize common letter strings.	Identify adverbs and understand their role.	Investigate the effect of substituting adverbs.

NB HOUR 5 (+2) = Number of hours in unit (plus number of follow-up hours)

OVERVIEW: YEAR 4
TERM 2

HOURS	UNIT	SPELLING/ VOCABULARY	GRAMMAR/ PUNCTUATION	COMPREHENSION/ COMPOSITION
HOUR 2	READING FICTION Short fantasy story: 'The Vampire Teacher'.	Collect and note new words. Investigate *-ight* endings.	Revise and consolidate previous work on capital letters, nouns, adjectives, verbs, types of sentence, paragraphs, punctuation of speech as appropriate to class needs. Identify possessive apostrophes.	Develop basic reading skills. Develop skills of prediction, inference and deduction.
HOUR 3 (+1)	WRITING FICTION School Cards.	Spell words with *al-* prefix. Use *-able* suffix to make adjectives from verbs.	Use first person narrative. Construct adjectival phrases.	Apply skills of story writing learned in 'Animal Adventure' unit (Term 1) but with more imaginative content. Use a planning grid.
HOUR 3	REDRAFTING SIMULATION 'Kanda, the Fisherman'.	Explore synonyms using a thesaurus.	Revise conventions of writing dialogue. Experiment with adding an adverb to the reporting clause. Revise nouns and adjectives.	Investigate how to redraft the content of writing.
HOUR 4	READING NON-FICTION Information genre: 'Body Facts'.	Explore compound words. Extend vocabulary related to information-book layout.	Revise simple present tense. Recognize and use temporal connectives.	Understand reference aids: contents, index and glossary, page design. Identify key features of explanatory text.
HOUR 2	WRITING NON-FICTION Explanation genre: Words in Windows.	Check spellings in own work. Revise terms: *title, illustration, caption, font, body text, subtitle, columns, text boxes, bold.*	Revise redrafting skills. Devise redrafting checklist for information writing.	Make short notes. Present information and explanations in the style of modern reference books using organizational devices.
HOUR 1	REFERENCE AND RESEARCH SKILLS Appraising Non-fiction Texts.	Understand and use vocabulary related to features of non-fiction texts.	Identify features of non-fiction texts.	Appraise non-fiction books. Raise awareness of need to be critical when choosing and using information books.
HOUR 1	READING POETRY Cultural variety: 'Old Praise Song of the Crocodile'.	Identify words and phrases which suggest poem is from a different culture. Collect and note new words from reading.	Mark up a text for reading aloud. Add own punctuation.	Focus on expressive and descriptive language. Respond orally and through drama.

NB HOUR 5 (+2) = Number of hours in unit (plus number of follow-up hours)

OVERVIEW: YEAR 4
TERM 2 (CONTINUED)

	UNIT	SPELLING/ VOCABULARY	GRAMMAR/ PUNCTUATION	COMPREHENSION/ COMPOSITION
HOUR 1	WRITING POETRY Limericks.	Identify stressed and unstressed syllables.	Revise capital letters for new lines of poetry.	Identify patterns of rhyme and rhythm in poetry. Write own poems based on structures of those read.
HOUR 5	READING FICTION Long-established fiction – fantasy adventure story: *The Snow Queen* by Hans Christian Andersen.	Learn the archaic terms and other new vocabulary in the text. Spell *ou* and *ough* words.	Revise and identify adjectives. Develop knowledge of similes. Recognize prepositions. Recognize conjunctions.	Understand how writers create imaginary worlds. Identify clues to when story was written. Study plot, character, setting. Appreciate descriptive language. Literal and inferential comprehension.
HOUR 2	WRITING FICTION Adventure game story: 'Hildebrand's Dungeons'.	Check own spellings.	Learn the present continuous tense. Compare with simple present tense. Revise first, second and third person.	Investigate features of the 'adventure game' genre. Write an adventure story in the adventure game format. Plan story carefully using a decision tree.
HOUR 2	READING NON-FICTION Explanation genre: 'Piggy Bank'.	Develop vocabulary from text. Understand the terms *summary* and *abridgement*.	Identify and understand how certain words and phrases are used to indicate sequence in texts.	Investigate features of explanatory text. Experiment with re-sequencing text in different ways. Abridge and summarize text.
HOUR 2	WRITING NON-FICTION Explanation genre: 'Wacky Mousetrap'.	Use prefixes and suffixes to generate a name for the invention.	Use appropriate connectives.	Write an explanatory text.
HOUR 1	REFERENCE AND RESEARCH SKILLS: Preparing for Research.	Understand the term *research* and investigate other words from the root word.	Formulate questions.	Prepare for research by reviewing what is known, what is needed, what is available, and where to search.
HOUR 1	WORD PLAY Figurative language: 'The Spring Wind' by Charlotte Zolotow.	Use appropriate language in adjectival phrases in poetry.	Extend skills in using adjectives. Punctuate own poetry.	Understand the use of figurative language in poetry.

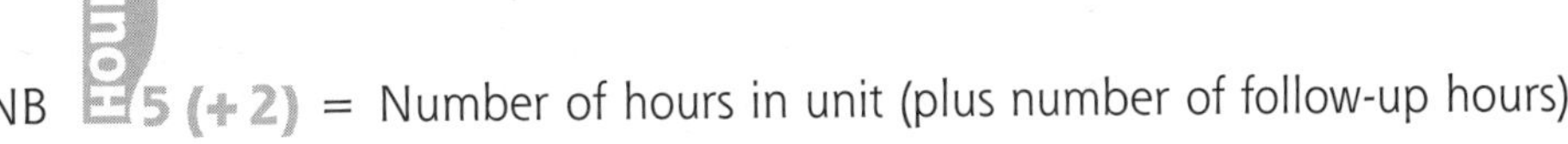
NB HOUR 5 (+ 2) = Number of hours in unit (plus number of follow-up hours)

OVERVIEW: YEAR 4
TERM 3

HOURS	UNIT	SPELLING/ VOCABULARY	GRAMMAR/ PUNCTUATION	COMPREHENSION/ COMPOSITION
HOUR 2	READING POETRY Modern free verse: 'Big Fears' by John Rice.	Investigate building words with similar patterns and meanings.	Investigate features of free verse. Revise third person narrative structure.	Read a poem with enjoyment. Respond by comparing own experiences. Explore pattern in free-verse poetry.
HOUR 2	WRITING POETRY 'The Prophecies of Mother Shipton'.	Investigate vocabulary in text.	Investigate the future tense.	Write a poem using rhyming couplets, based on model read.
HOUR 2	READING NON-FICTION Discussion text: '"I Feel Like a Scarecrow," Says Vicky'.	Investigate abbreviations.	Identify and understand use of discursive connectives.	Read and evaluate an article. Understand how it presents arguments to discuss issues.
HOUR 2	WRITING NON-FICTION Discursive/persuasive writing: 'Letter to the Editor'.	Explore abbreviations used in address.	Use discursive connectives.	Read and evaluate an article. Use a letter-writing frame to structure presentation of arguments and personal point of view.
HOUR 5 (+ 3)	READING FICTION *Cric Crac: A Collection of West Indian Stories* by Grace Hallworth.	Develop vocabulary from text. Spell words from common letter strings but different pronunciations – *ea* and *ou* words. Practise *-tion*, *-sion* suffixes.	Understand how nouns, verbs and adjectives can be changed by adding endings. Compare dialect with standard English. Explore concept of abstract nouns.	Read folk stories from other cultures. Identify morals, common themes, characters. Write own episode in the style of a story read.
HOUR 2	WRITING FICTION Pourquoi Stories.	Check spellings.	Revise items on the redrafting checklist.	Write a short 'pourquoi' story using one read as a model.
HOUR 1	REFERENCE AND RESEARCH SKILLS Using a Dictionary: Guide Words.	Use guide words in dictionaries to find more easily words needed for developing vocabulary.	Recognize and identify the guide words on a dictionary page.	Understand that guide words in a dictionary can help to find a word.

NB  5 (+ 2) = Number of hours in unit (plus number of follow-up hours)

OVERVIEW: YEAR 4
TERM 3 (CONTINUED)

	UNIT	SPELLING/ VOCABULARY	GRAMMAR/ PUNCTUATION	COMPREHENSION/ COMPOSITION
HOUR 5	READING NON-FICTION Recount (biography): *Hans Christian Andersen* by Andrew Langley.	Investigate the *wa* letter string. Practise extending words by adding prefixes and suffixes.	Identify dashes and hyphens and respond to them when reading. Investigate the past perfect tense.	Read non-fiction related to history. Identify problems faced by a subject and discuss how resolved. Understand features of biography. Summarize ideas in shortened form (postcard).
HOUR 3	WRITING NON-FICTION Recount (biography): Amy Johnson.	Develop vocabulary from text.	Summarize key ideas. Write from notes. Explore links between paragraphing and structure.	Research and write non-fiction related to history (biography), using a short biography read as a model.
HOUR 5	WRITING SIMULATION Ninevah.	Develop new vocabulary from text. Use dictionaries to investigate word origins. Extend work on synonyms.	Identify verb tenses. Identify common punctuation marks: colon, semicolons. Reinforce verb work.	Read a newspaper article. Research information linked to other curricular area (history). Write labels/captions, descriptions, stories, articles and letters.
HOUR 1	REFERENCE AND RESEARCH SKILLS Summarizing: Spiders.	Develop subject specific vocabulary from text.	Revise use of present tense for information texts.	Summarize key ideas from text. Use note-making strategies. Write information clearly and concisely.
HOUR 1	WORD PLAY Skipping and Action Rhymes.	Identify rhymes and syllables.	Exhibit knowledge of punctuation marks when reading.	Recognize simple forms of poetry and their uses. Investigate rhythm, rhyme and syllables.

NB  5 (+ 2) = Number of hours in unit (plus number of follow-up hours)

OBJECTIVES GRIDS: BLANK TEMPLATES

UNIT	SPELLING/ VOCABULARY	GRAMMAR/ PUNCTUATION	COMPREHENSION/ COMPOSITION

UNIT	SPELLING/ VOCABULARY	GRAMMAR/ PUNCTUATION	COMPREHENSION/ COMPOSITION

UNIT	SPELLING/ VOCABULARY	GRAMMAR/ PUNCTUATION	COMPREHENSION/ COMPOSITION

UNIT	SPELLING/ VOCABULARY	GRAMMAR/ PUNCTUATION	COMPREHENSION/ COMPOSITION

Term 1

It's Too Frightening For Me!

OBJECTIVES

UNIT	SPELLING/VOCABULARY	GRAMMAR/PUNCTUATION	COMPREHENSION/ COMPOSITION
READING FICTION Short novel: *It's Too Frightening For Me!* by Shirley Hughes.	Revise spelling of common verb endings. Extend knowledge of homophones. Extend vocabulary.	Revise and consolidate work on nouns and adjectives. Investigate verb tenses and use of descriptive verbs. Identify paragraphs. Identify key words to convey meaning for headlines.	Develop basic reading skills. Investigate how setting and characters are built up. Identify and describe key characters. Explore narrative order. Respond imaginatively.

ORGANIZATION (5 HOURS)

	INTRODUCTION	WHOLE-CLASS SKILLS WORK	DIFFERENTIATED GROUP ACTIVITIES	CONCLUSION
HOUR 1	Look at what the cover tells about the story. Shared reading from beginning to page 15, establishing setting and characters.	Revise nouns and adjectives.	1*: Guided reading and discussion with teacher. 2 & 3: Storyboard exercise. 4*: Guided reading and discussion with teacher.	Share points arising from discussion groups. Make predictions.
HOUR 2	Read pages 16 to 19. Ask class for predictions about what Jim will find when he opens the door.	Investigate use of the past tense and choice of descriptive verbs.	1–4*: Writing a 'follow-on' from page 19.	Ask selected pupils to read their follow-ons, then read pages 20 to 29. Draw attention to cliffhanger device and use of anticlimax.
HOUR 3	Read pages 30 to 43.	Revise spelling of common verb endings.	1: Storyboard exercise. 2 & 3*: Guided reading and discussion with teacher. 4: Storyboard exercise.	Select pupils from all groups to share their storyboards.
HOUR 4	Read pages 44 to 55. Investigate vocabulary. Discuss 'plan'.	Extend knowledge of homophones.	1–4*: Completion of the Character sheet according to ability.	Discuss work on characters.
HOUR 5	Read pages 56 to end, pausing to make predictions.	Identify paragraphs. Identify key ideas and words for headlines.	1–4*: Choose from writing: another adventure for Arthur and Jim; Mary's diary; a news report; a 'wanted' poster for Captain Grimthorpe.	Examples of different types of imaginative response are selected for reading and discussion.

RESOURCES

It's Too Frightening For Me! by Shirley Hughes (Young Puffin, ISBN 0-14-032008-3) – if possible, enough copies for half the class, photocopiable pages 24 (Storyboard), 25 (Nouns and Adjectives), 26 (Character sheet), scissors, paste, OHP and acetate (optional), board or flip chart, writing materials.

PREPARATION

Duplicate enough copies of photocopiable pages 24 (Storyboard) and 26 (Character sheet) for one per child (plus spares). A selection of illustrations from the book can be photocopied and pre-pasted onto one copy of the storyboard to support the storyboard exercise, although this is not essential. If possible, prepare an OHT of photocopiable page 25 (Nouns and Adjectives) and make enough copies for pairs of children.

SYNOPSIS

Jim and Arthur are drawn towards a scary, old house, despite having heard a ghostly voice coming from it. One day they go into the house and find that the 'ghosts' are just a little girl called Mary and her granny, who is the caretaker. They befriend Mary, and try to help when the owner of the house returns and ill-treats her and Granny. Eventually, the cruel owner is exposed as a fraud and the real owner decides to have the house turned into an old people's home, with Granny as its first resident. Mary is invited to live with the boys' family.

Introduction

Introduce the book by reading the blurb on the back cover. Discuss what kind of story the children think it will be. What do they think is meant by 'deliciously scary'? Display the front cover (on OHT, if available). What further information does it give? (Title, author, publisher, what Jim and Arthur look like and the fact that Arthur is younger, the use of speech bubbles which might be continued inside and so on.) Read from the beginning of the book to page 15. Draw attention to the fact that in this short beginning to the story, the author has established the setting, three of the characters and presented the boys with the first problem to solve. Who is the girl? What do the children think will happen in the story?

Whole-class skills work

Use photocopiable page 25 (Nouns and Adjectives) to revise the terms 'noun' and 'adjective'. Work through the sheet together. (Note that the focus is recognizing simple adjectives, that is, when an adjective is used just before a noun – attributive use. Adjectives used predicatively will be covered later.) When working on the extract from the novel, ask children to look out for pairs of adjectives used together. The effect of these pairs is a useful focus for discussion in group reading sessions.

Differentiated group activities

1*: Guided reading and discussion with the teacher. These questions will provide a starting point:

- What do you think is in the house? What makes you think that?
- How do Jim and Arthur feel about going inside the house?
- What do you think will happen if Jim and Arthur go inside?

If time allows, find and discuss more examples of nouns and adjectives.

2 & 3: Work on the Storyboard using photocopiable page 24. Children work in pairs within groups and use some of the illustrations from the story to devise their own story or scene. This should highlight what they think will happen in the story. Encourage them to make quick sketches in the 'film' boxes, and to write a description of what happens in the text boxes. Some children may enjoy writing under the following headings:

- Description of action
- Dialogue
- Sound effects.

Emphasize that the point of the exercise is to visualize the story as a film.

4*: Ask the children to re-read the passage, a paragraph in turn, to monitor basic reading skills. Then discuss the story using the questions above.

Conclusion

With the whole class, talk about the story so far, raising any appropriate points from the group discussions. Ask the children what they know of Jim and Arthur. What do they think their relationship is? Who do they think the girl at the window is? Talk about what the children would have done if they had been in Jim and Arthur's situation.

Introduction

Read pages 16 to 19. Ask the children again about the relationship between Jim and Arthur. How do they know? (Establish that the text on page 17 does not actually say they are brothers, but implies it: 'Jim's and Arthur's Mum...') What story do the children think Jim's and Arthur's Mum had read to them? Then ask the class for predictions about what Jim will find when he opens the door.

Whole-class skills work

Use the passage just read to focus on the use of verbs. Identify that the verbs are in the past tense and that this is a common feature of narrative fiction. Rework pages 18 to 19 into the present tense. How does this change the passage? Draw attention to the spelling of the regular verb endings (-s in the present tense; *-ed* in the past tense). Look also at how the author has used very descriptive verbs: *noticed* (rather than *saw*), *slithered* (rather than *slipped* or *slid*), *disappeared* (rather than *went*).

Differentiated group activities

1–4*: Write a follow-on from page 19. This activity follows on from the discussion in the introductory session. The author has built us up to expect something really scary and spooky – the children's follow-on work will, no doubt, reflect this. Explain that they should write a description of what Arthur sees when he peers into the room – they should not try to finish the story! The teacher should work with Group 4 and less able children in Group 3 to ensure that they write in a style which would fit into the story.

Conclusion

Ask one or two selected children to read out their follow-on (choose the scariest examples). Then read pages 20 to 29. Explain that Shirley Hughes has used an effect called *anticlimax*. A climax is a build-up and an anticlimax is a sudden let-down. She has described the house and Arthur's and Jim's reactions in a way that leads us to expect a very scary horror story, but what they find in the room is something quite ordinary! Ask them to look at pages 23 and 24 to see how the author has used format (the 'cliffhanger' at the end of page 23) to build up the suspense.

Introduction

Read pages 30 to 43.

Whole-class skills work

Remind children that homophones are words which sound the same but have different meanings. Focus initially on the 'It's' in the title (short for *It is*) and compare it with 'its' (belonging to it). Then discuss the following list, making sure the meanings of each word are clearly understood.

two/too/to	where/wear	for/four	heard/herd
there/their/they're	hair/hare	which/witch	here/hear

Brainstorm other words and write them on the board or flip chart.

Differentiated group activities

1 & 4: Storyboard exercise (see above).
2 & 3*: Guided reading and discussion with the teacher. The following questions can be used as a basis for discussion:

- What kind of man is Captain Grimthorpe?
- What is his dog like?
- How do they behave?
- What adjectives does the author use to describe him?

■ Can you think of some other suitable adjectives?
■ How do the illustrations add to your enjoyment and understanding of the story? Discuss in particular the use of speech bubbles.

Conclusion
Selected children from all groups share their storyboards. Recap on events so far and invite Groups 2 and 3 to share what they have discussed. Encourage predictions on how Captain Grimthorpe's arrival will change life for Mary, Granny and Uriah.

Introduction
Read pages 44 to 55, pausing at the end of page 48. What does the word 'grave' mean? Notice that in this context it is used as an adjective. What is another meaning of the word grave? What part of speech is it? What does the word 'resourceful' mean? Read to the end of page 55. Discuss the plan to rescue Uriah. What do the children think the boys were going to do with Uriah?

Whole-class skills work
Use pages 51 to 55 to focus work on paragraphs. Summarize each paragraph on the board, for example: 1. The plan. 2. Uriah greets Mary. 3. Cat is not happy. 4. Struggle.

Differentiated group activities
The class has now read enough of this story to be able to complete the Character sheet on photocopiable page 26.
1*: Use the sheet as a guide and write an essay entitled 'The Characters in *It's Too Frightening For Me!*' with one paragraph for each character.
2 & 3: Complete the Character sheet in sentences.
4*: Jot down notes on the Character sheet.

Conclusion
Share work on character descriptions. Which characters do the children like/dislike? Invite some of the children in Group 1 to read out their character essays. Recap on the section of the story read today. What do the children think will happen to Uriah?

Introduction
Read pages 56 to the end, pausing to invite children to say what will happen next. What do they think Grimthorpe will do once he has been unmasked? What do the people from the Council want? What will happen to Mary?

Whole-class skills work
Work on headlines. Remind children how headlines are constructed of key words with linking verbs often missed out, for example, 'Grimthorpe exposed in cat and wig drama', 'Hardlock House to have new lease of life'. Ask children to brainstorm more headlines that would be suitable for newspaper reports on the story.

Differentiated group activities
1–4*: A choice of task can be offered, but the teacher should guide their choice, bearing in mind the relative difficulty of the task. They are, in order of difficulty:
■ Write another adventure for Arthur and Jim.
■ Write what Mary might have written in her diary after the main events in the story.
■ Write a newspaper article based on part of the story using one of the headlines made up earlier.
■ Write a 'Wanted' poster for Captain Grimthorpe, giving a full description.

Conclusion
Examples of different types of imaginative response are selected for reading and discussion.

FOLLOW-UP (2 HOURS)

See page 204 (It's Too Frightening for Me! A Play) which provides a grid plan for a 2-hour follow-up unit on writing the story as a play.

STORYBOARD
Sketch of scene
Description

NOUNS AND ADJECTIVES

A **noun** is the name of a person, place or thing, for example *teacher, garden, tree.*

An **adjective** describes a noun, for example the *helpful* teacher, a *large* garden, a *tall* tree.

In Column 2 write a list of nouns (two have been given to start you off). Then, in Column 1, write some adjectives to describe them.

ADJECTIVES	NOUNS
	lawnmower bus

Read this extract from the story, and underline the adjectives in one colour and the nouns they describe in another colour.

Down by the railway footpath, quite near to where Jim and Arthur lived, was a big house. It was a gloomy old place with high brick walls. The windows were boarded up and the gates always kept padlocked. Nobody went in and nobody came out, except for a big tom cat, as black as a shadow.

On one of the gateposts, carved in stone, was the name 'Hardlock House'.

There were spooks in there. Jim and Arthur knew this for sure because they had heard the ghostly screams.

Sometimes they dared one another to squeeze through the gate, where the bars had rusted away, and creep up the overgrown drive. Thick bushes grew on either side, dripping and rustling.

Round the corner, the drive opened out into a bit of garden where a crumbling porch tottered over the front door. There were little windows on either side of it with cracked panes of coloured glass.

CHARACTER SHEET

Choose two adjectives for each character. Then write a short description of the character.

Jim

Adjectives

____

____

Description

Arthur

Adjectives

____

____

Description

Mary

Adjectives

____

____

Description

Capt. Grimthorpe

Adjectives

____

____

Description

ANIMAL ADVENTURE

OBJECTIVES

UNIT	SPELLING/VOCABULARY	GRAMMAR/PUNCTUATION	COMPREHENSION/ COMPOSITION
WRITING FICTION Guided writing: 'Animal Adventure'.	Identify synonyms of 'said'. Spell two-syllable words with double consonants. Revise *y-ies* plurals, *f-ves* plurals. Learn other plural forms.	Start a new paragraph for a new topic. Indent paragraphs. Identify paragraphs. Use paired adjectives and items separated by commas. Punctuate speech.	Write a story with a simple structure. Use paragraphs to structure and order the narrative. Build paragraphs with simple sentence patterns using paired adjectives and items in lists separated by commas.

ORGANIZATION (5 HOURS)

	INTRODUCTION	WHOLE-CLASS SKILLS WORK	DIFFERENTIATED GROUP ACTIVITIES	CONCLUSION
HOUR 1	Read 'Animal Adventure'. Explain story structure.	Revise how paragraphs are set out.	1*: Guided writing of beginning of story using sample story as a model. 2 & 3: Reading Comprehension part B. 4*: Guided writing of beginning of story using template.	Selected pupils from Groups 1 & 4 read their story beginnings, followed by brief discussion.
HOUR 2	Guided reading with the teacher of the story with children 'in role' speaking the dialogue.	Revise and consolidate conventions of setting out and punctuating dialogue.	1: Reading Comprehension part B. 2 & 3*: Guided writing of beginning of story using template as guide. 4: Reading Comprehension part A.	Selected pupils from Groups 2 & 3 read their story beginnings, followed by brief discussion.
HOUR 3	Discuss the development – the 'middle' – of the story, emphasizing the link between structure and paragraphing.	Identify synonyms of 'said'. Spell two-syllable words with double consonants.	1 & 4*: Guided writing of middle of the story. 2 & 3: Reading Comprehension part C.	Selected pupils from Groups 2 & 3 share answers to Reading Comprehension part C. Use these to help the class understand 'twist in the tale' endings.
HOUR 4	Read the ending of 'Animal Adventure'. Explain that this story ends with a 'twist in the tale'. Discuss other suitable endings.	Revise and consolidate *y-ies* and *f-ves* plurals. Learn *o-oes* plurals.	1: Reading Comprehension part C. 2 & 3*: Guided writing of part 2 of the story. 4: Reading Comprehension part B.	Selected pupils from Groups 1 & 4 read some comprehension answers and Groups 2 & 3 read their continuations.
HOUR 5	Recap on main points taught throughout the week relating to story structure.	Redrafting: explain what to look for when redrafting.	1–4*: Redrafting and finishing off.	Selected pupils read their complete story.

RESOURCES

Photocopiable pages 32 and 33 ('Animal Adventure'), 31 (Story Template – Animal Adventure) and 34 (Reading Comprehension), OHP and acetate (optional), lined paper with ruled margins, board or flip chart, writing materials.

PREPARATION

A set of all photocopiable resources should be prepared for each pair of children. Prepare enough copies of photocopiable page 31 (Story Template) with continuation notes blanked out for Group 4. It is useful, in addition, to make an OHT of the story text as a focus for whole-class discussion. Children should write on lined paper with a ruled margin (which helps with indentation and clear paragraph layout).

HOUR 1

Introduction

Read 'Animal Adventure'. Pause after 'They were bright yellow, and made a terrible roaring sound.' Ask the children what they think the monsters are. Read to the end.

Explain the story structure and write it on the board as follows:

Beginning: Description of a place and main character; description of other characters; introduction of a problem

Middle: Narration of a series of adventures which take place when trying to solve the problem

Ending: A solution, but a twist in the tale.

Ask the class which parts of the story fit into which section.

Whole-class skills work

Revise paragraphing conventions with reference to the story and ensure children understand the terms *indent* and *indentation*. Explain to children that they should indent the first line of a paragraph approximately 1cm, or a 'finger space'. No blank lines should be left between paragraphs. Using a coloured marker, help them to pick out the paragraphs. As dialogue is also indented, paragraph divisions are not always clear! Children in Group 1 could be asked to differentiate new speaker indentations from indentations that show a new idea or topic.

Differentiated group activities

1 & 4*: Guided writing with the teacher of *beginning* of a story based on sample story. Encourage children in Group 1 to use the sample story as a model for structure, use of adjectives, paragraphs, speech marks, use of commas in lists and so on. Work with Group 4, encouraging them to begin their story directly onto the Story Template sheet (page 31). See notes below.

2 & 3: Work through part B of the Reading Comprehension sheet.

Notes on the story template sheet:

Explain that the first paragraph begins with a description of the forest, the second describes a key character and the third introduces a problem. A continuous line is for the name of a place or an animal; dotted lines are for other words, phrases and sentences.

Sentence 1: choose a name for the forest, add two adjectives to describe it.

Sentence 2: add two phrases of description linked by 'and'.

Sentence 3: choose an animal and a name for the animal.

Sentence 4: begin with the name of the animal and add two adjectives to describe it.

Sentence 5: this sentence is a three-item list, with one adjective for each item, for example *He had pointed ears, a bushy tail and bright eyes.*

Sentence 6 requires only the name of the key character.

Sentence 7: describe what the animal saw.

Finally, complete the conversation. Notes for completion of the story (in later sessions) are given at the bottom of the template. These should have been deleted for Group 4 (see Preparation) who will write onto the template itself.

Conclusion

Selected children from Groups 1 and 4 read out their story beginnings, followed by discussion: Is the setting clearly and vividly described? Is the main character clearly described? Is the problem stated and interesting enough to make you want to read on?

Introduction

Allocate different groups in the class to play the parts of the speaking animals. Re-read the story, letting the children join in in their appropriate groups with the dialogue.

Whole-class skills work

Display the story on OHP and investigate how the dialogue is set out and punctuated, marking the text as the children identify different aspects. All children should know how to use speech marks before and after words actually spoken and should be making progress in placing a comma, full stop, question mark or exclamation mark before the final speech marks. More able children should be aiming to set out dialogue with a *new indented line for each new speaker*.

Identify synonyms for 'said' in the story. Make a list of them and brainstorm others to use as a reference when writing.

Differentiated group activities

1: Work on part B of the Reading Comprehension sheet.
2 & 3*: Write their story beginnings as described in Hour 1, but using the template *as a guide*. In other words, children follow it closely, but can expand sentences, and add extra description. Encourage children to use dialogue in paragraph 3 remembering what they learned in the skills session.
4: Work on part A of the Reading Comprehension sheet. This exercise is designed to develop reading fluency. Allow children time to read at least part of the story in their groups, even if they have not finished marking it up.

Conclusion

Selected children from Groups 2 and 3 read their story beginnings, followed by brief discussion.

Introduction

Guided reading with the teacher of the section beginning 'Scamp and Mole summoned all the animals to a meeting...' to '...the other side of the road'. Explain that this is the *middle* of the story, in which the situation described in the first few paragraphs is worked out. Point out that in a longer story, the animals would have many more problems and adventures along the way. Here, they only have one – crossing the road. Make explicit the link between story structure and paragraphing by splitting this story middle into smaller chunks: for example, *Scamp and Mole summoned... They all started talking at once... So the birds flew out... They soon left the shelter... It was a long time...*

Whole-class skills work

Use words from the story to focus on the spelling of two-syllable words containing double consonants. Write the following words on the board or chart: *litter, squirrel, little*. Ask the children what they have in common. Find other examples of double consonant words in the story: *summon, happen, flutter, yellow, burrow, berries, scurried, biggest, buzzing* (*happily* and *terrible*, too, although they are three-syllable words). Explain that it is often difficult to hear any difference in sound between a single or double consonant and that makes spelling difficult. But one useful way to see if a word needs a double consonant is to listen to the sound of the vowel before it. Write *later, polite* and *secret* on the board or chart. What do they notice about the vowel sound? (It is long, whereas the vowel sound in the double-consonant words is short.)

Differentiated group activities

1*: Children plan and write the 'middle' section of their stories. Each problem faced by the animals should be a separate paragraph. Aim for three paragraphs.
2 & 3: Work on part C of the Reading Comprehension sheet which explores the 'twist in the tale' ending.
4*: As for 1, but aim for one or two paragraphs only.

Conclusion

Selected children from Groups 2 and 3 read some of their answers to part C of the Reading Comprehension sheet. Use these to help the class understand the concept of 'twist in the tale' endings.

Introduction

Shared reading of the ending of 'Animal Adventure'. Remind the class that this kind of ending is called 'a twist in the tale'. Explain the pun 'tale/tail'. Discuss other ways of ending the story and emphasize that the most straightforward ending will usually be the best. In this ending, the animals find a new home which is as good as their old one.

Whole-class skills work

Revise *y-ies* and *f-ves* plurals. Remind children of the rules:

RULE: Words ending in *y* change the *y* to *i* and add es if the letter before *y* is a consonant.
NOTE: If you apply the rule wrongly the word will *look* wrong, for example *railwaies*.
Test the application of the rule with these words. Note that one of the words does *not* take an *-ies* plural. Write the plural of *story, bully, army, aunty, birthday, balcony.*

RULE: Words ending in a single *f* have the plural ending *-ves*.
EXCEPTIONS: *beliefs, briefs, chefs, chiefs, clefs, dwarfs, gulfs, handkerchiefs, reefs, roofs.*
Test the application of the rule with these words. Note that one of the words does *not* take a *-ves* plural. Write the plural of *half, leaf, reef, wolf.*

About 30 words ending in o change to oes in the plural. There is no satisfactory rule for this. Ask the children to write out and learn the commonest ones: *goes, potatoes, cargoes, heroes, tomatoes, dominoes, mosquitoes, volcanoes, echoes.*

Differentiated group activities

1: Work on Reading Comprehension sheet part C.
2 & 3*: Children plan and write the 'middle' section of their stories. Each problem faced by the animals should be a separate paragraph. Aim for three paragraphs.
4: Work on Reading Comprehension sheet part B.

Conclusion

Selected children from Groups 1 and 4 read some comprehension answers and children from Groups 2 and 3 read some story continuations.

Introduction

In a question and answer session, recap on the main points taught throughout the week:

- What is the structure of the story we have been writing?
- What have we learned about paragraphs?
- What have we learned about dialogue?

Jot down the points made by the children on the board or flip chart.

Whole-class skills work

Give guidance on redrafting. Ask children to work with a partner in a two-stage process:
- Stage 1: Read through the story and look for places where the description can be made more detailed and improved.
- Stage 2: Proofread the story for spelling, grammar and punctuation mistakes. Look particularly for the skills covered during the week as listed on the board or flip chart.

Differentiated group activities

1–4*: All groups redraft their story. The teacher should work briefly with all groups, but give particular attention to Group 4 and some of the less able children in Groups 2 and 3. This is an opportunity for them to rewrite the story and add more of their own ideas.

Conclusion

Invite volunteers to present readings of their stories. Evaluate, noting positive achievements.

STORY TEMPLATE

Animal Adventure

_____________ Forest was a(n) ....

place. In the forest there were

.... and

....

One of the animals in the forest was a .... called

_____________. _____________ was a(n) ....,

.... creature. He had ....,

...., and ....

One day _____________ saw something terrible.

....

....

He ran to tell his friends.

'......................!' cried _____________.

'......................,' replied _____________.

'......................,' agreed _____________.

Continue the story by describing how the main character leads the animals to a new home. They could face two or three problems on the way. Each problem, and how the animals solve it, should be a separate paragraph.

The last paragraph could be a description of their new home leading to the final line:
'It was even better than _____________ Forest.'

ANIMAL ADVENTURE

Fiveways Forest was a wonderful place for animals to live. It was miles from the nearest town so there were not many human visitors to drop litter, start fires, or frighten the animals with their badly behaved dogs. The trees were mainly huge old oak trees, which provided acorns for food and shelter from wind and rain.

One of the animals who lived in the forest was a squirrel called Scamp. He was a lively little character with bright, sparkling eyes, pointed ears and a bushy tail. He lived in a hole in the biggest oak tree, and could usually be seen darting around the branches looking for acorns.

One day, when Scamp was looking for acorns at the edge of the forest, he saw something terrible. Three strange monsters were coming down the track towards the trees. They were bright yellow, and made a terrible roaring sound. As Scamp watched, one of them crashed right into a tree and pushed it over. Then he saw a team of humans with huge buzzing things in their hands start to cut up the tree. Scamp ran at once to tell his friends.

The first animal he saw was Mole, who had just come up from making a new burrow.

'Mole!' gasped Scamp. 'I've just seen something terrible!'

'Calm down, Scamp,' said Mole.

Scamp took a few minutes to get his breath back, then described what he had seen.

Mole frowned. 'Those yellow monsters,' he said, 'I think I know what they are. Humans call them *bulldozers*.'

'That's all very well,' said Scamp impatiently, 'but what does it all *mean*, do you think?'

Mole spoke solemnly. 'It means they are going to cut down the forest and build something – houses, perhaps, or a road.'

'Then we must do what we can to save the animals!' cried Scamp.

Scamp and Mole summoned all the animals to a meeting at the biggest oak tree. Scamp told them what he had seen, and Mole told them what he thought would happen.

'I flew that way just a minute ago,' said wise old Owl 'and they've cleared a huge space already. We haven't got long!'

'What are we going to do?' squeaked the mice.

'We'll all be bulldozed!' wailed the voles.

'We must make a plan,' advised Scamp.

They all started talking at once as they told each other their ideas. Then Owl hooted to silence them and said, 'We must find a new home. I will send all the birds to look for one, and they will tell us which way to go.'

'Yes, yes, yes!' chorused the mice.

'Let's start straight away!' agreed the voles.

So the birds flew out in all directions. After about half an hour they began to return. There was noisy cheeping and chirping as they told their news to Owl. Then, at last, he turned to the other animals and announced, 'We have found a new forest two miles north of here. I will lead the way.' With that he fluttered towards the next tree.

Scamp saw him go and shouted encouragement to the others. 'Come on. Let's follow him!'

They soon left the shelter of Fiveways Forest and were marching across an open field. Everything went well until they came to a huge river of concrete along which mighty monsters roared and thundered at tremendous speeds.

'I think humans call this a *road*,' ventured Mole.

'Yes,' said Scamp, 'but how are we going to get across!'

It was a long time before they could think of anything, but suddenly Mole said, 'I know, I'll get all my friends and relatives to dig a tunnel!'

It took the whole of the next day to do this and all the moles were exhausted, but the animals were able to walk safely through the tunnel to the other side of the road.

They had many other problems and adventures along the way, but at last they came to their new home which they called New Forest. It was a lovely place, full of tall green trees with lots of nuts and berries to eat. In fact, it was just as nice as their old home!

Scamp found himself another tall oak tree, and Mole burrowed happily into the soft rich soil. The mice and voles scurried into the undergrowth to make their homes. Owl, perched on top of a tall elm tree, looked around happily and said to himself, 'All's well that ends well!'

He hadn't seen the three yellow monsters in the distance.

READING COMPREHENSION

PART A

In twos or threes, prepare the text for reading aloud to the class. You could prepare the text by:

- looking up the meanings of any words you are not sure about
- marking up all punctuation in red
- underlining words which you will emphasize
- marking who reads each section.

PART B

In twos, talk about these questions, then write your answers.

- What kind of animal was Scamp?
- What were the three strange monsters that Scamp saw?
- What were the buzzing things that the humans had in their hands?
- Make a list of the adjectives used to describe Scamp.
- Why were the humans cutting down the forest?
- What did the animals plan to do?
- How did they manage to get all the animals across the road safely?
- Why was Owl wrong when he said, 'All's well that ends well!'

PART C

- Explain in your own words the meaning of 'twist in the tale'. What is the 'twist' in this story?
- Write a continuation of the story, describing what happens next.

GREETINGS, I AM A ZILLON

OBJECTIVES

UNIT	SPELLING/VOCABULARY	GRAMMAR/PUNCTUATION	COMPREHENSION/ COMPOSITION
READING NON-FICTION Procedural genre (instructions): 'Greetings, I am a Zillon'.	Understand technical language in text.	Recognize the imperative form of the verb. Identify common adverbs with *-ly* suffix.	Identify different purposes for and features of instructions text. Skim and scan for information.

ORGANIZATION (2 HOURS)

	INTRODUCTION	WHOLE-CLASS SKILLS WORK	DIFFERENTIATED GROUP ACTIVITIES	CONCLUSION
HOUR 1	Read and identify different types of instructions text.	Read the text on the Zillon Instructions Leaflet. Demonstrate how to skim the leaflet for a particular topic, then scan a section to find a particular piece of information.	1–4: Skim and scan text to answer questions. All groups should do as many as they can in the time allowed. *Teacher works with Group 4.	Discuss the answers to the questions and the processes (eg skimming and scanning) by which they were found.
HOUR 2	Shared reading with the teacher of the Zillon Instructions Leaflet. Discuss how features of text, layout and design aid meaning and retrieval of information.	Revise the imperative form of the verb. Identify common adverbs with *-ly* suffix.	1: Identify imperative verbs and adverbs in text. Write a glossary of difficult terms. 2 & 3*: As above with teacher support. 4: Identify imperative verbs and adverbs in text.	Present and share answers to group work. Recap on information retrieval skills.

RESOURCES

Photocopiable pages 37 and 38 (Zillon Instructions Leaflet), 39 (Reading Comprehension) and 40 (Adverbs), collection of instructional texts (for example recipes, directions on how to get somewhere, instructions for how to use some medication, instructions for using a home appliance, how to fill in a form, how to play a game, what to do in an emergency), board or flip chart, OHP and acetate (optional), dictionaries, writing materials.

PREPARATION

The two photocopiable resource sheets on pages 37 and 38 are designed to be photocopied back to back and folded in half lengthways, which recreates the format of an instructions leaflet. The page numbers will act as a guide to correct folding. Make enough copies for one between two children. If possible prepare an OHT of pages 2 and 3 of the Instructions Leaflet and photocopiable page 40 (Adverbs) – or enlarge to A3. Make enough copies of photocopiable page 39 (Reading Comprehension) for one between two children.

Introduction

Read out, in turn, the examples of instructional texts you have collected (or extracts from them). For each one, ask the children to say what kind of instruction the text is and write it on the board or flip chart. You should have a list of about five or six different types and purposes of instructional text. Ask the children if they can think of any other situations which require reading instructional text and add them to the list.

Whole-class skills work

Give out copies of the Zillon Instructions Leaflet and establish that it provides instructions on how to use a children's toy. Demonstrate skimming and scanning by saying: 'Suppose I wanted to put in the batteries, but did not know how – where would I look?' Show how you would skim the instructions looking for the word battery, possibly in a subheading. Then, using the OHT, demonstrate how you would scan the section until you found the information you wanted. Explain that you would then re-read it carefully. Ask the children to skim the leaflet to find out where they would find information about the warranty. Having established that it is on the back page, ask them to scan the text to find out what a warranty is. Look the word up in the dictionary to confirm the meaning.

Differentiated group activities

Give out copies of photocopiable page 39 (Reading Comprehension). Part A is a list of questions. These are in three sections, 'stepped' in difficulty. Encourage all groups to answer as many as they can. Allow exactly 10 minutes to encourage speed in the skimming and scanning processes. Work through the questions verbally with Group 4. Part B should be done by all groups in about 10 or 15 minutes.

Conclusion

Discuss the answers to the questions, and emphasize the skimming and scanning processes by which they were found.

Introduction

Shared reading with the teacher of the Zillon Instructions Leaflet. Discuss how the features of text layout, design and diagrams help to convey different kinds of information, for example the use of a speech bubble and first-person text to talk directly to the child, clear headings to direct the reader through the text, and diagrams to show how to operate the cassette player in case the reader cannot fully understand the text.

Whole-class skills work

Discuss the fact that the purpose of instructions is to tell the reader what or how to do something. The instructions are written as a set of command sentences. The subject of the commands is assumed to be the reader and is therefore not mentioned in the sentence. Therefore, command sentences usually begin with the verb. Write on the board or flip chart: *Read this leaflet carefully*. Ask the children to find this instruction on the front page of the Zillon leaflet. Explain that 'read' is called an imperative verb and is an example of the kind of command language used in instructions. Then look at the sentence again and ask the children what the sentence tells them about *how* they should read the leaflet – *carefully*. Teach the term 'adverb' as a word that tells us more about the verb. An adverb usually answers the questions how, when, where or why. Most adverbs are formed by adding *ly* to an adjective: careful + ly = carefully. Display photocopiable page 40 (Adverbs) on the OHP and work through the exercise as a class.

Differentiated group activities

1: Re-read the Zillon Instructions Leaflet, underlining imperative verbs and ringing adverbs. Then write a glossary for the difficult terms in the leaflet, using a dictionary.
2 & 3*: As above with teacher support. Make sure they have found these words: *warranty, comprehensive, defects, attached, registration, purchase, receipt, abuse, unreasonable, require, statutory, alkaline, operating, distorted, depressed.*
4: Re-read the Zillon Instructions Leaflet, underlining imperative verbs and ringing adverbs.

Conclusion

Discuss children's answers for marking up the leaflet for imperative verbs and adverbs. Select children to define some of the difficult vocabulary.

Play Safe with the Zillon 90-day Warranty and Service Agreement
Zillons have their own comprehensive warranty which cover, them against any defects in material or workmanship for 90 days. To benefit from this warranty, send your name and address along with details of where and when you purchased your Zillon and proof of purchase* to: the Inter-Galactic Healthcare Centre at the address below.

Should your Zillon need care and attention after the 90-day warranty period, we will service and repair it upon receipt of your cheque or postal order for £10 and proof of purchase*. This service agreement does not apply to defects from abuse, alteration or unreasonable use and does not apply should your Zillon require service two years after the date of purchase.

IMPORTANT
To send your Zillon to the Inter-Galactic Healthcare Centre, please remove its spacesuit and space pack, batteries and cassette. Pack it in a strong carton. DO NOT wrap in newspaper. Enclose your name, address and a description of the problem. Send to:

Zillon Inter-Galactic Healthcare Centre
PO Box 1357
Toytown TT2 4ZL

This in no way affects your statutory rights.

*Till receipt or similar

This product is not suitable for children under 3 years of age.

4

Zillon

Greetings, Earthling!
I am a Zillon and I come from the planet Tharg to talk and play with you. But before I can do that, there's something *you* must do. Read this leaflet carefully. It tells you how to look after me and what to do if I won't play.
ZILLON HOTLINE
TELEPHONE (01234) 567890 EXT 008
DURING WORKING HOURS

Help

If your Zillon will not play, read this leaflet first before telephoning the Zillon Hotline for help. Most problems can be fixed at home, but if this is not possible, follow the instructions on the back page. Send your Zillon to the Inter-Galactic Healthcare Centre where it will be mended and returned to you within 28 days.

1

GETTING TO KNOW ME

1. Put in my batteries (carefully).
Remove my space pack and spacesuit. Open the battery compartment. Put in four C batteries and one 9-volt battery exactly as the diagram shows you. Take care to fit batteries correctly. Use alkaline batteries only.

2. Insert my cassette (slowly).
I have an instruction tape, so play this for operating and safety tips (one side is blank). When you want to change my tape, push the red button to open the door – but be careful not to force it open too far. Take out the tape and put in a new one. Make sure that the exposed tape is at the bottom. Now close the door.

3. Press the buttons (gently).
To hear my tape, press my green button. Press my red button to stop the tape and open the door. If you want to hear something again, press my blue button to rewind. Press my yellow button to fast forward.
My voice can be made louder or quieter by turning the volume wheel.
I can play any cassette, but my mouth moves best with my own tapes.

2

HEALTH TIPS

- When you aren't playing with me, keep me in a cool, dry place. I don't like DIRT, HEAT or WATER – and PLEASE don't use any sharp objects, pens or pencils near me.
- Never put me in water. We don't have water on Planet Tharg so I can't swim and I will drown.
- Clean my tape player once a month. Ask an adult to help you. You can buy a cleaning kit from a shop that sells tapes. If you do this, I will last longer and so will my tapes.
- If you're not going to play with me for a long time, please take out my batteries.

GROOMING TIPS

- I can be cleaned with mild soap and a damp cloth, but remember – NEVER put me in water.
- I like my fur to be brushed, but please don't use a hairdryer, curling iron or hair spray.
- To keep my spacesuit looking its best, wash it by hand with mild soap and let it dry naturally.

THE INTER-GALACTIC DOCTOR SAYS

- If your Zillon's voice is distorted, or its mouth won't move, change its 9-volt battery.
- If it is too quiet, adjust the volume wheel. If it is still too quiet, change its 9-volt battery.
- If your Zillon won't work at all, make sure its tape is not at the end, the tape door is closed and the green play button is pressed down. You can play one side of its instruction tape in any cassette player for more tips.
- Replace the whole set of batteries at one time.
- IMPORTANT – Do not leave the blue (rewind) or the yellow (fast forward) buttons depressed. The motor will continue to run after the tape stops, causing the batteries to run down quickly.

3

READING COMPREHENSION

PART A

You have 10 minutes to answer as many of the following questions as possible. Your answers can be written quickly in note form in the space below each question.

■ You have to buy some batteries for your Zillon. What type of battery and how many will you need?

■ You can hardly hear the sound from the Zillon's cassette. How can you make it louder?

■ What must you do if your Zillon is still too quiet?

■ What must you do if you are not going to play with the Zillon for a long time?

■ Name three things which could damage the Zillon.

■ If your Zillon's mouth won't move, what must you do to make it work?

■ If you have to send your Zillon to the Inter-Galactic Healthcare Centre what must you do?

■ How much will it cost to have your Zillon repaired?

■ How long is the warranty period?

■ What must you do to benefit from the warranty?

PART B

■ *Discuss:* From reading the instructions, can you guess what kind of creature the Zillon is? What special things can it do?

■ Design an advertisement for the Zillon from Planet Tharg.

ADVERBS

The burglar crept **quietly** into the house.

The adverb **quietly** tells us *how* the burglar came into the house.

Add **-ly** to each of these adjectives to change them into adverbs.

quick	careful	loud
safe	kind	rude
clear	slow	soft

Think of a sentence using each one. (You can use the back of this sheet.)

When **ly** is added to words ending with **y**, the **y** is changed to **i** before adding **ly**.
bus**y** → bus**ily** easy → eas**ily**

When **ly** is added to words ending in **e**, drop the **e** before adding **ly**.
gentl**e** → gent**ly** tru**e** → tru**ly**

Change each of these adjectives to adverbs:

greedy	proud	noisy
terrible	bitter	lucky
angry	sensible	happy
hungry	glad	grim

Choose **five** of the adverbs you have made and think of sentences for them. (You can use the back of this sheet.)

WRITING AN INSTRUCTIONS LEAFLET

OBJECTIVES

UNIT	SPELLING/VOCABULARY	GRAMMAR/PUNCTUATION	COMPREHENSION/ COMPOSITION
WRITING NON-FICTION Procedural genre (instructions): Writing an Instructions Leaflet.	Review the use of apostrophe when spelling contractions. Use and spell appropriate technical language.	Use the imperative form of the verb.	Write clear instructions. Use style of procedural genre.

ORGANIZATION (2 HOURS)

INTRODUCTION	WHOLE-CLASS SKILLS WORK	DIFFERENTIATED GROUP ACTIVITIES	CONCLUSION
HOUR 1 Display an OHT of the inside pages of the Zillon Instructions Leaflet. Explain that the class will be writing a similar leaflet using the same format.	Remind pupils of the imperative form of the verb. Ask pupils to brainstorm a list that would be useful in writing instructions.	1 & 2: Write a draft of the instructions. Plan the format of the leaflet. 3 & 4*: As above, but working with the teacher and using the Zillon Instructions Leaflet as a template.	Share ideas and draft layouts. Selected pupils present their instructions.
HOUR 2 Use the Zillon leaflet to show how the leaflet is created by making a single fold. Briefly explain the template.	Discuss layout conventions: title, subheadings, labelling of diagrams, use of bullet points.	1–4: Write a final version of instructions. *The teacher supports Groups 1 & 2.	Evaluate by actually using the instructions with products.

RESOURCES

Photocopiable pages 37 and 38 (Zillon Instructions Leaflet) from previous unit, OHT and acetate (optional), writing materials.

PREPARATION

If possible, prepare an OHT of photocopiable pages 37 and 38. Ask the children to bring in a product for which they can write 'how-to-use' instructions. It could be a toy or some other product. If they cannot bring in a product, they could bring a picture of one instead. Make sure that you have available in the classroom a mail-order catalogue which is a ready source of pictures.

Introduction

Display an OHT (or enlarged version) of the Zillon Instructions Leaflet on photocopiable pages 37 and 38. Remind the children of the format of the leaflet, reviewing the features of text, layout and design discussed in the previous unit. Explain that they will be using the same format to write an instructions leaflet for the product they have brought in to school.

Whole-class skills work

Pick out the contractions in the Zillon Instructions Leaflet to review the use of the apostrophe when spelling shortened forms. Write the following contractions on the board or flip chart, and ask children to come up and write the two words from which they are formed: *there's, aren't, can't, don't, you're, won't*. In each case ask them what the apostrophe stands for. Ask them to find examples in the leaflet and to read out the sentences in which they occur.

Remind children of the activity they did previously on the imperative form of the verb. Ask them to cite some of the imperative verbs in the Zillon Instructions Leaflet. Ask them to brainstorm imperative verbs they think might be useful in writing instructions for their products. Write these on the board or flip chart.

Differentiated group activities

1 & 2: Write a draft plan of their instructions. Children in Group 1, and perhaps some in Group 2, should be encouraged to devise other formats if they wish.
3 & 4*: Work with these groups at this critical drafting stage, ensuring that they use the correct form of the verb and that their instructions are well-formatted, clear and easy to follow.

Conclusion

Good examples of clear writing from any group can be shared with the rest of the class.

Introduction and whole-class skills work

Use this combined session to focus attention on the design features of the Zillon Instructions Leaflet. Display the leaflet again and ask the children to pick out aspects of the design which help to make the meaning of the text easier to read and understand, for example the typeface used and the size of the text, the use of graphic devices such as speech bubbles, a flash for the hotline number, boxes to separate text and illustrations, headings, subheadings, use of capital letters, underlining, bulleted text and diagrams. Ensure the children use the correct terminology for these features and write them on the board or flip chart for reference.

Differentiated group activities

1 & 2*: Write a final version of their instructions. As many children may be using their own format, they will need support at this stage to ensure that their design is effective.
3 & 4: Write the final version of their instructions, using the Zillon Instructions Leaflet as a template.

Conclusion

Select two or three examples of the instruction leaflet to be read. Evaluate them by asking someone to follow the instructions to use the products.

DICTIONARY WORK

OBJECTIVES

UNIT	SPELLING/VOCABULARY	GRAMMAR/PUNCTUATION	COMPREHENSION/ COMPOSITION
REFERENCE AND RESEARCH SKILLS Dictionary Work: alphabetical order.	Use third and fourth place letters to locate and sequence words in alphabetical order.	Use knowledge of sentence construction to check for grammatical sense and accuracy.	Understand purpose of alphabetical order. Practise alphabetical order.

ORGANIZATION (1 HOUR)

INTRODUCTION	WHOLE-CLASS SKILLS WORK	DIFFERENTIATED GROUP ACTIVITIES	CONCLUSION
HOUR 1 Review purpose of knowing alphabetical order. Order jumbled words and sentences by alphabetical order up to fourth letter.	Oral practice of alphabetical order. Recognize that alphabet can be divided into parts to help in finding information.	1*: Practise finding words in dictionary. Complete all parts of photocopiable sheet. 2 & 3: Complete parts A, B & C of photocopiable sheet. Complete part D if time. 4*: Complete parts A & B of photocopiable sheet independently. Complete part C with teacher support.	Share sentences from part D of photocopiable sheet. Extend sentences with adjectives and adverbs within parameters of alphabetical order and context.

RESOURCES

Photocopiable page 45 (Dictionary Work: Alphabetical Order), board or flip chart, dictionaries, writing materials.

PREPARATION

Write the following on the board or flip chart:

1. *in Adam Grandma's yard hat found the*
2. *to her nursery whistle give rhymes*
3. *cats for all eat fish supper*
4. *This __________ is a __________ of art that deserves to be __________ up on the wall.*

   (pinned, piece, picture)
5. *__________ or you will become __________ and miss your __________.*

   (connection, concentrate, confused)

Introduction

Recall with the children the need for knowing the alphabet and for being able to recognize and arrange words in alphabetical order.

Point to 'sentence' 1 written on the board or flip chart and ask the class what is wrong with the sentence. Can they put it in the correct order to make sense? (*Adam found Grandma's hat in the yard.*) Can they tell you anything interesting about the order of the words in the sentence? If they do not, explain that the words are in alphabetical order.

Point to the second 'sentence' and ask the children to make sense of it (*Give her nursery rhymes to whistle.*) It should have been easier this time!

Now point to the third 'sentence' and ask them to do the same. (*All cats eat fish for supper.*) Which letters did they need to use to put *fish* and *for* in alphabetical order? Review the need to look at the second letters if the first letters are the same.

Ask the children to complete 'sentence' 4 by putting the three words in brackets into the sentence in alphabetical order. Draw attention to the need for looking at the *third* letter. (*This picture is a piece of art that deserves pinning on the wall.*)

Finally, ask them to complete 'sentence' 5 in the same way. Which letter of the 'c' words did they need to look at? (The fourth letter – *Concentrate or you will become confused and miss your connection.*)

Whole-class skills work

Begin this session with a rapid question-and-answer quiz, testing knowledge of alphabet order. For example:

- What letter comes after h?
- What letter comes before j?
- What is the twenty-fifth letter?
- Which letter comes between k and m?
- Which letters are on either side of v?
- Which letter is the third from the last?

Then explain that in addition to knowing letter order, it is helpful to know which part of the alphabet a letter is in. Dividing the alphabet into, say, four parts means that we can open the dictionary (or any reference book that is organized alphabetically) to roughly the right spot, rather than having to go through it from front to back. Write the alphabet on the board or flip chart and ask for suggestions about how it might be divided into four parts (quartiles), for example:

First: A, B, C, D, E, F, G
Second: H, I, J, K, L, M
Third: N, O, P, Q, R, S
Last: T, U, V, W, X, Y, Z

Then ask the children in which part of a dictionary you would find, for example, the following words or topics: *volcano, kangaroo, hemisphere, quartet, dinosaur, witch, bulldozer, microscope*. Ask them to check by looking up the word as quickly as possible in their dictionaries and putting their hands up as soon as they have found it.

Differentiated group activities

1*: Ask children to find particular words in the dictionary as quickly as possible after you say them. Encourage them to build up speed in finding the right page and then scanning the page for the right word. They should then complete photocopiable page 45 (Dictionary Work: Alphabetical Order) independently.
2 & 3: Work on photocopiable page 45 – at least parts A, B and C. If they are able and have time, they could try part D. They could work in pairs.
4*: Work on parts A and B of the photocopiable sheet on their own or in pairs. Then complete part C and, if time, part D with teacher support.

Conclusion

End the hour by asking the children to share their own jumbled sentences. See if the sentences can be extended by adding perhaps adjectives or adverbs that fit in alphabetically and contextually.

DICTIONARY WORK: ALPHABETICAL ORDER

PART A

The letters in these words are all jumbled up. Put the letters in alphabetical order to find out what these words are. Then put the words in alphabetical order.

otgsh ____________ owlf ____________ hpoc ____________

letb ____________ nkto ____________

iytc ____________ dtapo ____________

ryorl ____________ rtof ____________

PART B

Write each group of words in alphabetical order. Be careful! For words that begin with the same letters you may need to look at the second, third or even fourth letters!

want	____________	operate	____________	groan	____________
arrow	____________	octopus	____________	green	____________
fight	____________	oboe	____________	grumble	____________
angel	____________	opposite	____________	group	____________
weave	____________	only	____________	grocer	____________
fable	____________	once	____________	grunt	____________

PART C

These sentences are all jumbled up. Put the words in alphabetical order to find out what they say.

1. for seats arrive good early
2. dogs pets cuddly nice big make
3. tasty all grocers vegetables green sell
4. on floated a the feather beautiful water bird's lightly
5. saw scorpions Sally scowling scary

PART D

Write two sentences with the words in alphabetical order. Then jumble them up and ask your partner to work out what they say.

HIGHWAYMAN'S HOLLOW

OBJECTIVES

UNIT	SPELLING/VOCABULARY	GRAMMAR/PUNCTUATION	COMPREHENSION/ COMPOSITION
READING POETRY Classic historical poem: 'Highwayman's Hollow' by Gilbert V Yonge.	Investigate new vocabulary in poem. Identify syllables.	Explore grammar of poetry. Practise use of possessive apostrophe.	Read a poem with a historical theme. Study the verse form and rhyme pattern. Respond through drama. Explore figurative language.

ORGANIZATION (2 HOURS)

	INTRODUCTION	WHOLE-CLASS SKILLS WORK	DIFFERENTIATED GROUP ACTIVITIES	CONCLUSION
HOUR 1	Shared reading of poem, followed by discussion of historical context.	Demonstrate how to count syllables and stresses.	1*: Dramatic response to the poem. 2 & 3: Study of the verse form. 4*: Dramatic response to the poem.	Selected pupils from Groups 1 & 4 present their dramatic scenes.
HOUR 2	Re-read the poem. Explore figurative language.	Explain how to indicate rhyme schemes with letters of the alphabet. Practise use of possessive apostrophe.	1: Study of the verse form. 2 & 3*: Dramatic response to the poem. 4: Work on rhyme pattern and rhyming words.	Selected pupils from Groups 2 & 3 present their dramatic scenes.

RESOURCES

Photocopiable pages 49 ('Highwayman's Hollow' poem) and 50 (Investigating Verse Form – 'Highwayman's Hollow'), OHP and acetate (optional), an atmospheric sound effects tape or CD (for example, wind) and player, acting space, board or flip chart, writing materials.

PREPARATION

Prepare enough copies of the poem and the investigating verse form sheet for at least one between two. If possible, copy the illustration only from the poem sheet onto an acetate so that it can be projected on a wall or screen to provide a dramatic backdrop.

Introduction

Distribute copies of the poem and read it aloud as expressively as you can. For added effect, you could use the overhead projector to project the image on the photocopiable sheet onto a wall.

Ask the children to offer their initial responses to the poem. What is the poem about? What is the mood of the poem? What words or phrases are used to convey the mood?

Discuss what highwaymen were and place them in their historical context. What is the meaning of the phrase 'Stand, deliver' which is specifically associated with highwaymen? (*Highwaymen were thieves on horseback who robbed travellers on the highway in the 17th and 18th centuries. Dick Turpin was probably the most notorious. 'Stand and deliver' was what the highwaymen said to their victims which meant 'stand up and give me your money and other valuables'.)*

Whole-class skills work

Prepare children for their group study of verse form by modelling how to count syllables. Use individual words from the first line, and then the whole line as an example. Explain how to hear and mark stresses by slow, emphatic reading. Place a diagonal line over stressed syllables (see line 1, below). Explain how to mark rhymes with letters of the alphabet. Use a different letter for each different rhyme.

/ / / / / / Where the cliff hangs hollow, where the gloom falls chill,	a
You hear something, follow, follow, follow down the hill;	a
Where the horses sweat and lather and the dusk begins to gather	b (with internal rhyme)
It is there that I will meet you and will greet you,	c (with internal rhyme)
You, Sir Traveller.	d

Differentiated group activities

1*: Groups of between four to six children work out a dramatic scene based on the poem, for example the encounter between the highwayman and his supposed victim when, in fact, the highwayman became the victim. Suggest that, for the final presentation, they could perform in front of the projected image (photocopiable page 49) and choose suitable sound effects from a tape or CD. Depending on the size of the group, roles can be allocated, for instance, as follows: director, effects operator, narrator, victim, highwayperson. Move among the groups to provide support as they are preparing their dramatic scenes. You could ask them to 'freeze-frame' the action at any point and ask them questions such as: What are the two characters feeling at this point? What are they thinking? What will they do next?

2 & 3: Complete the investigating verse form sheet on photocopiable page 50. Children should work individually where they are able. Those who need support could be paired with more able children. Allow the group time to come together at the end to share their ideas.

4*: As Group 1, but set a simpler task, for example act out the story in the poem or prepare a choral reading of the poem.

Conclusion

Selected children from Groups 1 and 4 present their dramatic scenes to the whole class. Ideally, this should be done at the front of the classroom, in a drama studio or on the hall stage, with the image from photocopiable page 49 projected behind them. For best effect, try to project the image at floor-to-ceiling size. The projector also acts as a spotlight (the fact that the actors' bodies will make shadows on the screen is a small price to pay for such easily achieved and effective scenery!).

Introduction

Display and re-read the poem. Draw attention to the fact that the whole poem is contained in speech marks. Who is speaking the poem? Is there more than one speaker? *(No. The speaker is the ghost of a highwayman who was killed while trying to rob a traveller.)* Discuss the use of figurative language – in particular, the phrases 'the night falls blind' and 'the dark firs frown'.

Whole-class skills work

Use the title of the poem to revise the possessive apostrophe. Explain that the apostrophe + s indicates ownership or possession. So 'Highwayman's Hollow' shows that the hollow belongs to the highwayman. Ask the children to come up with other examples of their own and write them on the board or flip chart. Then ask the children to work in pairs to play the 'Apostrophe Game' as follows:

- Child 1 thinks of a name or role.
- Child 2 thinks of an object.
- They tell each other what they have thought of.
- They then write it down as a phrase with the apostrophe in the right place.

The game can be fun, as some unexpected combinations arise, for example *the policeman's antler, Dr Marshall's teddy bear*. Leave some time at the end of the session to share some of these.

Differentiated group activities

1: Verse form study.
2 & 3*: Drama activity (as Group 1 above).
4: Find the rhyming words in the poem. Brainstorm and write down other words that belong to those rhyme families.

Conclusion

Selected children from Groups 2 and 3 present their dramatic scenes to the class in the way described above.

FURTHER IDEA

The same technique can be used to explore other poems, for instance 'The Highwayman' by Alfred Noyes. The edition illustrated by Charles Keeping is an excellent one to use, as the illustrations provide evocative backdrops.

HIGHWAYMAN'S HOLLOW

"Where the cliff hangs hollow, where the gloom falls chill,
You hear a something, follow, follow, follow down the hill;
Where the horses sweat and lather and the dusk begins to gather
It is there that I will meet you and will greet you,
You, Sir Traveller."

"Where the leaves lie rotting and the night falls blind,
You hear a someone trotting, trotting, trotting down the wind,
And you listen all a-shiver to my ghostly 'Stand, deliver,'
Yes, although my bones have whitened, you are frightened
Yet, Sir Traveller."

"'Twas a traveller who slew me where the dark firs frown,
'Twas his small sword through me and the blood dripped down.
Where the horses sweat and lather and the dusk begins to gather,
It is there I ride behind you to remind you,
You, Sir Traveller."

Gilbert V Yonge

HIGHWAYMAN'S HOLLOW

■ Choose some words from the poem and clap out the syllables.

■ Choose a line from the poem and count the syllables in the whole line. Write down your answer next to the line.

■ Do the same with another line, then a whole verse.

■ Choose a line. Read it aloud slowly and emphatically. Read it again and tap out the stressed syllables. Mark the stressed syllables with a diagonal line.

■ Work out which lines rhyme and mark out the rhyme pattern with letters of the alphabet.

■ Do you think lines 3 and 5 rhyme? Give reasons for your answer.

■ Write down all the words that rhyme in the first verse. Do they all occur at the end of lines? What do you notice? Look at the second verse. Is it the same?

■ Think of more rhyming words to match those in the poem. How many different spellings are used for the same rhyme?

■ Find out what a **refrain** is. Which line in the poem is the refrain?

HAIKU

OBJECTIVES

UNIT	SPELLING/VOCABULARY	GRAMMAR/PUNCTUATION	COMPREHENSION/ COMPOSITION
WRITING POETRY Haiku.	Practise tapping out syllables. Use a thesaurus to find synonyms with required number of syllables.	Learn how to bend rules of grammar for poetic purpose. Use punctuation to clarify meaning.	Read and write haiku to develop understanding of verse format and economy of expression.

ORGANIZATION (1 HOUR)

INTRODUCTION	WHOLE-CLASS SKILLS WORK	DIFFERENTIATED GROUP ACTIVITIES	CONCLUSION
Explain the Japanese origin of haiku and read the examples. Briefly discuss how each one creates its effect. Emphasize economy of expression.	Revise how to count syllables. Show pupils how to use a thesaurus to find alternative words or to say things in a different way in order to keep the syllable pattern.	1–4: In pairs, all pupils experiment with haiku. They should be encouraged to help each other and to redraft frequently. *The teacher supports the less able.	Each pupil reads out one haiku.

RESOURCES

Photocopiable page 53 (Haiku Poems), OHP and acetate (optional), thesauruses, writing materials.

PREPARATION

Make enough copies of photocopiable page 53 for at least one between two children. If possible, prepare it also as an OHT.

Introduction

If possible, display photocopiable page 53 (Haiku Poems) on an OHP. Read aloud the examples of haiku poetry, some of which were written by children. Explain to the children that haiku (pronounced *high-coo*) is a Japanese form of unrhymed poetry, which is highly valued for its economy of expression. Each poem is about a single idea and consists of only 17 syllables. (Remind children that a syllable is a part of a word that you can say on its own.) In Japan these are represented by 17 Japanese characters, each of which represents a syllable. (Some of these characters are illustrated on the photocopiable sheet.) In English, the haiku is written in three lines with five syllables in the first line, seven in the second line and five again in the third line.

Whole-class skills work

Remind the children how to count syllables. The best way to do this is to say a word or line slowly and emphatically and clap or tap each sound. Ask the children to count the syllables in words of different length, for example *butterflies*, *feather*, *crash*. Then ask them to tap out the pattern of one of the haiku on the photocopiable sheet. Now ask them to think of alternative words for some of those in the poems on the sheet. Demonstrate how using a thesaurus is useful to help find words which keep to the syllable pattern. Encourage experimenting with trying to say the same thing in different ways.

Differentiated group activities

Children should work in pairs to write their own haiku. They should be encouraged to experiment freely and revise frequently. Above all, they should strive to say something worthwhile within the constraints of the form. Support less able children by offering ideas for subjects for their poems and by helping them to brainstorm relevant words and descriptive phrases.

Conclusion

Aim to enable each pair of children to read out their haiku. Draw attention to those poems which are particularly successful such as those that say something well or contain a striking image.

FURTHER IDEA

Japanese haiku were beautifully presented in Japanese characters on illustrated scrolls. The children could prepare their best haiku for presentation using the Japanese characters on the photocopiable sheet for decoration.

FOLLOW-UP (1 HOUR)

See page 205 which provides a grid plan for a 1-hour follow-up unit on writing a haiku sequence as a class.

HAIKU POEMS

Spring
Warm April sunrise –
Tender green shoots pierce the soil
Aiming for the sun.
Anonymous

A silvery world
All the fields and hills
have been captured by the snow
and nothing is left.
Joso

Fear
Shivers down the spine,
Butterflies in the stomach,
Cold sweat on the brow.
Steven Scogings

Ghosts
Ghosts, ghouls, all whirring,
Scaring us out of our house,
Slamming doors deftly.
Steve Crane

Candle
That feather of flame
melting the window's ice skin
guides us through the night.
Wes Magee

Robin
As heavy snow falls
he's a red-vested Batman
on the garden fence.
Wes Magee

Summer
The sun's shining face
beams down on seaside swimmers
as foamy waves crash.
Unknown

ZARG ENTERS

OBJECTIVES

UNIT	SPELLING/VOCABULARY	GRAMMAR/PUNCTUATION	COMPREHENSION/ COMPOSITION
READING PLAYS 'Zarg Enters'.	Understand and use vocabulary related to drama conventions.	Mark up text to support reading aloud. Identify statements, questions, orders and exclamations.	Read a playscript with expression. Respond imaginatively to character and plot. Compare organization of a playscript with stories – how are settings indicated, storylines made clear?

ORGANIZATION (3 HOURS)

	INTRODUCTION	WHOLE-CLASS SKILLS WORK	DIFFERENTIATED GROUP ACTIVITIES	CONCLUSION
HOUR 1	Look at the script with pupils, explaining how to use it.	Explain the importance of expression in reading. Practise this in pairs. Identify statements, questions, orders and exclamations.	Read the play in mixed-ability groups of four or five.	One group should be chosen to read part 1 and another to read part 2.
HOUR 2	Revise the term 'blocking'.	Pupils discuss ideas and plan their blocking on paper.	Try out their blocking and then rehearse the play.	The rest of the class evaluates the readings. Two different groups present their blocked version of the play.
HOUR 3	Discuss how the play might end.	Explain improvisation skills.	Allocate each group an improvisation.	Discuss differences between plays and stories.

RESOURCES

Photocopiable pages 57–61 ('Zarg Enters' Playscript), a large space (drama studio or hall, if available, otherwise a classroom with tables pushed out of the way), OHP and acetate (optional), simple 'props' such as three exercise books, a pair of glasses, odds and ends to dress up an alien, a school register, a lunch box with something revolting inside, a pocket calculator (to use as the alien's computer), writing materials, some photographs.

PREPARATION

Make enough copies of the play on photocopiable pages 57–61 to allow one for each child. Prepare a performance area at the front of the studio, hall or classroom. This should contain some children's desks and chairs facing a teacher's desk and chair.

Introduction

Explore the script with the children, explaining how to use it. Explain that the scene description and stage directions are printed in italics (the stage directions are also in brackets) and should not be read out. Remind the children how the words spoken by each character are written exactly as they are spoken, without the use of the words 'said', 'asked' and so on.

Whole-class skills work

Remind the children of the importance of expression in reading, particularly in plays. Ask different children in turn to look out of the classroom window and to describe what they see in different ways – as if they are disappointed, delighted, jealous, surprised. Emphasize the need to use voice expression, facial expression and gestures to communicate. Suggest that as they look out of the window they discover the classroom is flying through space. Choose a couple of children to communicate what they see and how they feel.

Revise the four types of sentence: statements, questions, orders and exclamations:

- Statements end with a full stop and a *falling* intonation (tone of voice).
- Questions end with a question mark and a *rising* intonation.
- Orders end with a full stop or exclamation mark and have a *level, 'clipped'* intonation.
- Exclamations end with an exclamation mark and have a *high, rising* intonation.

Ask children to identify some of each in the playscript and to practise reading them with the correct intonation.

Differentiated group activities

Groupings for this unit are mixed-ability groups of five. If a group of six is necessary because of total numbers, the sixth person should be a narrator and read all the text in italics. Tell the children not to try to match gender. Groups should then allocate parts and read the play a number of times, concentrating on developing realistic expression. Encourage them to mark their text with reminders to help expression. They could also underline or highlight their part, just as real actors do. During the session, give organizational support to all groups. Differentiation can be provided by allocating the parts of Zarg and Mrs Scratchit to more able children as the roles are a little more challenging.

Conclusion

One group should be chosen to read the first part (up to the point of 'take off', where the script is marked with asterisks) and another to read the second part. The rest of the class should evaluate the readings by commenting on how true to life the reader's expression was and giving suggestions for improvement.

Introduction

Explain to the class that they are now going to plan out the movements for their play and that this process is called 'blocking'. When movements are being planned, they need to keep in mind the position of the audience to ensure that they have a clear view of everything that happens and that the actors are facing the audience as much as possible. The front of the classroom could be arranged as a simple performance area and, although only one group will be able to rehearse in it, all groups should plan with that space in mind.

Whole-class skills work

Ask the whole class to brainstorm and list ideas for the movements performed by the actors throughout the play. First they should look at what the script already provides in the way of blocking information. Then they should try to come up with ideas for enhancing/expanding this. Remind the class that the characters need to be looking at the person they are speaking to, that movements and gestures need to reflect what is being said, that they should try to avoid turning their backs to the audience and so on. Discuss how the blocking ideas might be indicated on the script. Suggest the uses of notes and/or symbols: for example, move ➔; X to window; FX knock (FX is standard 'jargon' for effects, as in sound effects!).

Differentiated group activities

Each group should plan its ideas and make notes on paper before beginning to try them out in the space allocated. All groups should try out their blocking and then rehearse the whole play a number of times. Give support where required, particularly advising on how enactment can reflect and add to the meaning of the script.

Conclusion

Two different groups present their version of the fully blocked play in the performance area. Other children should be encouraged to evaluate the blocking: Can they see what is happening? Do the movements help to put across the meaning of the words? Can all actors be heard clearly? Did the expression of the actors make the audience believe that the classroom was flying through space?

Introduction

Revise the term 'improvisation'. It means: 'making it up as you go along'. It is a technique often used by actors when they practise and also in performance as a way of creating true-to-life dialogue.

Whole-class skills work

Model the technique for the whole class by inviting two children to the front of the class. Give them a scenario to improvise, for example: 'You have promised to meet a friend after school to play, but your mum is saying that you need to come home and do your homework.' Prompt them when necessary, ask for suggestions from other children and make it clear that improvisation requires careful listening as partners have to respond realistically to what each says. Then ask children to practise in pairs the following improvisation: 'Try to persuade somebody that you have just seen a flying saucer'.

Differentiated group activities

Allocate one of the following 'What if...' improvisations to each group:
- Mrs Scratchit finds her glasses when the alien first comes into the classroom.
- Bof's computer programming does not work.
- Zarg takes them to the museum on Krell.
- The classroom is attacked by an alien spaceship.
- Zarg falls in love with Karen.
- Mrs Scratchit puts Zarg in detention.

Conclusion

Select a group who have not performed previously to present their improvisation. Follow it up by translating it into the beginning of a playscript on the board or flip chart. Discuss which elements of the improvisation constitute the 'dialogue' and what would need to be written as scene setting and stage directions.

FOLLOW-UP (2 HOURS)

See page 206 which provides a grid plan for a 2-hour follow-up unit that investigates the difference between stories and plays and involves children in writing the 'Zarg Enters' play as a story.

'ZARG ENTERS' PLAYSCRIPT (1)

CAST
Mrs Scratchit – a teacher
Zarg – an alien
Bof – a schoolboy (real name Billy, but a computer boffin)
Kirsty – a schoolgirl
Karen – a schoolgirl

SCENE: *A typical morning in an English primary school. Mrs Scratchit turns from the handwriting lesson which she is writing on the board to find the pupils staring out of the window.*

Mrs S: Billy, what are you staring at?
Bof: An alien spaceship, Miss.
Mrs S: Don't talk rubbish, Billy. Now turn round and get on with your work.
Bof: But, Miss, there really is an alien spaceship!
Kirsty: He's right Miss, and it's huge!
Karen: It must be at least 15 miles wide!

(Mrs Scratchit goes to the window to see what all the nonsense is about, but she can't see very far without her glasses.)

Mrs S: (*Trying to see*) Just as I thought, there's nothing there!
Pupils: (*Together*) Miss, you forgot to put your glasses on!
Mrs S: Nonsense. I can see perfectly well, thank you.
Kirsty: (*Whispering*) That's what she thinks!
Mrs S: Now get on with your work, or you'll stay in at break.

(They work quietly for a few moments. Suddenly there is a knock at the door.)

Mrs S: That must be the new boy we've been expecting. Come in.

(Zarg enters.)

Bof: (*Whispering to Kirsty*) Uh oh, it's an alien!
Kirsty: Uurrgghh!!! He's got stick-out eyes, green skin and eight tentacles!

'ZARG ENTERS' PLAYSCRIPT (2)

Karen: You never know, he might have a nice personality.
Mrs S: (*Trying to see*) Hello, what's your name?
Zarg: (*In a metallic voice*) Zarg.
Mrs S: (*Writing in the register*) My, what an unusual name! Where are you from?
Zarg: Krell.
Mrs S: I've never heard of it. Is it far?
Zarg: 122 light-years away.
Mrs S: No jokes, please. My register must be correct. What I really need to know is – do you come on the school bus?
Zarg: There is no bus service from Krell.
Mrs S: Are you a school dinner or a packed lunch?
Zarg: A packed lunch.

(He opens a small box he is carrying. The pupils crane their necks to see inside. The food looks disgusting.)

Pupils: Uurgghh!!
Mrs S: That will do for now. Sit down.
Zarg: I will not obey the orders of an earthling.
Mrs S: How dare you contradict me!
Zarg: I am the commander of a spaceship which could blow you to pieces in an instant. All I have to do is press one button on my computer.

(He holds up a small computer. Bof looks interested. Mrs Scratchit tries to find her glasses, but fails.)

Mrs S: Nonsense! You're as bad as the rest of them. Now, sit down before I lose my temper.

(Zarg sits next to Bof and starts tapping keys on his computer.)

Mrs S: Zarg, you naughty boy, what are you doing now?
Zarg: I am commanding my ship to take this classroom back to Krell.
Mrs S: What a silly excuse! You are not allowed to use a computer for a handwriting lesson. Get out a pen at once!
Zarg: I do not have the device you call a 'pen'.
Mrs S: (*Sighing with exasperation*) I suppose

'ZARG ENTERS' PLAYSCRIPT (3)

I'll have to lend you one from my stock cupboard.

Karen: (*Alarmed*) The classroom's going all wobbly!

Kirsty: We're taking off!

* * * * * * * * * * *

(Mrs Scratchit goes to the stock cupboard to find a spare pen for Zarg. While her back is turned, Kirsty and Karen rush to the window.)

Karen: Hey, we're in space!

Kirsty: Look, that's the moon. You can see the craters.

Karen: Look at that funny red planet.

Bof: That's Mars.

Kirsty: Wow, look at Saturn! Aren't those rings beautiful?

Karen: We seem to be going faster and faster.

Kirsty: Jupiter... Uranus... Neptune... Pluto...

Karen: Hey, I don't recognize that planet. What is it called, Bof?

Bof: Don't know, I've never seen it before! (*To himself*) Come to think of it, I've never seen any of the planets before...

Zarg: That is Krell. Soon we will be there.

Bof: What are you going to do with us?

Zarg: This classroom will be placed in the Krell Museum of Primitive Life Forms.

Kir/Kar: (*Together*) You mean, we'll be like animals in a zoo?

Zarg: That is correct.

Kir/Kar: (*Together*) Aaarrrggghhh!!!

Mrs S: What is all this noise about? Now get back to your handwriting practice. Zarg, here's a pen.

(Zarg takes the pen, examines it carefully, shakes it, puts it to his ear and so on, trying to figure out what it is.)

Karen: (*Whispering to Bof*) What can we do?

Bof: Er... panic?

Kirsty: You're the computer whizz kid, can't you do something to his computer?

Bof: That's a good idea! I'll try.

(Bof carefully sneaks the computer away from Zarg who is engrossed in trying to figure out what to do with the pen. Bof taps on the keyboard for a while.)

Bof: (*Shaking his head*) I've got into the program but I can't

'ZARG ENTERS' PLAYSCRIPT (4)

understand it. The only computer language I know is Q-Basic and this is nothing like it!

Karen: (*Wailing*) I don't want to spend the rest of my life in a zoo!

Kirsty: We've got to think of something.

(They think for a few moments. Karen is still wailing.)

Kirsty: Listen, suppose you just copy it back into the computer, only *backwards*. Would it get us home again?

Bof: It's worth a try. (*Bof taps at the keyboard while Kirsty and Karen look on anxiously.*) Done it! Oh, and I'll just add one more thing. Here we go! *(He presses a key.)*

(Kirsty and Karen rush to a window.)

Karen: It's working! We're going backwards!

Kirsty: You're right – there's Pluto!

Bof: Shh! Come over here and make sure he doesn't notice.

(Kirsty and Karen sit down just in time, because Mrs Scratchit has finished what she's writing on the board. She goes back to her desk to look for her glasses. Zarg soon gets tired of trying to use a pen.)

Zarg: (*Throwing pen on floor*) What a stupid thing!

Karen: Never mind that, Zarg. Would you like to see my holiday photographs?

Zarg: What is a holiday?

Karen: It's when you go away from home and have fun.

Zarg: You mean, like I'm doing now? Destroying other people's planets and that sort of thing?

Karen: Not really. Look, this is me swimming in the sea, this is my brother building a sandcastle... (*and so on until Zarg falls asleep through boredom*).

(Suddenly there is a bump and everyone nearly falls over.)

Kirsty: We're back safely! Thank goodness.

Bof: Look! The program's still working!

(They watch in amazement as Zarg walks out backwards. Then they run to the window.)

'ZARG ENTERS' PLAYSCRIPT (5)

Karen: His ship's taking off!
Kirsty: I hope we never see it again!
Bof: We won't. I programmed all their bombs to go off in... (*He looks at his watch.*)
Kir/Kar: (*Together*) ...Four, three, two, one...

(There is a sound like thunder and a brilliant flash of light.)

Pupils: (*Shouting with joy*) WOWEE!!
Mrs S: (*Looking up from her desk and putting her glasses on*) Wasting time again! I've found my glasses and I'm coming to see how much you've done!
Pupils: Uh oh!
Mrs S: As I thought – nothing! You'll all have to stay in at break!
Kirsty: But Miss, there was an alien spaceship.
Karen: And the alien came into our classroom.
Kirsty: And took us to the planet Krell.
Bof: And I fixed his computer and brought us back again.
Karen: And blew them all up!
Kirsty: And saved the human race!
Mrs S: (*Staring*) Well, really! (*To audience*) And they say that children today have no imagination!

WOLF IN THE WOODS

OBJECTIVES

UNIT	SPELLING/VOCABULARY	GRAMMAR/PUNCTUATION	COMPREHENSION/ COMPOSITION
WRITING PLAYS 'Wolf in the Woods'.	Develop vocabulary related to television scripts.	Write a television script using layout conventions correctly. Identify and classify adverbs.	Write a television script with convincing dialogue. Compare features of a playscript and television script.

ORGANIZATION

INTRODUCTION	WHOLE-CLASS SKILLS WORK	DIFFERENTIATED GROUP ACTIVITIES	CONCLUSION
HOUR 1 Show video extract and then identify scenes. Display and read photocopiable sheet 'Wolf in the Woods' television script extract.	Compare stage and television scripts. Explain key features and terms of a television script.	1–4: Plan a continuation of script using a storyboard. Pupils work in pairs. *Teacher works with Groups 2 & 3.	Selected pupils display and discuss their storyboards. Review features of television script and layout.
HOUR 2 Re-read 'Wolf in the Woods'. Discuss what makes convincing dialogue.	Examine layout conventions. Identify and classify adverbs.	1–4: Write television scripts based on their storyboard plans. *Teacher works with Groups 1 & 4.	Selected pupils read out their work and display their scripts. Compare them with the storyboard plans.

RESOURCES

Photocopiable pages 64 (Television Script) and 24 (Storyboard from 'It's Too Frightening For Me!' unit), 5–10 minute video extract from a television play/drama (an extract showing several short scenes from a currently popular soap opera would be ideal), television, video recorder, OHP and acetate (optional), board or flip chart, writing materials.

PREPARATION

Prepare a video extract as described above. If possible, make OHTs of photocopiable pages 64 (Television Script) and 24 (Storyboard). If an OHP is not available, make enough copies for one between two children and one enlarged copy (to at least A3 size).

Introduction

Tell the children you are going to show them a short video extract of a television drama. Explain that you want them to jot down in note form the different scenes as they watch it. Show the extract, then make a list of the scenes (of which there should be several).

Display the 'Wolf in the Woods' television script and explain that it is just the beginning of a television script. Read it through as a preparation for explaining the layout conventions in detail. (Note that the photocopiable resource uses a simplified set of conventions which are suitable for use by children.)

Whole-class skills work

Using the model provided by the 'Wolf in the Woods' script, discuss how a playscript differs from a television script. Make a list of the children's suggestions on the board or flip chart, ensuring that the following key points are brought out.

■ Television scenes are usually much shorter and there are more of them.
■ Television enables the scenes to move quickly in time and place. Writers for the stage have to allow for scenery being moved!
■ Television makes use of carefully planned camera angles. Explain some key terms: *close up* (showing head or head and shoulders), *zoom* (the camera moves in quickly on the subject), *pan* (the camera moves 'panoramically' from side to side).
■ Television usually makes more use of music and sound effects.

Finally, explain to the children that they will be writing a continuation of the 'Wolf in the Woods' television script, and that the first step is to plan their script. Show a copy of the storyboard photocopiable sheet (taken from the first unit 'It's Too Frightening For Me!'). Explain that storyboards are used by television and film producers to plan out the main scenes.

Differentiated group activities

With children working in pairs, all groups should use the storyboard frame to plan their script. The first two frames should be filled in using the scenes already written in the 'Wolf in the Woods' script. The children should then think of two more scenes that will continue and then end the script. Children in Group 1 may wish to plan more than two scenes, in which case give them extra copies of the storyboard. Support Groups 2 and 3.

Conclusion

Select children from each group to show and talk about their storyboards. Discuss how aspects might later be translated into the television script.

Introduction

Shared reading of the 'Wolf in the Woods' script. Discuss the importance of realistic dialogue. Display a copy of 'Wolf in the Woods'. Point out that real television scripts are very much more complicated than the one displayed, but the children should follow the simple conventions in the example. Character names, Camera and Sound FX (FX is short for 'effects') should be written in the margin. Dialogue begins immediately to the right of the margin. Note that there are no stage directions. These should be written as instructions for the camera.

Whole-class skills work

Remind the children what an adverb is and identify the adverbs in the 'Wolf in the Woods' script. Classify them according to whether they describe how someone speaks, how the camera moves or how the sound is heard. Brainstorm examples for each category.

Differentiated group activities

All groups should write their television scripts based on the storyboard plans they made. Begin working with Group 4, supporting them as they write out their scenes. Explain that the important thing is not length, but ideas, realistic dialogue, and *imagining* the play in the television medium. Then work with Group 1 who should be encouraged to exploit the television medium to the full.

Conclusion

Selected children read out their work and display their scripts. Compare them to the storyboard plans and evaluate how well they have translated their ideas into the formal conventions of a television script.

FURTHER IDEA

If the school has access to a camcorder, this exercise could be followed by genuine planning and scripting to make a film. The following guidelines will help:
■ Encourage children to write a play set in familiar surroundings, for example the classroom, the school grounds and so on.
■ The main characters should be children and adults in the school.
■ Keep it short. Three scenes from a play would be a more realistic target than a whole play.
■ Write the storyboard and script in two hours as described above.
■ Actual filming could take place on a rota basis over the following week.

TELEVISION SCRIPT

CAST	Mr Martin, Tim, Andy, Amy, Kylie, other pupils.
SCENE 1	*MR MARTIN'S CLASSROOM*
CAMERA	*Long shot of Mr Martin's classroom. Zoom in quickly on Mr Martin's face. He is looking worried.*
SOUND FX	*Spooky music, fading slowly to silence.*
MR MARTIN:	Where's Kylie?
ANDY:	Gone, Sir.
MR MARTIN:	Gone? Gone where?
ANDY:	Gone home, Sir.
MR MARTIN:	Why would she want to do that?
ANDY:	'Cause Tim was teasing her, Sir.
MR MARTIN:	Is this true, Tim?
TIM:	No, Sir. Absolutely not, Sir!
OTHER PUPILS:	*(Shouting loudly)* Yes, Sir!
CAMERA	*Close up of Tim's face. He blushes with embarrassment. Then cut sharply to close up of Mr Martin.*
MR MARTIN:	Which way did she go?
ANDY:	She always goes through the woods, Sir.
MR MARTIN:	I've heard strange stories about those woods. I hope she's all right!
CAMERA	*Follow Mr Martin's gaze through the classroom window and out into the woods.*
SOUND FX	*Fade up spooky music.*
CAMERA	*Cut.*
SCENE 2	*WILLOW WOODS*
CAMERA	*Shot of gloomy, damp wood. After a while, Kylie, wearing a red anorak with the hood up, walks nervously into the scene.*
SOUND FX	*Noise of howling wind and spooky music. Both fade to silence as Kylie stops and looks round frantically.*
CAMERA	*Pans the scene jerkily, following Kylie's gaze.*
SOUND FX	*Twig snaps suddenly.*
KYLIE:	*(Whispering fearfully)* Who's there?
SOUND FX	*Sudden crash of spooky music (organ chords).*
CAMERA	*Spins wildly round behind Kylie to focus on the shadowy outline of a wolf.*
KYLIE:	*(Screams chillingly.)*
CAMERA	Cut.

The School Times

OBJECTIVES

UNIT	SPELLING/VOCABULARY	GRAMMAR/PUNCTUATION	COMPREHENSION/ COMPOSITION
READING NON-FICTION Report genre: 'The School Times'.	Revise work from Year 3 on common homophones.	Recognize layout features: headline, subheading, columns, illustrations, captions. Investigate the grammar of headlines.	Identify different types of text. Identify main features of newspapers.

ORGANIZATION (2 HOURS)

	INTRODUCTION	WHOLE-CLASS SKILLS WORK	DIFFERENTIATED GROUP ACTIVITIES	CONCLUSION
HOUR 1	Read 'The School Times'. Discuss differences in style compared to other kinds of texts.	Ask pupils to find the following layout features: headline, subheading, columns, illustrations, captions.	1: Find examples of the key layout features in real newspapers. 2 & 3* (pairs within groups): Re-read the school newspaper. 4: Label the layout features in the school newspaper.	Recap on layout features: how do they help you to read the newspaper?
HOUR 2	Read an extract from the front page of a real newspaper.	Investigate the grammar of headlines. Revise and extend understanding of homophones. Identify examples in 'The School Times'.	1*: Read a real newspaper and explore vocabulary and style. 2 & 3: Find examples of the key layout features in real newspapers. 4*: Re-read the school newspaper.	Compare the layout of the school newspaper with the real newspaper. What features do they have in common? What additional features does the real newspaper have?

RESOURCES

Photocopiable page 67 ('The School Times') and a selection of newspapers, including tabloids and broadsheets (a children's newspaper such as 'The Early Times' would be preferable for close study as there is no danger of unsuitable language or illustrations, and the text will be better suited to the age group), OHP and acetate (optional), board or flip chart, sheets of A3 paper, writing materials.

PREPARATION

Make enough copies of photocopiable page 67 ('The School Times') for at least one between each pair of children. If possible, prepare also an OHT of the front page (or extract) from a real newspaper. Make a list of the key layout features (headlines, subheads, photographs and captions, text in columns) on an OHT, board or flip chart.

Introduction

Read 'The School Times' together and talk about the nature of the stories. Can the children think of similar stories about their own school? Look at the layout of the page – how is it different from the way in which pages of a book are presented?

Whole-class skills work

Display the list of key layout features and ask the children to identify examples in the school newspaper. Check that they know the meaning of each term.

Make a list of about six different headlines, using headlines and subheadings from 'The School Times' and examples from the other newspapers. Investigate the grammar of headlines. The following characteristics should be noted:

- They are in the present tense.
- They are short and to the point. Key words are used and non-essential words omitted to keep them short, for example 'Titanic Sinks – Great Loss of Life'.
- They are usually written in upper case (all capital letters) or title case (lower case with capital letters at the beginning of all words except connectives).

Differentiated group activities

1: Identify and label key layout features in real newspapers. Discuss how these features help the reader.
2 & 3*: Subdivide the groups into pairs of children to read 'The School Times' to each other. Work with these groups to support basic reading skills. Discuss page layout and the content of the articles.
4: Label the layout features in 'The School Times'. An effective way to do this is to stick the newspaper onto an A3 sheet and draw labels with lines to the various features.

Conclusion

Begin by checking that children have understood and remembered the terms taught. Then discuss each in turn and the key question: how did it help you to read the newspaper?

Introduction

A real newspaper front page should be displayed (on OHP if possible) and one or two articles read out to the class while they follow. Talk about the kind of language used, particularly in headlines and captions. How does it differ from spoken language? How does it differ from the language used in books? Talk about the level of formality used.

Whole-class skills work

Revise the term 'homophones' which means 'words which sound alike'. These words have different meanings; the spellings are often different as well. Several homophones are the cause of common errors in writing. In the list below, read each sentence aloud twice. Ask the children to listen carefully and to identify the homophones. Then ask them to spell the appropriate homophone correctly. Make a list of the homophones on the board or chart.

- We wondered (whether, weather) the (weather, whether) would improve.
- She looked for (there, their, they're) photographs.
- It is (too, two, to) cold!
- I must not forget to (write, right) that letter.
- Why don't you (where, wear) that red tie?
- We went to (buy, by) a CD player.
- The mouse nibbled at a (piece, peace) of cheese.
- The (hole, whole) class enjoyed the story.

Finally, ask the children to look again at 'The School Times' and to find other examples of homophones. Add these to the list.

Differentiated group activities

1*: Read some articles in the real newspapers. Underline homophones and highlight any interesting vocabulary. Look out for words and phrases the journalist has used to convey information and those that make the article exciting. Examine opening sentences that set scenes or capture interest. Discuss the intended audience. Help with tasks and ask questions to test understanding of the content of the articles.
2 & 3: Find and label examples of key layout features in real newspapers (see above).
4*: Guided reading of 'The School Times' with teacher support. Less able readers should concentrate on just one section of the newspaper.

Conclusion

Compare the layout of 'The School Times' with the real newspaper, looking for features they share in common and additional features in the real newspaper. This will reinforce knowledge of basic page design and terminology and will enable many children to learn about additional layout features to use when writing their own newspapers.

THE SCHOOL TIMES

June 1998 No. 10 Free to all pupils

NO BLUES FOR THE BLUES

Sports Day draws record-breaking crowds

A record number of parents came to watch and cheer at our summer sports day.

Fortunately, the weather was fine, although the forecast had predicted rain. The fun-filled day featured an egg and spoon race, a sack race and a mountain-bike race. Later on there were two football games, a rounders game and a tension-filled tug of war. Team points were given to the winners of each event. The Blue Team beat the Red Team by just one point! The photograph shows the Blue Team winning its final victory.

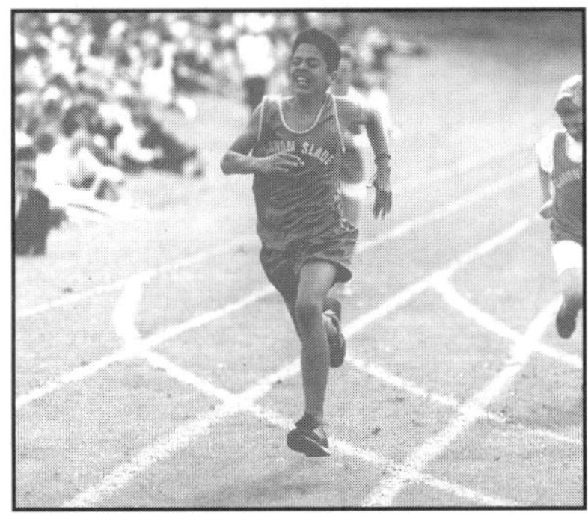

The Blue Team's victory

SCHOOL GETS FACELIFT

During the summer, while we are all having fun in the sun, *some* people will be hard at work at school.

Two new classrooms will be added to the school this summer. There will also be improvements to the library, computer centre and the school office. Most important will be a new school drive and parking area so that children can be picked up and dropped off safely.

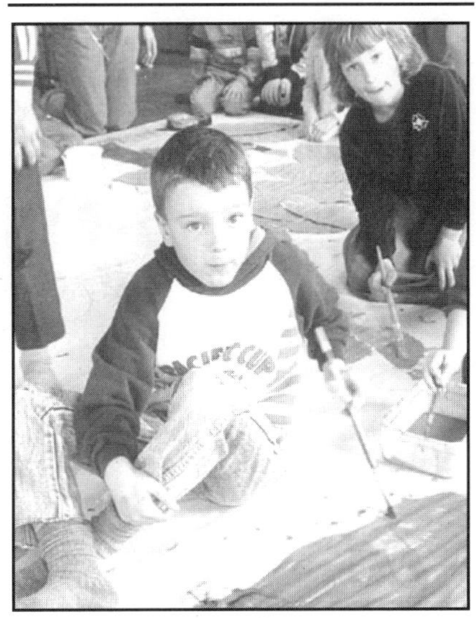

Neil McIntosh working on one of the wall-hangings

BUSY BEAVERS ON GROUNDS DAY

We had our very first 'Grounds Day' on 2nd May.

First we collected all the litter and weeded the borders. Then we painted wall-hangings showing animals and birds which belong to endangered species. Some of us marked out games on paving stones. We also planted new plants in the borders. At the end of the day we held an outdoor concert to which parents were invited. Let's hope we can make this an annual event.

PUT AN END TO BULLYING

All children in the Junior department have been asked to fill in a questionnaire on bullying.

This is the start of an effort to find out what is really happening. Part of the questionnaire is a plan of the school grounds so that children can mark where most bullying takes place. We think this is a great idea, and we think all children should fill it in honestly so that we can help the teachers to help us.

IT'S PLAYTIME!

The school play will be 'Ali Baba'.

This has been written by two teachers, Mrs Darrel and Mr Smith. It includes lots of well-known songs, and there will be a chance to dress up in fancy costumes.

Can you help?

If you can't sing, then why not be a dancer? We need at least forty thieves! If you can't sing or dance, you could always join the backstage crew to paint scenery or make costumes. Contact Mrs Darrel if you would like to be part of the great world of theatre!

NEWSPAPER CONSTRUCTION KIT

OBJECTIVES

UNIT	SPELLING/VOCABULARY	GRAMMAR/PUNCTUATION	COMPREHENSION/ COMPOSITION
WRITING NON-FICTION Recount genre: Newspaper Construction Kit.	Identify and use 'news' words.	Use layout features: headline, subheading, columns, illustrations, captions.	Develop note-taking skills. Write newspaper-style reports about school events.

ORGANIZATION (3 HOURS)

	INTRODUCTION	WHOLE-CLASS SKILLS WORK	DIFFERENTIATED GROUP ACTIVITIES	CONCLUSION
HOUR 1	Shared reading of 'The School Times'. Discuss what makes an interesting article.	Explain note-taking skills. Short practice session.	1–3: Practise note-taking in pairs (teacher support where needed). 4*: Teacher models the process for the group.	Pupils describe events using notes. Recap on note-taking skills.
HOUR 2	Read an example of reporter's notes and demonstrate how they can be turned into an interesting article.	Model turning notes into article.	1–4*: Add words to 'News Words' sheet. Write first draft of a newspaper article from notes and using 'News Words' where appropriate.	Pupils asked to interview someone and take notes at break or after school.
HOUR 3	Discussion on redrafting and proofreading.	Explanation of how to use newspaper templates.	1–4: Redraft, proofread and present final copy of newspaper. *Teacher works with Groups 2 & 3 after initial support for Group 4.	Share some first drafts. Discussion on awareness of audience and suggestions for redrafting. Groups share their finished work. Recap on key skills and concepts.

RESOURCES

Photocopiable page 67 ('The School Times' from previous unit) and pages 71–74 (Note-taking Skills, News Words, Newspaper Front Page template, Newspaper Columns template), examples of real newspapers, sheets of A3 paper, OHP and acetate (optional), flip chart or board, scissors, glue, writing materials.

PREPARATION

Prepare enough copies of photocopiable page 67 ('The School Times') to allow for one between two children. Either prepare an OHT of photocopiable page 71 (Note-taking Skills) or prepare photocopies for children's use with parts 3 and 4 blanked out. Prepare enough copies of photocopiable page 72 (News Words) for one for each child. Prepare sets of the 'Newspaper Construction Kit' as follows: photocopiable page 73 (Newspaper Front Page template) should be duplicated (enlarged to A3) to provide one sheet for each of Groups 2 and 3; photocopiable page 74 (Newspaper Columns template) should be duplicated (enlarged to A3) to provide enough sheets for one between two children for Groups 2 and 3, plus some extra copies; photocopiable page 73 (Newspaper Front Page template) should be duplicated (A4 size) to provide one for each child in Group 4.

Introduction

Explain to the children that they are to work in groups to write a newspaper, and that they are going to use 'The School Times' as a model. Re-read 'The School Times' with the children. Ask them which articles are most interesting and why. What makes them interesting? Which phrases bring the articles to life and make them exciting to read?

Whole-class skills work

Explain how journalists gather their news by taking notes and help children to develop their own note-taking skills. This can be done by using the 'Note-taking Skills' sheet: *Either* display parts 1 and 2 on the OHP (keeping parts 3 and 4 covered); *or* give the children a photocopy of parts 1 and 2 only.

- Read through the explanation in part 1 and explain what is meant by *shorthand*.
- Read through the interview with Mrs Darrel (part 2) while children follow the text. Then ask them to work through the points below it.
- Discuss the points with them. The key points in the interview are the name of the teacher, the musical and the dates and times given by the teacher. In sentences 2, 3 and 4 the teacher is just 'chatting' and the information is not essential.
- Display (on OHP or board) the examples of how it could be done (part 3) and discuss.
- Finally, ask the children to try it out again, but this time in a more realistic way, by *listening* to the interview with Mr Beetham (part 4). *Note:* children should not see the text.
- Ask the children to report back on their notes and discuss how they could be improved.

Differentiated group activities

1–3: Children now repeat the process in pairs: one child describes an event that has happened recently in school, for example a school trip, a telling off, an interesting lesson, while his or her partner makes notes. Roles are then reversed.
4*: Repeat the modelling process for Group 4, such as describe an event slowly and elicit suggestions about what children might jot down.

Conclusion

Ask selected children to use their notes to talk about the event their partner described. Discuss: What techniques were used to speed up note-taking? Were the notes legible? Did the notes help the writer to remember the event described? Finally, ask children to use their note-taking skills to gather news items for their newspaper. They could be asked to interview teachers or other children at break or lunchtime.

Introduction

Display some examples of children's notes from the previous hour on the OHP (or write them up on a flip chart or board). Read them out to the class then use them as a basis for a discussion of how they can be turned into an interesting article. Ask the children to identify the main point of the news story. What sort of headline might they use? What words might they use to make the story particularly exciting?

Whole-class skills work

Explain to the children that they are going to write up the notes on their interviews with children and teachers from the previous day as a news article for readers of their own age, and that it should be *interesting*. Stress that this is a journalist's skill – to make everyday news sound exciting. Discuss the words and phrases on the 'News Words' photocopiable sheet and other ways of making an article exciting.

Model this process, using the interview with Mrs Darrel. Display the sample notes, and show how they can be built up into the following text:

Mrs Darrel, who is Class 3's form teacher and the school music co-ordinator, told me about her plans for the next school production. She plans to stage a production of the musical 'Bugsy Malone' at the end of this term. Anyone who would like to be in the musical should go to her room for an audition at 3.30pm next Thursday. Full rehearsals for those given parts will start on the Wednesday after half term. The performance dates will be Tuesday, Wednesday and Thursday of the last week of term.

Point out that further improvements could be made as follows:

- Looking up the exact dates in a calendar, for example '...for an audition at 3.30pm on Thursday 24th September'.
- Looking at the 'News Words' photocopiable sheet for ideas, for example 'Mrs Darrel, who is Class 3's form teacher and the school music co-ordinator, made an *announcement* or *gave me an exclusive interview* about the next school production'.
- Adding some extra comments or sentences to make it more interesting, for example: 'plans to stage a *spectacular* performance...'; '*Bugsy Malone could be the best and most exciting production the school has ever done, so do go along for an audition and encourage your parents to buy tickets for the performance.*'

Differentiated group activities

1–4*: Give all children a copy of the 'News Words' photocopiable sheet. Ask them to spend the first five minutes of this session adding their own words. They could use examples from newspapers to help them.

The children then decide as a group who is going to write which article and begin their first drafts, working at their own level and using their 'News Words' for support.

Conclusion

Select some promising first drafts to be read out and explain to the class what is good about them. Invite suggestions for making them even better. Encourage the children to refer and add to the 'News Words' sheet when doing this.

Introduction

Tell the children that they are now going to use the news stories they have prepared to make their own newspaper pages. The first step is to redraft and proofread their articles.

- Redrafting involves changing words and sentences to make the article more interesting to read. To do this, children should repeat the process of the previous hours' skills sessions.
- Proofreading is checking for mistakes and correcting them. This is best done in pairs, with children helping each other.

Whole-class skills work

The next step is to present their redrafted work neatly in a newspaper format. Explain how to do this by modelling the process using copies of the Front page and Columns templates (photocopiable pages 73 and 74).

Step 1: Groups 2 and 3 should cut up the A3 Columns template sheets so that each group member has one column. Children should write a neat copy of their article onto that column, filling each line as fully as possible (with no margins). They can continue their articles into another column if necessary, although they should be aware of the space they have to fill and be disciplined in the length of their article.

Step 2: Children then decide which article or articles should go on the Front Page template sheet and move the copy around to find the best order. The space left for illustrations is optional. The other articles should be placed onto whole Columns templates to form the subsequent pages of the newspaper.

Step 3: When everyone is satisfied with the layout, paste down the work and add headlines, subheadings and illustrations.

Differentiated group activities

The aim is for each group to have produced a mini newspaper by the end of the session.

1: Can be given a free hand to design their own more sophisticated front page using real newspapers as a model.

2 & 3*: Use the templates to support the layout of their articles. The teacher will need to work with these groups to help with management of the templates. They may wish to think of their own title for their newspaper.

4: Children in this group should write directly onto the Front Page template at A4 size, which provides a framework for their writing. They can then decide whose article will be the actual front page and delete the 'School Times' title from the subsequent pages.

Conclusion

Ask the children to swap their newspaper pages and read and discuss each other's articles.

NOTE-TAKING SKILLS

PART 1

When journalists take notes they:

■ write quickly

■ use abbreviations, for example they write full names just once, then write the initials only, use the symbol **+** for the word **and**, miss vowels out of common words and so on.

■ jot down key points only – single words are sometimes enough.

Note that many journalists achieve all these requirements by using *shorthand*.

PART 2

Imagine that you interview Mrs Darrel about the next school production. This is what she says:

Next term I am hoping to put on the musical 'Bugsy Malone'. I saw it done by a school in Overhill and it's really good for a school performance – all the characters are kids. That's true – even in the film version all the adult characters are played by kids. The songs are easy to learn too. I am going to hold auditions next Tuesday and Wednesday at 3.30pm in my room. Rehearsals will begin on Wednesday after half-term, and the performances will be on Tuesday, Wednesday and Thursday evening of the week before we break up for the Christmas holidays.

■ What are the key points?

■ Think of quick ways of jotting the key points down.

■ Compare your notes with a partner. Have you got all the key points?

Can you read your quick notes and abbreviations?

PART 3

Here is an example of how it could be done:

Mrs Darrel
Bugsy Malone
aud. next Thurs in Mrs D rm 3.30
Reh. start Wed aft. 1/2 trm
Perf. Tue–Thur last wk trm

PART 4

Try it again with this interview with Mr Beetham, the head teacher:

I am very concerned about litter in the playground. The school looks a mess – and it is getting worse. I am going to talk to the whole school about it in tomorrow's assembly. At break time I am going to get the whole school to go out and pick up litter. Starting next Monday I am going to have a litter detention for any pupil caught dropping litter. They will have to stay behind for half an hour to pick up litter in the playground.

NEWS WORDS

Journalists know how to use language to 'pep up' a story. This chart shows how they do it. Read the chart, find some more examples in newspapers, then use your 'news words' to give spice to your own news stories:

IF YOU WANT TO...	CALL IT...
Make a small fire sound serious	a blaze
Make an ordinary event sound exciting	a drama
Blow up a disagreement	a battle or war
Make an unimportant comment sound important	an announcement
Make news out of good or bad weather	the best (or worst) since records began
Make a minor criticism sound really harsh	a tongue-lashing
Turn a minor improvement in science or medicine into a news scoop	a breakthrough
Make a small increase in prices sound huge	soaring
Make a small reduction sound huge	plummeting
Continue a story from yesterday's paper	a saga

NEWSPAPER FRONT PAGE

THE SCHOOL TIMES

NEWSPAPER COLUMNS

USING A RHYMING DICTIONARY

OBJECTIVES

UNIT	SPELLING/VOCABULARY	GRAMMAR/PUNCTUATION	COMPREHENSION/ COMPOSITION
REFERENCE AND RESEARCH SKILLS Using a Rhyming Dictionary.	Use a rhyming dictionary to compose jingles.	Investigate rhymes and jingles.	Write rhymes and jingles.

ORGANIZATION (1 HOUR)

INTRODUCTION	WHOLE-CLASS SKILLS WORK	DIFFERENTIATED GROUP ACTIVITIES	CONCLUSION
HOUR 1 What is a jingle?	Discuss previous examples. Explain the use of a rhyming dictionary.	1*: Make a class rhyming dictionary. 2: Create a school jingle. 3: Create an advert for a food magazine. 4*: Create a short rhyming adventure.	Share and evaluate group work.

RESOURCES
Rhyming dictionaries, magazine and videoed television advertisements, taped radio jingles, flip chart or board, paper, tape recorder, TV, video player, writing materials.

PREPARATION
Prepare some taped jingles and video some television advertisements. Cut-out magazine advertisements which use rhyme.

Introduction
Ask the children if they know what a jingle is. Explain that they hear them when they listen to the radio. Play some examples, possibly from a local radio station. Tell the children that jingles are usually musical but they differ from songs as they are used to advertise something. Show the video of the television adverts.

Whole-class skills work
Discuss the examples shown or heard in the introductory session. Ask the children why they think advertisers use jingles. What do they notice about the words in the jingles? Do they remember any stories with pairs of rhyming words, such as *Each Peach Pear Plum?*

Collect pairs of words that rhyme and list them on the flip chart or board. Explain how a rhyming dictionary could be used to provide other rhymes. Tell the children that they will be using pairs of rhyming words for a range of activities.

Differentiated group activities
1*: Make a class rhyming dictionary, starting with the rhymes that have been collected.
2: Make a jingle to advertise something to do with school life.
3: Create an advertisement for a food magazine.
4*: Create a short rhyming adventure for one of the characters discussed earlier.

Conclusion
Share and evaluate each group's work.

PLAYING WITH ADVERBS

OBJECTIVES

UNIT	SPELLING/VOCABULARY	GRAMMAR/PUNCTUATION	COMPREHENSION/ COMPOSITION
WORD PLAY Playing with Adverbs: 'Thumping, stumping, bumping, jumping'.	Recognize common letter strings.	Identify adverbs and understand their role.	Investigate the effect of substituting adverbs.

ORGANIZATION (1 HOUR)

INTRODUCTION	WHOLE-CLASS SKILLS WORK	DIFFERENTIATED GROUP ACTIVITIES	CONCLUSION
HOUR 1 Establish knowledge of verbs.	Make a class list of adverbs.	1: Write a simple verse incorporating adverbs appropriately. 2 & 3*: Working in pairs, supply own adverbs to given verse. 4: Use adverbs on flip chart to make own sentences.	Selected member from each group shares work, followed by class evaluation.

RESOURCES

Photocopiable page 78 ('Thumping, stumping, bumping, jumping' poem), OHP and acetate (optional), flip chart or board, chalk or felt-tipped pen.

PREPARATION

If possible, prepare an OHT of photocopiable page 78, otherwise copy the poem to A3 size.

Introduction

Establish the children's previous knowledge of verbs. Explain that verbs are words such as *walking, listening, being, playing.* Invite the children to suggest other verbs. Tell them that they are going to look at a short poem which contains mostly verbs. Display the poem and read it slowly, *emphasizing* the verbs.

Thumping, stumping, bumping, jumping

Thumping, stumping, bumping, jumping,
Ripping, nipping, tripping, skipping,
All the way home.

Popping, clopping, stopping, hopping,
Stalking, chalking, talking, walking,
All the way home.

Anonymous

Whole-class skills work

Explain that the poem is about going home. Invite the children to suggest words which describe *how* they might walk home – *happily? hungrily? slowly?* Try some examples, putting them into phrases, for example '*lazily* walking home'. Write the words on the board or flip chart. Explain that these words are called adverbs and they are used in sentences next to verbs to give more detail to the sentence: they describe the verb. Reinforce the concept by giving some more examples: *I sang sweetly. He wrote untidily. The crowd roared loudly.* Ask the children for other examples and write them on the board or flip chart.

Ask the children to think of adverbs which they could add while you are re-reading the poem. Read the poem and then read the first part again. Ask for ideas and list them.

Differentiated group activities

1: Write a poem of their own about going somewhere, choosing appropriate adverbs.
2 & 3*: Work in pairs, putting their own choice of adverbs into the poem.
4: Use the adverbs on the flip chart or board to make a collection of sentences with adverbs.

Conclusion

Ask one member of each group to share his or her work, revising and consolidating what an adverb is. Discuss with the class how they would like to display their work.

PLAYING WITH ADVERBS

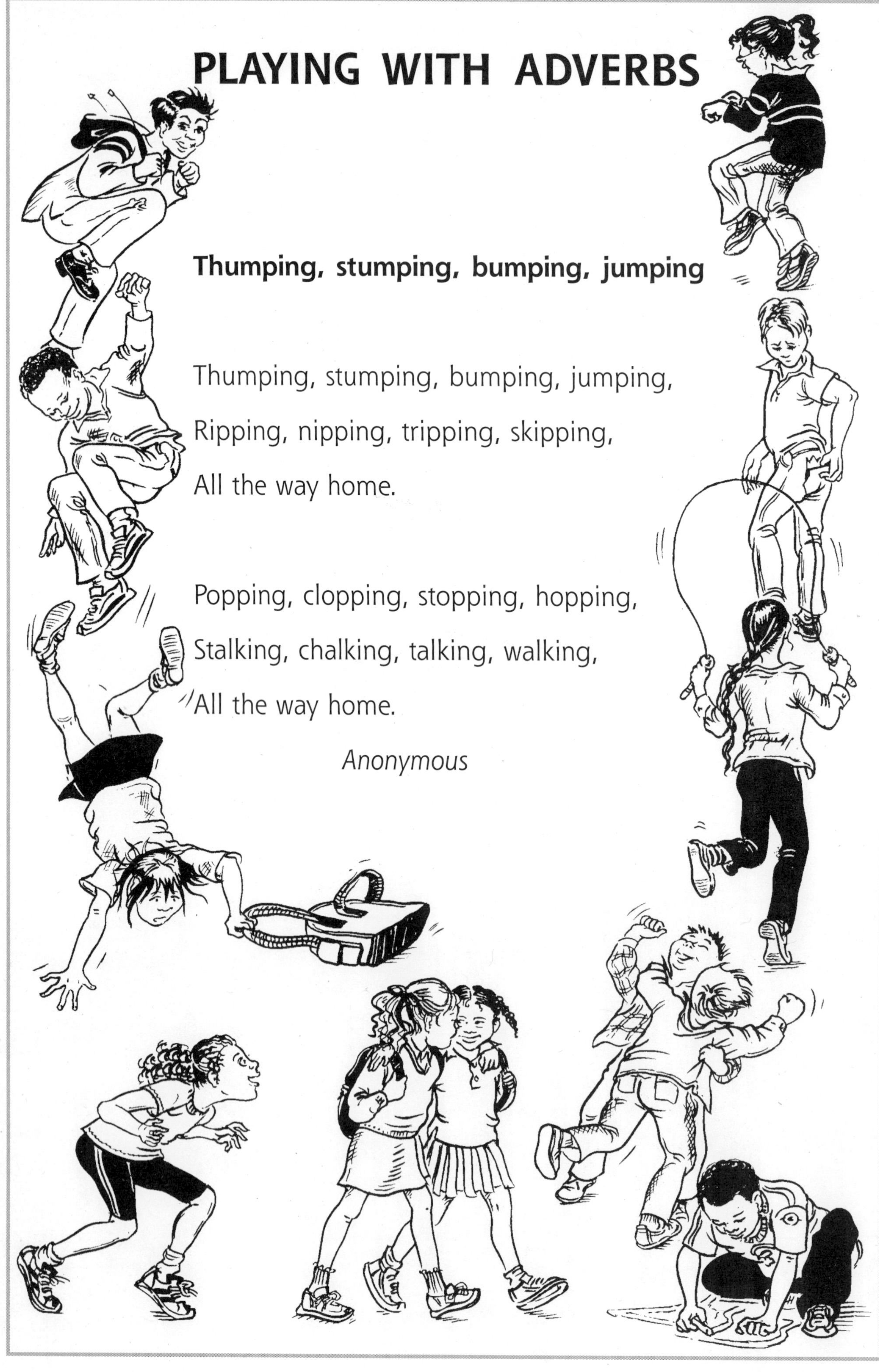

Thumping, stumping, bumping, jumping

Thumping, stumping, bumping, jumping,
Ripping, nipping, tripping, skipping,
All the way home.

Popping, clopping, stopping, hopping,
Stalking, chalking, talking, walking,
All the way home.

Anonymous

Term 2

THE VAMPIRE TEACHER

OBJECTIVES

UNIT	SPELLING/VOCABULARY	GRAMMAR/PUNCTUATION	COMPREHENSION/ COMPOSITION
READING FICTION Short fantasy story: 'The Vampire Teacher'.	Collect and note new words. Investigate *-ight* endings.	Revise and consolidate previous work on capital letters, nouns, adjectives, verbs, types of sentence, paragraphs, punctuation of speech as appropriate to class needs. Identify possessive apostrophes.	Develop basic reading skills. Develop skills of prediction, inference and deduction.

ORGANIZATION (2 HOURS)

	INTRODUCTION	WHOLE-CLASS SKILLS WORK	DIFFERENTIATED GROUP ACTIVITIES	CONCLUSION
HOUR 1	Shared reading of 'The Vampire Teacher'. Identify new vocabulary. Discuss what might happen next.	Use the story as a basis for revision of skills covered to date: capital letters, nouns, verbs, adjectives, types of sentence, paragraphs, punctuation of speech.	1*: Guided reading and Reading Comprehension – parts A, B and C. 2 & 3: Write own ending to the story. 4*: Guided reading and Reading Comprehension – parts A and C.	Selected pupils from Groups 2 & 3 read their endings to the class.
HOUR 2	Recap on story and read author's own ending.	Identify possessive apostrophes. Investigate words with *-ight* endings.	1: Write own ending to the story. 2 & 3*: Guided reading and Reading Comprehension parts A, B and C. 4: Write own ending to the story.	Share story endings. Discuss Reading Comprehension answers.

RESOURCES

Photocopiable pages 83 and 84 ('The Vampire Teacher'), 85 (Reading Comprehension), dictionaries, OHP and acetate (optional), board or flip chart, writing materials.

PREPARATION

Make enough copies of the story and Reading Comprehension sheet for one between two children. If possible, prepare an OHT of the story for use in the skills session.

Introduction

Read 'The Vampire Teacher' with the class. Identify new vocabulary (for example *vampire, retirement, threadbare, disapproved, detention, frog-marched, jovial, riveted*). Ask the children to try to guess the meaning from the context and then to try to confirm the meaning using a dictionary. Ask for suggestions about what might happen next in the story. What do they think has really happened to Trev? Do they think the boys were brave to follow Mr Pyre?

Whole-class skills work

Talk about how the story has been set out, reminding the children of the use of paragraph indents and the punctuation of speech. Use the opportunity to revise other skills such as the use of adjectives by drawing the children's attention to the descriptions of Mr Pyre and the headmaster.

Write the following on the board or flip chart:

Mr Pyre's grave
the headmaster's face
boys' complaints

Identify the possessive apostrophe and explain that an apostrophe used in this way shows ownership or possession. The thing owned is usually the next word (sometimes preceded by adjectives or adverbs). If the owner is singular, add an apostrophe + s; if the owner is plural and already ends in 's', just add an apostrophe, as in *boys'*. Ask who is the owner and what do they own or possess in the above examples. Ask for what other purpose are apostrophes used. (To replace letters in a contraction.) Find some examples in the story. Write a few sentences on the board or flip chart and ask where the apostrophes should go. Which are possessive apostrophes? For example: *Shes driving her fathers car, isnt she? The teachers smile certainly wasnt friendly. The childrens tests hadnt been marked.*

Differentiated group activities

1*: Guided reading and Reading Comprehension parts A, B and C. Use comprehension questions as a basis for discussion, particularly those in part B (higher-level comprehension) and part C (for discussion only). Children then produce written answers to parts A and B.

2 & 3: Write own ending to the story. Any ending which fits the characters and plot is acceptable. Explain that the ending will need to fit in with what the boys have found out during the story: Is Mr Pyre a vampire? If not, how do you explain the blood on Trev's neck, and the gravestone? Stress that the ending should be *short* – one paragraph is ideal, but not more than three.

4*: Guided reading and Reading Comprehension parts A and C. Support children in re-reading the text and use the questions on the sheet as a basis for discussion. Children write answers to part A only.

Conclusion

Invite children from Groups 2 and 3 to read their endings to the class. The rest of the class evaluate how well the endings fit in with the characters and plot.

Introduction

Recap on the story and read out the author's ending to it, given below. However, it is important to emphasize that it is not necessarily better than the endings that they have written. What is important is that the ending fits the characters and plot that have preceded it – and that it is a satisfying ending.

'Lots of teachers are old – but it doesn't prove that they are vampires!' said the headmaster.
'But the blood on Trev's neck...' muttered Tim.
'Just a rumour,' interrupted the headmaster.
'But the name on the gravestone...' pleaded Tom.
'Ah...' said the headmaster, 'that was very nearly a good piece of evidence, but you did not research it well enough.'
Tim and Tom looked surprised.
'If you'd have taken the trouble to investigate, you would have found out that Mr Pyre's real name is William – which does not begin with 'V'! 'Victoria', however, does. Victoria Mary Pyre was his wife's name. She died a few years ago and he visits her grave regularly. That explains what you saw.'
'Then Mr Pyre is not a vampire after all!' exclaimed Tom.
'No,' said the headmaster, drawing back his lips to reveal his sharp, pointed fangs, 'but I am!'

Discuss the way in which the author has ended the story. Was this what the children expected to happen? When did they begin to suspect that the headmaster might not be what he seemed?

Whole-class skills work

Investigate words ending in *-ight*. Write the words *tight* and *fight* on the board or flip chart. Ask children how to pronounce them, establishing that they sound like *white* and *quite* (long 'i'). Explain that the letters *gh* in the words are now silent, but until four centuries ago people did pronounce them (try it!). Brainstorm other *-ight* words and make a list, for example *bright, delight, fight, flight, fright, light, might, night, right, sight*. Then write these words: *eight, freight straight weight*. How are they pronounced? Ask children to suggest reasons for their different pronunciation (another vowel before 'i'). What about the word *height*?

Differentiated group activities

1: Write own ending to the story. This group could be encouraged to write a more extended ending of between one and two pages.
2 & 3*: Guided reading and Reading Comprehension parts A, B and C (see above).
4: Write own ending to the story. This group should keep their ending to one paragraph and concentrate on making it as good as possible.

Conclusion

Encourage the children to share their story endings. Discuss comprehension answers. Focus particularly on part C and encourage the children to share their own ideas.

FURTHER IDEA

Take the story one stage further. Ask the children to think about how the boys might escape from the headteacher. Perhaps Mr Pyre might rescue them. Perhaps the headteacher had only been playing a joke on them. What was the 'blood' they saw on Trev's collar? Had he been hurt in the playground fight? Perhaps the fight had broken out because someone had squirted tomato sauce on his clean shirt in the canteen at lunchtime. Or was Mr Pyre a vampire after all? Encourage the children to think of as many possibilities as they can. They could then work in groups to perform plays of their story endings.

THE VAMPIRE TEACHER

Mr Pyre, the new history teacher, looked like a piece of history himself. Though he must have been under the age of retirement, he looked 80 at least. His tiny black eyes were sunken in deep dark sockets, and his bloodless lips were drawn tight over large white teeth. His threadbare suit was cut in a style that was years out of date.

And he was strict. Within minutes of walking through the door, he had the classroom rearranged like those in Victorian photographs with everyone sitting in rows.

'Sit up straight!' he growled.

Everyone sat up straight – even Trev.

'Now get out your exercise books!'

Everyone looked blank, until Lucy croaked nervously, 'W-w-we haven't got any, S-s-sir. W-w-we usually write on p-p-paper.'

Mr Pyre frowned. He disapproved of modern teaching methods, but for the time being, he had no choice. He gave out some paper. Then he wrote a list of dates on the board and asked the class to copy them down in silence.

The lesson ground on for what seemed like hours until at last the bell went. Trev grinned at Tom, but Mr Pyre's next words soon wiped the smile from his face.

'I want you to learn all those dates for homework. I shall test you tomorrow, and anyone who gets even one wrong will stay behind after school for an hour!'

'What're you doing, Trev?' asked Tom as they trooped out into the yard.

Trev's attention was focused on his piece of paper. 'Trying to learn these – what do you think!'

Tom was amazed. He had never known Trev to try willingly to learn anything in all the time he had known him.

'What for?'

'Do you think I want a detention with that... that...'

He couldn't think of a suitable insult, but suddenly it came to him, '...that VAMPIRE!'

Tom laughed.

'Well, you've got to admit he looks like one!' said Trev.

But the joke turned sour when, next morning break, Mr Pyre caught Trev fighting in the playground. He grabbed him by the shirt collar and frog-marched him into school. Trev didn't come to school next day, and there was a rumour that he was last seen leaving Mr Pyre's classroom with blood on his neck and shirt collar.

'I reckon he really is a vampire,' said Tim when he heard about it.

'If he is, it's not fair,' complained Tom. 'I know there's a shortage of teachers, but they can't go digging up vampires and sending them in to teach kids.'

'Well at least he knows his history!'

'That's because he is history!'

They giggled at this, but then Tim became serious again. 'Come to think of it, I've never seen him eat school dinners!'

'Yeah, and his hands are really cold!'

They frowned at each other for a moment, then Tim said, 'I think we should complain to the Headmonster.'

The Headmonster (or '-master' to give him his official title) couldn't have been more different to Mr Pyre. He was plump, rosy-cheeked and quite jovial – for a headmaster.

However, as he listened to the boys' complaints, his usual cheerful smile faded. Finally, he said, 'Boys, rumour is a terrible thing. It is cruel and unfair. You must always look for evidence before making a judgement. And anyway – can't you use your common sense? A vampire indeed! I'm surprised at you!'

'He's right,' said Tom afterwards. 'I feel a stupid fool!'

'He's right,' echoed Tim. But his thoughts were along a totally different track. 'We've got to get more evidence. Let's follow Mr Pyre home tonight. If he's a vampire he'll live in a coffin. If he's not, he'll live in a house.'

It was not the best evening for a vampire hunt. The gloom and fog would have looked great in a film, but were a bit scary in real life. Still, Tim and Tom managed to keep their spirits up. Until, that is, Mr Pyre turned in the direction of the church.

They followed him as far as the churchyard gate – which was as far as they dared to go. They watched from a safe distance as he walked along a narrow path between the graves and stopped near one of the headstones. What happened next was difficult to see because of the gloom and fog, but he seemed to sink down out of sight, as though the grave had swallowed him up.

That was enough evidence for Tim and Tom. They ran faster than they ever did in games lessons, and spent the night haunted by visions of Mr Pyre rising from his grave to drink their blood.

Next day, before going to school, Tim and Tom decided to look again at Mr Pyre's grave. In the bright morning light, it all seemed like a foolish nightmare, and they half expected to find an ordinary explanation – but what they found sent shivers down their spines. On the gravestone were written these words:

HERE LIETH
THE MORTAL REMAINS
OF V.M. PYRE
WHO DEPARTED THIS LIFE
ON 15TH SEPT. 1990
R.I.P.

'It's true!' gasped Tim. 'Our history teacher's been dead for years! No wonder his suit looks out of date!'

'Never mind his suit,' said Tom, 'what if he gives us a vampire bite instead of detention!'

'We've only one chance,' said Tim. 'We must present this evidence to the Headmonster!'

The headmaster couldn't see the boys until 4.30. He showed them in and invited them to sit down. As they did so he locked the door to his study. 'I know what you want to see me about,' he explained, 'and we wouldn't want to be disturbed, would we? Now why don't you tell me all about it...'

Tim did the talking while Tom scratched nervously at a spot on his trousers. The head seemed to be listening sympathetically, but the way he rubbed his hands together over and over as he listened made Tom feel uneasy.

At last Tim finished his tale. The headmaster stood up, smiled a closed-lipped smile, and said, 'My, my, what foolish boys you are, after all. You can't see the evidence even when it's staring you in the face!'

'Er... what do you mean, Sir?' stammered Tim, his gaze riveted on the headmaster's face...

READING COMPREHENSION

PART A

- When was Mr Pyre first called a vampire?
- What gave Trev the idea of calling him a vampire?
- What rumour went around the class next day?
- What happened when Tim and Tom went to see the headmaster?
- What happened when Tim and Tom followed Mr Pyre to the churchyard?
- What did it say on the gravestone?
- What did Tim and Tom think it meant?

PART B

- Make a list of all the evidence collected by Tim and Tom that suggested that Mr Pyre was a vampire.
- Why do you think the headmaster locked the door of his study at the end of the story?
- What was the explanation of Mr Pyre's visit to the churchyard?
- What feature of the headmaster's appearance is emphasized at the end of the story?

PART C

- What is a vampire? Piece together everything you know about the vampire legend. How did you find out this information?
- Can you think of a time when you had strange or frightening ideas about something that turned out to be perfectly ordinary?

SCHOOL CARDS

OBJECTIVES

UNIT	SPELLING/VOCABULARY	GRAMMAR/PUNCTUATION	COMPREHENSION/ COMPOSITION
WRITING FICTION School Cards.	Spell words with *al-* prefix. Use *-able* suffix to make adjectives from verbs.	Use first person narrative. Construct adjectival phrases.	Apply skills of story writing learned in 'Animal Adventure' unit (Term 1) but with more imaginative content. Use a planning grid.

ORGANIZATION (3 HOURS)

	INTRODUCTION	WHOLE-CLASS SKILLS WORK	DIFFERENTIATED GROUP ACTIVITIES	CONCLUSION
HOUR 1	Introduce oral storytelling activity using School Cards. Give tips for oral presentation. Revise use of first-person narrative.	Spell words with *al-* prefix.	1–4: Play the School Cards game and tell orally composed stories to each other. * Teacher works with Groups 1 & 4.	One pupil from each group is chosen to tell his or her oral story to the whole class.
HOUR 2	Display the Story Planner. Relate to stories previously read: 'Animal Adventure (Term 1) and 'The Vampire Teacher' (previous unit).	Use the planner to write a plan for the oral story. Change verbs to adjectives with *-able* suffix.	1–4: Begin to turn oral story into a written story. * Teacher works with Groups 2 & 3.	Selected stories are read out and evaluated.
HOUR 3	Display 'The Vampire Teacher' story and discuss the way dialogue is handled.	Introduce the concept and use of the adjectival phrase.	1–4: Finish and redraft their stories. * Teacher works with Group 4.	Selected pupils read out examples of redrafted stories.

RESOURCES

Photocopiable pages 89–92 (School Cards), 93 (Story Planner), 83 and 84 ('The Vampire Teacher' from the previous unit) and 32–33 ('Animal Adventure' from Term 1), sturdy card, lamination materials (optional), scissors, OHP and acetate (optional), board or flip chart, writing materials.

PREPARATION

Photocopiable pages 89–92 (School Cards) should be printed onto card, laminated and cut into sets. One set per group of four or five children is needed. Prepare enough Story Planners for one per child. If possible, prepare OHTs of the Story Planner and the stories 'The Vampire Teacher' and 'Animal Adventure'.

Introduction

The main aim of this unit is to revise key writing skills introduced in the 'Animal Adventure' unit (Term 1). The School Cards act as a stimulus for ideas, the skills sessions provide revision of key skills, and the Story Planner is a reminder of the story structure developed in 'Animal Adventure'. Begin by arranging the class into groups of four or five children, broadly within ability groups but overlapping where necessary to create groups of the required size. Then model the oral storytelling activity using the set of cards prepared from photocopiable pages 89–92. Demonstrate the procedure by taking one group of children through the following process while others watch:

- Shuffle each set of cards (places, people, objects and situations) separately and place the sets face down in the middle of the table.
- The first player takes the top card from each set and places it face up in front of him or her.
- The player must make up an oral story using all the cards (the teacher should do this during the demonstration session). The story should be told in the first person. (Remind children what telling a story in the first person means. In this case it means that the storyteller (the child) is a key character in the story. He or she will tell the story from his or her point of view, using 'I'.) For example, the child picks the following cards: place – the library; person – Ms Sharp, Head teacher; object – laptop computer; situation – your lunch has gone mouldy. The child might relate how she was in the library when she realized that her lunch had gone mouldy. Ms Sharp came by with her laptop computer and was quickly able to calculate a new scientific formula for restoring mouldy food. The stories can be as fanciful as the children choose, but they must use all four cards and should try to include as much imaginative detail as possible.
- Continue the game clockwise around the table.

Whole-class skills work

Write the following list of words on the board or flip chart: *almost, along, also, always, altogether, although, already*. Ask the children what the words have in common. They all begin with the prefix *al-*. The words have been formed by adding *all* to other words and dropping one 'l' (or two in the case of *along*). Tell the children to use the words in sentences, and write these up as well. Explain that these words occur frequently in reading and writing and children should learn how to spell them. They could write them in their word books and learn the list for homework.

Differentiated group activities

All groups play the School Cards card game and tell their orally composed stories to each other. When everyone has had a turn, decide whose was the best story. The rest of the group should then work together to help that person to prepare the story for presentation to the class or other groups. The teacher works with Groups 1 and 4.

Conclusion

One child from each group is chosen to tell his or her oral story to the whole class. The rest of the class should listen carefully and positive comment should be invited. Ask the class questions such as: 'What did you like about that story?'

Introduction

Explain that the oral stories from Hour 1 are going to be developed into written stories, and that you wish to revise and extend the skills taught previously, for example during the unit 'Animal Adventure'. The first key skill is planning a story with an effective structure, that is, a good beginning, middle and end. Display the Story Planner and go through the different sections, reminding children how it applied to 'Animal Adventure'. (You could also apply it to the structure of 'The Vampire Teacher'.) Talk about the children's stories that they listened to in Hour 1. Ask them to help you fill in the Story Planner for one of the stories. Then give them each a planner and tell them to fill in their copies in the same way for their own stories.

Whole-class skills work

Demonstrate how to change verbs into adjectives by adding the suffix *-able*. Write the following table on the board or flip chart.

VERB	ADJECTIVE
break	breakable
change	changeable
enjoy	enjoyable
read	readable
sink	sinkable

Ask the children to brainstorm more verbs, and adjectives derived from them. Then explore spelling patterns, noting that some words ending in 'e' drop the 'e' while others retain it. For words ending in a consonant, the suffix is added without changes being made to the root word.

Finally, have fun! Ask children to brainstorm a random list of verbs, then add *-able* and try to explain them. Two examples would be: *run* (verb), *runable* (adjective), *a course that is not too long or difficult to run* (explanation); *watch* (verb), *watchable* (adjective), *a TV programme that is good enough to watch* (explanation).

Differentiated group activities

Children in all groups can then begin to turn their oral story into a written story. Explain to all children that they can develop or change their oral stories in any way, and can borrow ideas from the stories they heard at the end of Hour 1. Remind them of the ending of 'Animal Adventure'. What was it called? (A twist in the tale.) Can they adapt their school stories to end in a similar way?

1: Children should be encouraged to adapt the structure freely, or to write a plan in a completely different way, if they wish.

2 & 3*: The teacher works with Groups 2 and 3 with particular focus on the key skills being revised and developed in this unit. Children in Group 2 should be encouraged to follow the basic structure but write several paragraphs in each section.

4: Children should follow the planner closely, writing one paragraph for each section.

Conclusion

Read out good examples of stories written by children in Groups 2 and 3. Invite other children to say what they liked about them. Comment on effective features and encourage other children to use them.

Introduction

Display 'The Vampire Teacher' story (on OHT or enlarged photocopy) and use it to revise and consolidate the punctuation and layout of dialogue. The attention of more able children should be drawn to the indentations for each change of speaker. Teach them the rule: *every time the speaker changes, start a new line and indent.*

Whole-class skills work

Explain that an adjectival phrase is simply a group of words (phrase) which describes a noun in the same way as a single adjective does, for example: The teacher *with the loud voice* teaches in the next room. Another kind of adjectival phrase is made by placing an intensifying adverb before the adjective, for example: The *very* strict teacher. The comparative or superlative form of the adjective (that is, with suffix *-er* or *-est*) is often used to begin an adjectival phrase, for example: Your class teacher is *friendlier than mine.*

As a class, create some sentences with adjectival phrases. Encourage children to look for opportunities to add adjectival phrases in their stories during redrafting.

Differentiated group activities

Children in all groups finish off and redraft their stories. This should be done by reading through the stories in pairs, and looking for four things:

- places where description could be made more vivid, for example by adding adjectives or adjectival phrases
- consistent use of first-person narrative
- correct punctuation and setting out of dialogue
- correct spelling.

* The teacher works with Group 4.

Conclusion

Selected children from all groups read out their first draft followed by discussion and suggestions for further revision from the teacher.

FOLLOW-UP (1 HOUR)

See page 207, which provides a grid plan for a 1-hour follow-up unit. This enables finishing off the stories and publishing a class collection of school stories.

SCHOOL CARDS: PLACES

PLACE

Outside the Head teacher's office

PLACE

Dinner hall

PLACE

School hall

PLACE

Outside the school gates

PLACE

Caretaker's cupboard

PLACE

Library

PLACE

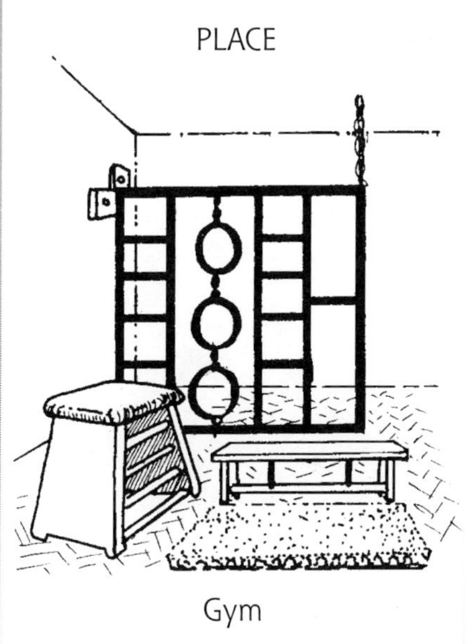

Gym

PLACE

Classroom

PLACE

Playground

SCHOOL CARDS: PEOPLE

PERSON  Ms Sharp, Head teacher	PERSON  Mr Fielding, Y4 teacher	PERSON  Miss Galen, Y6 teacher
PERSON  Mr Bolton, school caretaker	PERSON  Mrs McDuff, dinner lady	PERSON  Cathy Cokes, pupil
PERSON  Craig Andrews, pupil	PERSON  Dean James, pupil	PERSON  Nasha Aziz, pupil

SCHOOL CARDS: OBJECTS

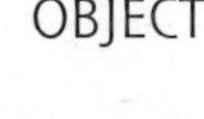

OBJECT	OBJECT	OBJECT

Bubblegum	Pocket dictionary	Photograph
OBJECT	OBJECT	OBJECT
	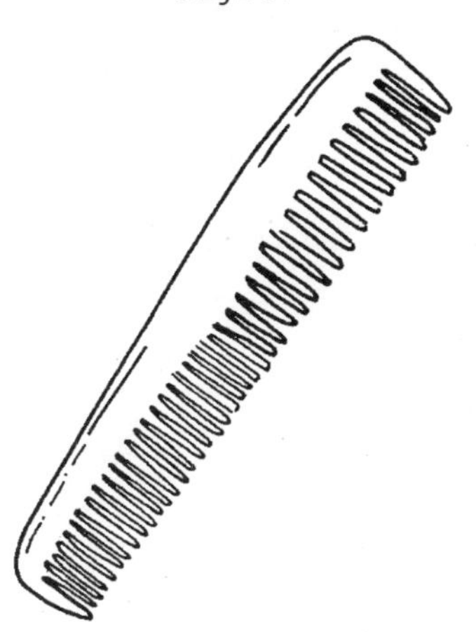	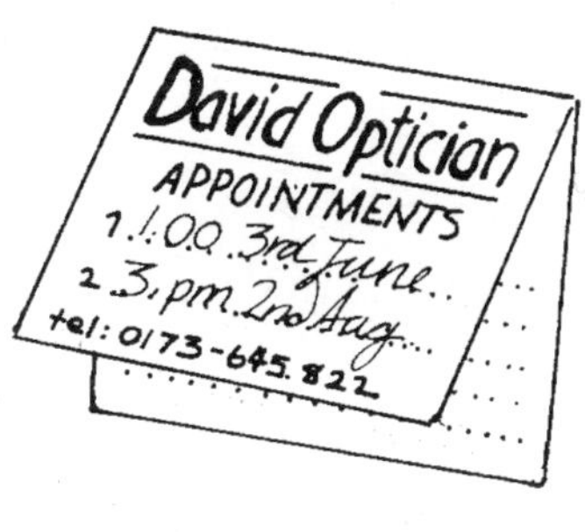
Audio cassette	Comb	Optician's appointment card
OBJECT	OBJECT	OBJECT

Laptop computer	Packet of birdseed	Pen

SCHOOL CARDS: SITUATIONS

SITUATION

Your lunch has gone mouldy.

SITUATION

You have forgotten your school bag with your pencil case and all your books.

SITUATION

You have a fight with your best friend.

SITUATION

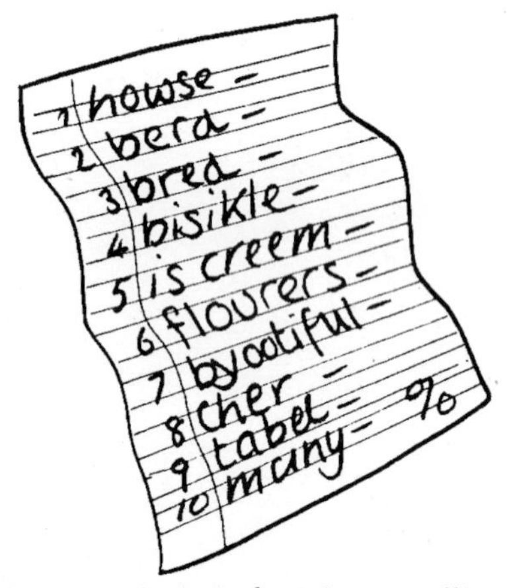

You get 0 out of 10 in a spelling test.

SITUATION

You stayed up too late last night and can't keep awake.

SITUATION

You are bullied by someone.

SITUATION

You were supposed to be picked up after school but no one has come.

SITUATION

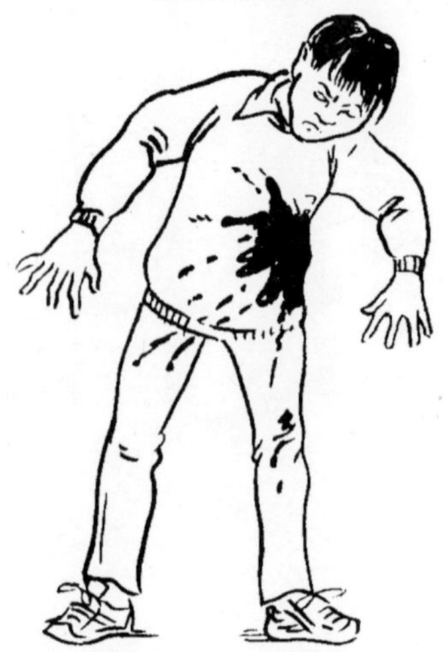

Somebody spills red paint all over your new uniform.

SITUATION

You lose your secret diary and your worst enemy finds it.

STORY PLANNER

This grid shows the plan for two different stories.

Beginning	Description of main character(s).	Description of place.
Middle	Description of place. Setting out a problem. Attempts to solve the problem.	Description of main character(s). Setting out a problem. Dialogue about the problem. Attempts to solve the problem.
End	Problem solved.	A twist in the tale.

Use this grid to plan your own story.

Beginning
Middle
End

REDRAFTING SIMULATION

OBJECTIVES

UNIT	SPELLING/VOCABULARY	GRAMMAR/PUNCTUATION	COMPREHENSION/ COMPOSITION
REDRAFTING SIMULATION 'Kanda, the Fisherman'.	Explore synonyms using a thesaurus.	Revise conventions of writing dialogue. Experiment with adding an adverb to the reporting clause. Revise nouns and adjectives.	Investigate how to redraft the content of writing.

ORGANIZATION (3 HOURS)

INTRODUCTION	WHOLE-CLASS SKILLS WORK	DIFFERENTIATED GROUP ACTIVITIES	CONCLUSION
HOUR 1 Shared reading and discussion of the story beginning, 'Kanda, the Fisherman' *before* giving out pupil copies.	Explore synonyms using a thesaurus.	1–4*: Work in pairs within groups to redraft the story.	Pupils provide suggestions for dealing with each of the 'editor's' comments.
HOUR 2 Explain that the 'editor' has placed the best of the revisions into the manuscript and it now reads as follows. Read the revised script.	Revise conventions of writing dialogue and experiment with adding an adverb to the reporting clause.	1–4*: Guided writing of continuations of the story.	Pupils read out examples of continuations.
HOUR 3 Display the 'Kanda' story on OHP and focus discussion on the editor's comments.	Revise nouns and adjectives.	1–4*: Work in pairs within groups role-playing 'editor' and 'author'.	Pupils brainstorm a list of points which would make a helpful prompt for future redrafting. Introduce 'Redrafting Checklist'.

RESOURCES

Photocopiable page 97 ('Kanda, the Fisherman') and 98 (Redrafting Checklist), a set of thesauruses, board or flip chart, OHP and acetate (optional), writing materials.

PREPARATION

Prepare enough copies of photocopiable page 97 ('Kanda, the Fisherman') for one between two children. If possible, prepare the sheet as an OHT, or enlarge it to A3 size.

Introduction

Read the story beginning given on photocopiable page 97, before giving out pupil copies. Ask children: Did you think this was a good story beginning? Many will say 'yes' without thinking, so ask them to think again using the following questions.

- Was there enough detail? What would you have liked to know more about?
- Was the shark attack described in an exciting way?

Finally, ask them to imagine that this is the manuscript of a story which you have sent to a publisher. The story has been sent back to you, the author, with the editor's suggestions for improvement. If you can make the improvements she suggests, she will publish the story.

Whole-class skills work

Most children find it relatively easy to proofread for technical errors, but are not sure what is expected of them when it comes to redrafting for content. Explain to them that the purpose of this unit is to teach them how to redraft for *content* – there are no technical errors in the story. The main thing they will be looking for is to use alternative words and expressions which are more precise than the first things that they think of. The 'editor's' comments will show the aspects that need improvement, and a valuable tool to help them is a thesaurus. Revise the use of the thesaurus by giving this example:

'The word *boat* is used in the story. Let's look up the word in a thesaurus and see how many synonyms we can find.' (The *Oxford Children's Thesaurus* contains over 50 synonyms!) The next step is to pick out ones which are suitable. For this story, the following synonyms are worth considering: *canoe, dinghy, rowing-boat, yacht, sailboat*. Ask children to discuss the list. They should arrive at an accurate description of each one, then choose one which best fits the story. Encourage them to use the thesaurus when redrafting 'Kanda, the Fisherman' in their groups.

Differentiated group activities

Children work in pairs within groups to redraft the story. They should discuss possibilities for revision but should each write their own version of the redrafted story. It does not matter if a pair of children produce exactly the same redraft.

* The teacher supports all groups as needed.

1: Children should be able to work quickly enough to redraft the whole passage.

2 & 3: Children should aim to do as much of the passage as they can but should be told that it is better to do part of the passage to a high standard than rush on to the end.

4: Children in this group should concentrate on the first half only (to '...and carried on.'). It is important that they focus on enhancing the detail and improving the vocabulary and are not worried about finishing the whole story.

Conclusion

Go through each of the editor's comments in turn and ask children for suggestions as to how to deal with it. Jot these down quickly for later use. After the lesson, incorporate the best of these suggestions into the story.

Introduction

Explain that the 'editor' has incorporated the best of the revisions into the manuscript and it now reads as follows. Read the revised script.

Ask children to comment on how much they think it has improved. Where appropriate, re-read sections of the earlier version for comparison.

Explain that the editor now wants the story to be finished off. Read and discuss her comments with the class.

Whole-class skills work

Children should by now be able to punctuate dialogue reasonably accurately, should use synonyms of *said* where appropriate and should be beginning to set out dialogue with a new indented line for each change of speaker. Revise and consolidate the conventions of punctuating and setting out dialogue as appropriate. Then introduce a new element: adding an adverb to the reporting clause, as in the following example:

SIMPLE REPORTING CLAUSE	REPORTING CLAUSE WITH ADVERB
'Sit down,' *said Sarah.*	'Sit down,' *said Sarah quickly.*

Ask the children to copy the example and experiment with other adverbs, for example: 'Sit down,' *said Sarah crossly*. More able children could be asked to try combining a synonym of *said* with an adverb, for example: 'Sit down,' *suggested Sarah helpfully*.

When you have a list of about ten examples, ask the children to comment on how the adverb helps us to understand the character's feelings about what she is saying. Finally, ask children to use some dialogue in the continuation of the story and suggest that they should try to use the ideas above.

Differentiated group activities

All children write continuations of the story.

* The teacher supports all groups as necessary.

1: Children should be encouraged to write freely and develop the story in their own way, departing from the suggestions on the sheet if they can think of better ideas. Ask them to try to use some reporting clauses with synonyms of *said* and adverbs.

2 & 3: Children should follow the editor's suggestions but could be expected to expand them fully. They should use some reporting clauses with adverbs.

4: Children should use the editor's three continuation suggestions as paragraph guides. Ask them to include a few lines of dialogue. They could also be asked to add an adverb to some reporting clauses as this is not all that difficult if they follow the pattern.

Conclusion

Read and discuss selected story continuations. Ask the class to judge how well each continuation follows on from the beginning (Who forgot that Kanda lost an arm in his fight with the shark?).

Introduction

Display the 'Kanda, the Fisherman' story on the OHP and focus on the editor's comments. Ask children: What kinds of things has she commented on? What kind of improvements does she want? Explain that during group work they are going to play the role of editor and author in pairs. They will swap continuations and comment on them in exactly the same way.

Whole-class skills work

Revise nouns and adjectives as follows. Display the 'Kanda, The Fisherman' text and ask children to identify the nouns. Circle them. Next they should look to see if any adjectives are linked to those nouns. There aren't many and this is a sign of the paucity of the writing. Ask the children to find two or three nouns which would benefit from being described by an adjective, for example '*menacing* shark fins'. Tell children to apply this process when acting as 'editor'.

Differentiated group activities

All children work in pairs within groups, role-playing 'editor' and 'author'. They should begin by swapping their story continuations and making comments on their partner's work, then swapping back to redraft on the basis of the comments.

Less able children will need support during this session to help them identify areas for improvement in their partner's work and to make appropriate and helpful comments.

Conclusion

Ask children to read out examples of the following:

- a section of their original text which was later revised
- the comments made by a partner
- the revised section.

Discuss which areas needed most improvement and what kind of comments were most helpful. Ask children to brainstorm a list of points which would make helpful prompts for future redrafting. These points could include matters of content and technical accuracy. A sample 'Redrafting Checklist' is given on photocopiable page 98. You could use it in this session as follows:

- Incorporate children's suggestions, or reword points on the checklist to reflect children's wording so that they recognize their contribution.
- Prepare three different versions. Each version could be targeted at a specific ability range. (The version on the photocopiable sheet is a fairly full version, appropriate for children in Group 1; select fewer points for Groups 2 and 3 and Group 4.)

Display the checklist as a classroom resource to support the children's future redrafting activities.

KANDA, THE FISHERMAN

"nice"! – you can do better than that! Tell us what Laana is like!

Kanda was a fisherman on Laana, which was a really nice island.

He worked very hard, but didn't earn much money.

Give an idea of how hard he worked – e.g., describe a typical day

This didn't matter when he was single, but

when he met Tamara, he knew he would have to

What is she like?

work even harder to save up for their future.

How does he feel when he sees the fins?

One day when he was out fishing he saw some

shark fins near the boat. He knew that he

ought to stop fishing for the day because of the

danger, but he thought of Tamara and carried on.

Can you think of a better word?

He was pulling in his net for the last time

when his foot slipped and he fell in the water.

He felt very worried about this because of

Can you think of something a bit stronger?

the sharks. Then he saw a fin coming towards

Say more about his feelings! good!

him. He felt very frightened. He swam away as

Describe the shark here. Choose a better word

fast as he could. But the shark got him. He

Describe the fight. Describe the blood etc.

tried to fight the shark off, but it bit his arm

off. Kanda shouted with pain. Just then, some

Is that all!

friends arrived and helped him out of the water.

What did they say?
What did they do next?

Some things to think about when you finish the story:
- What does Tamara say and do?
How does he earn a living with only one arm?
Do they get married in the end?

REDRAFTING CHECKLIST

PART 1: CONTENT

- Find descriptions of people and places. Is there enough detail to help the reader imagine what they were like?
- Find the action in the story. Is it described in enough detail? Investigate synonyms for some of the verbs to find better alternatives. Could adverbs be added to good effect?
- Is the reader kept informed about how the characters feel?
- Find the nouns. Add adjectives where appropriate.
- Look at the dialogue. Would a synonym of **said** be more effective? Would it be effective to add an adverb to the reporting clause?

PART 2: GRAMMAR, PUNCTUATION & SPELLING

- Is the story written in sentences and paragraphs?
- Have capital letters been used for beginning sentences, names, places, days, months, and special occasions?
- Are speech marks used before and after words actually spoken?
- Does speech begin with a capital letter?
- Is there a comma, full stop, question mark or exclamation mark before final speech marks?
- Have apostrophes been used to show missing letters in contractions?
- Is an apostrophe + s used to show ownership?
- Check the spelling.

Body Facts

OBJECTIVES

UNIT	SPELLING/VOCABULARY	GRAMMAR/PUNCTUATION	COMPREHENSION/ COMPOSITION
READING NON-FICTION Information genre: 'Body Facts'.	Explore compound words. Extend vocabulary related to information-book layout.	Revise simple present tense. Recognize and use temporal connectives.	Understand reference aids: contents, index and glossary, page design. Identify key features of explanatory text.

ORGANIZATION (4 HOURS)

INTRODUCTION	WHOLE-CLASS SKILLS WORK	DIFFERENTIATED GROUP ACTIVITIES	CONCLUSION
HOUR 1 Shared reading of double-page spread: 'Body Framework'. Investigate layout features.	Revise the terms: title, illustration, caption, font, body text. Teach new terms: subtitle, columns, text boxes, bold.	1*: Guided reading and discussion of whole text. 2: Glossary exercise. 3*: Analysis of information genre. 4: Reading Comprehension based on 'Body Framework'.	Discuss the contents page to gain an overview of the book.
HOUR 2 Shared re-reading of the sections of 'Body Framework' in a different order and discuss whether it makes any difference to our understanding.	Study the features of information genre, for example use of simple present tense, non-chronological.	1: Reading Comprehension based on 'Body Framework'. 2*: Guided reading and discussion of whole text. 3: Glossary exercise. 4*: Analysis of information genre.	Review and summarize basic features of information genre.
HOUR 3 Examine the contents, index and glossary. Discuss their uses. Re-read 'Name those Bones' in the 'Body Framework' chapter.	Carry out an exercise on alphabetical order based on 'Name those bones'.	1*: Analysis of information genre. 2: Reading Comprehension based on 'Body Framework'. 3*: Guided reading and discussion of whole text. 4: Glossary exercise.	Display and discuss the glossary. Relate to the glossary exercise.
HOUR 4 Examine the book as a whole: look at cover design, introduction, 'blurb' and a range of page layouts.	Explore compound words.	1: Glossary exercise. 2*: Analysis of information genre. 3: Reading Comprehension based on 'Body Framework'. 4*: Guided reading and discussion of whole text.	Go over the answers to the Reading Comprehension questions with the whole class.

RESOURCES

Group set of *The Usborne Book of Body Facts* (ISBN 0-7460-0948-8), photocopiable pages 102 and 103 (Body Framework), 104 (Reading Comprehension) and 105 (Information Genre), OHP and acetate (optional).

PREPARATION

Make enough copies of all photocopiable sheets for one per pair. If possible, photocopy pages 102 and 103 side-by-side onto A3 to reflect the double-page spread layout and make OHTs of the contents and glossary pages of *The Usborne Book of Body Facts.*

Introduction

As a class, read the double-page spread 'Body Framework'. Involve children in the reading by asking for volunteers to read different sections. Draw attention to the three-column layout, text boxes and so on.

Whole-class skills work

Revise the terms: title, illustration, caption, font, body text. Teach new terms: subtitle, columns, text boxes, bold. Ask children to find examples in the text of 'Body Framework'.

Differentiated group activities

1*: Read and discuss the whole text using the group set. The following task can be used as a starting point.

Use the contents and index pages to find out where you would look for information on the heart. Try to answer these questions about the heart:

- Where in the body is it situated?
- How can you find out if your pulse rate is healthy?
- What is heart disease?

Ask the children to pose their own questions about the human body and go through the same process.

Examine the book as a whole including the front and back cover, the blurb, the page layout (Which features are standard throughout the book? Which vary?), the contents, glossary and index.

2: Glossary exercise. Tell the children to pick out 20 of the most difficult words in 'Body Framework' (do not use the Latin terms in the 'Name those Bones' box). They should then place them in alphabetical order in a column and write an explanation in a second column (using a dictionary to check/look up explanations).

3*: Analysis of information genre activity outlined on photocopiable page 105. Children in this group should attempt all parts of the sheet except part C.

4: Reading comprehension activity on photocopiable page 104, part A only. Point out that there is one question on each section of 'Body Framework' (except the sections in boxes). This will help them to find the information they need more easily.

Conclusion

If available, use an OHT of the contents page to discuss it and to gain an overview of the book. If an OHP is not available, ask the children what they would expect such a book to include and cross-check with the contents page. Read out the list of contents. Discuss how the contents page should be used.

Introduction

Re-read the sections of 'Body Framework' in a different order and discuss whether it makes any difference to our understanding. The answer is that it doesn't, thus demonstrating one important feature of information genre – it is non-chronological. Explain the last term by saying that *chrono-* means 'to do with time' (from Greek); hence, another word for clock is *chronometer*. In other words, information can be given in any order, it does not depend on a time sequence like a story.

Whole-class skills work

Study the features of information genre, using this list as a starting point:

- Use of layout to aid clarity: title, illustration, caption, font, body text, subtitle, columns, text boxes, bold.
- Non-chronological – explored and explained in the introduction.
- Use of simple present tense. Ask the children to explore this for themselves. Using the 'Body Framework' text, ask them to pick out verbs in the 'Bone brawn' section (where they will find examples of the verb 'to be'). If you sense any doubt in their minds, write out the present tense of the verb 'to be' for them to copy:

	SINGULAR	PLURAL
1st person	I am	We are
2nd person	You are	You are
3rd person	He/she/it is	They are

Differentiated group activities

1: Reading Comprehension – all parts.
2*: Reading and discussing the whole text (see above).
3: Glossary exercise (see above).
4*: Analysis of information genre, part A only.

Conclusion

Review the basic features of information genre: use of layout, use of simple present tense, non-chronological.

Introduction

Examine the index and glossary. Discuss their uses. Re-read 'Name those bones' in the 'Body Framework' chapter and explain that this is a short, specific glossary to help with the scientific terms of the bones mentioned on the page.

Whole-class skills work

Use this session to practise alphabetical order based on 'Name those bones'. Ask the children to put the list into alphabetical order. Begin with the common names and, if there is time, go on to do the same with the scientific names. This can be done with the whole-class working together, or pairs of children could work together for a timed period, then share results at the end.

Differentiated group activities

1*: Analysis of information genre – all parts.
2: Reading Comprehension based on 'Body Framework' – all parts.
3*: Reading and discussing the text (see above).
4: Glossary exercise – as above, but based on ten words from the passage.

Conclusion

If available, use an OHT of the Glossary on page 46 of *The Usborne Book of Body Facts*. Relate to the glossary exercise by asking the following questions: Is your glossary in alphabetical order? Does it contain a clear explanation?

Introduction

Examine the book as a whole: look at cover design, introduction, 'blurb' and a range of page layouts. One copy of the book could be given to each group, and OHTs (if available) used to look more closely at the 'blurb' and some additional pages.

Whole-class skills work

Explore compound words. Explain to children that *framework* (from the chapter title) is a compound word because it is made by putting two shorter words together. This is a way of making new words out of old ones and is very common. Compound words rarely change their spelling when they are put together. Ask children to scan the text and find at least five more. The compound words they might find are *newborn, breastbone, thighbone, topmost, backbone, cheekbone, kneecap, shinbone, collarbone* and *jawbone*.

Brainstorm some other compound words and write them on the board or flip chart. Explain that some compound words are not fully joined together and are written with a hyphen, for example: *double-jointed*. Can they think of others? (For example *all-round, bull's-eye, do-it-yourself, play-off*.)

Differentiated group activities

1: Glossary exercise (see above).
2*: Analysis of information genre – all parts (see above).
3: Reading Comprehension based on 'Body Framework' (see above).
4*: Reading and discussing the whole text (see above).

Conclusion

Go over the answers to the Reading Comprehension questions with the whole class and sum up the main objectives of the unit.

BODY FRAMEWORK (1)

Body framework

Skeleton scaffold

Without a skeleton, your body would collapse in a heap. Your skeleton holds your body up and gives it shape. It provides firm anchorage for your muscles so you can move. It also protects delicate organs, such as your heart, lungs, brain and spinal cord.

How many bones?

Most adults have 206 separate bones in their skeletons. A newborn baby has over 300 bones, but some of them join, or fuse, together as it gets older. Over half your bones are found in your hands and feet. There are 26 bones in each foot and 27 in each hand. These bones allow you to make very small, precise movements.

What's in a bone?

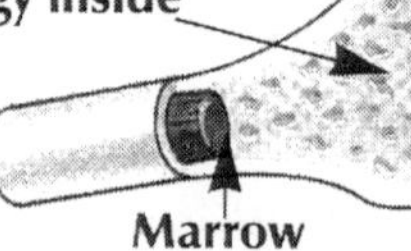

A bone is a living structure made up of water, minerals such as calcium, and a tough protein, collagen. The outer part is very hard, but the inside is softer and spongy. Some bones contain a substance called marrow which makes red blood cells.

Brain box

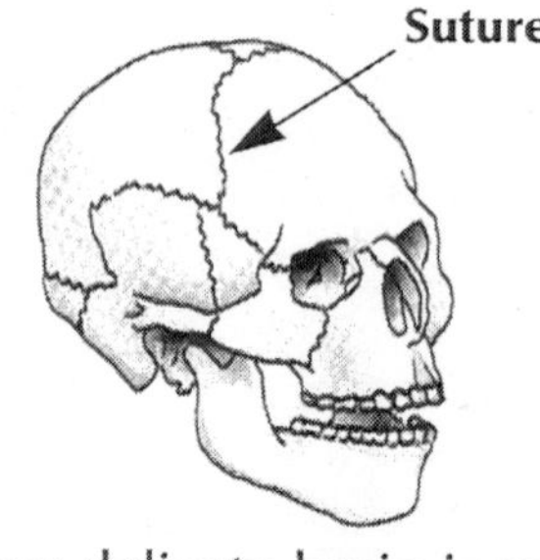

Your delicate brain is well protected inside your cranium, the main part of your skull. This "brain box" is actually eight separate bones. As you get older, the bones gradually join together to make your skull stronger. The places where the bones join are visible as wiggly lines, called sutures.

Amazing But True

Your rib cage is made up of 12 vertebrae, 24 ribs and a breastbone in three parts. It protects your heart and lungs from knocks and bumps. Your rib cage moves each time you breathe – about 5 million times a year.

Flexible backbone

Animals which have backbones and skeletons inside their bodies are called vertebrates. Your backbone is a flexible chain of 26 bones. The topmost bone supports your skull. It is called the atlas bone after the Greek god, Atlas. In legend, he carried the world on his shoulders.

Record-breaking bones

Longest bone	Femur (thighbone)
Strongest bone	Femur (thighbone)
Smallest bone	Stapes (stirrup-shaped bone inside the ear)
Largest joint	Knee joint
Smallest joint	Between bones inside ears

BODY FRAMEWORK (2)

Name those bones

All the bones in your body have a scientific name. Many also have a common name.

Scientific name	Common name
Cranium	Skull
Zygoma	Cheekbone
Mandible	Jawbone
Clavicle	Collarbone
Scapula	Shoulder blade
Sternum	Breastbone
Vertebrae	Backbone
Pelvis	Hips
Carpals	Wrist bones
Phalanges	Finger and toe bones
Femur	Thighbone
Patella	Kneecap
Tibia	Shinbone
Tarsals	Ankle bones

Bone brawn

Bone is one of the strongest materials. Bones are much lighter than steel or concrete, but, weight for weight, they are much stronger. A bone is five times stronger than a steel bar of the same weight. Bones make up about 14% of your body weight.

Multi-jointed

Many of your bones meet at joints. These allow you to bend and move. At a joint, the bones are held in place by strong straps, called ligaments. The ends of the bones are covered in pads of tough gristly cartilage, to prevent wear and tear. They are kept "oiled" by a special fluid, called synovial fluid. If you are "double-jointed", it just means that you have extra long ligaments in your joints and can bend them farther than usual.

Types of joints

There are about 100 joints in your body. They can be divided into five main types:

1. Hinge – knees, elbows and fingers.

2. Ball and socket – shoulders and hips.

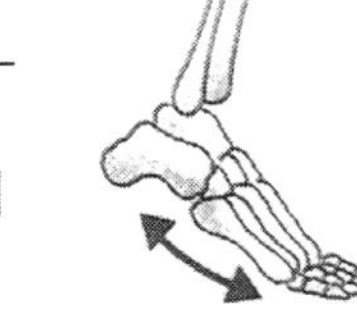

3. Sliding – between ankles and toes.

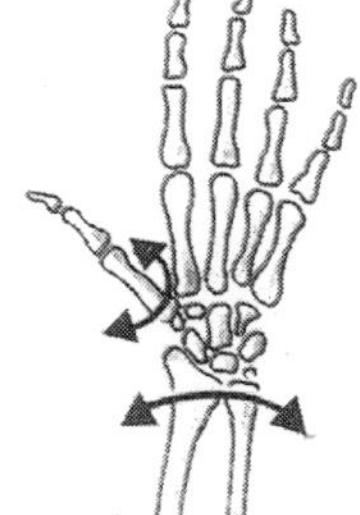

4. Saddle – at bases of thumbs.

5. Pivot – in wrists.

DID YOU KNOW?

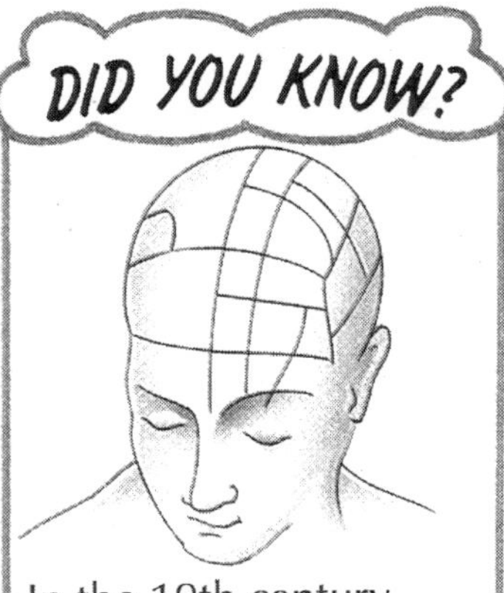

In the 19th century, some people believed that you could tell a person's character and special talents by feeling the bulges and bony lumps in their skull. This study is called phrenology. The skull is divided up into 37 areas. Each is said to represent a particular talent or characteristic.

READING COMPREHENSION

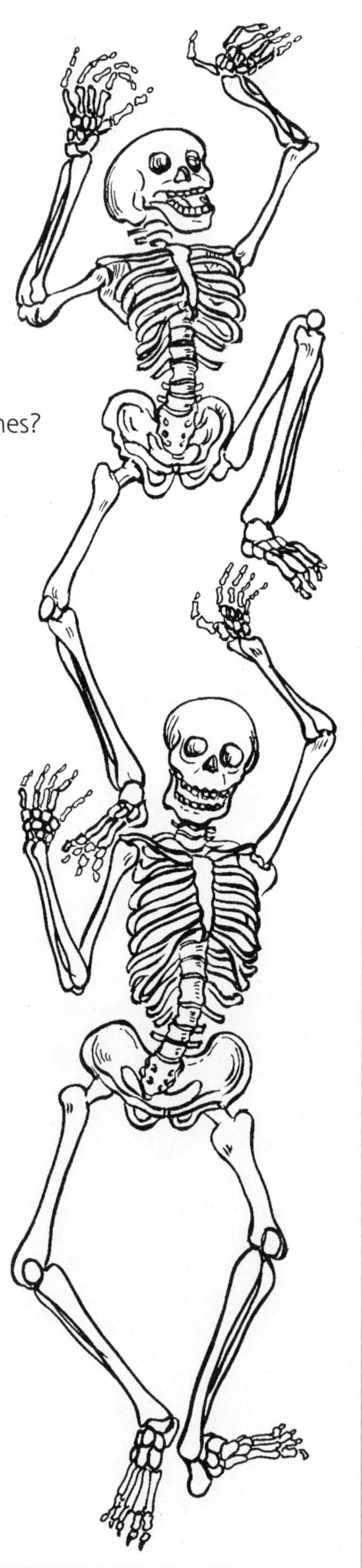

PART A

(Note: there is one question per section of text.)

- What is the skeleton for?
- How many bones are there in an adult skeleton?
- What is a bone made of?
- What is the scientific name for the 'brain box'?
- What is the scientific name for animals with backbones?
- What can you do if you are 'double-jointed'?
- Give an example of a 'hinge' type of joint.
- Which is stronger, a bone or a steel bar?

PART B

- Give the scientific names for: shoulder blade, hips, thighbone, kneecap.

- Give the common names for cranium, mandible, vertebrae, tibia.

PART C

- The skeleton does three things. What are they?

- A newborn baby has 300 bones, but adults have only 206. Why?

- Which bone is named after a Greek god and why?

- List three things that you have learned about bones that you didn't know before.

INFORMATION GENRE

PART A

■ Four sections of the text have a box around them. Why do you think the designer has done this?

■ Two of these boxes have headings with special fonts in specially drawn boxes. Why do you think the designer has done this?

■ Write out two examples of bold text. Explain what 'bold' means.

■ Why do you think the designer used cartoons for some of the illustrations?

■ Read the section 'Brain box' and find three verbs in the present tense.

■ Write out the present tense of the verb 'To join' in full.

PART B

■ Read the section 'Did you know?' Find three verbs in the present tense and one verb in the past tense. Explain why this verb is in the past tense.

■ Simple words and phrases are used to explain difficult scientific ones. Find four examples.

PART C

■ 'Brain box' gives scientific information about the brain. 'Did you know?' gives information about a belief which is unscientific. Pick out some phrases which show that the writer does not intend the reader to accept the information as fact.

PART D

■ Read carefully the information about phrenology in 'Did you know?' and then discuss whether you think there could be any truth in this idea.

Words in Windows

OBJECTIVES

UNIT	SPELLING/VOCABULARY	GRAMMAR/PUNCTUATION	COMPREHENSION/ COMPOSITION
WRITING NON-FICTION Explanation genre: Words in Windows.	Check spellings in own work. Revise terms: *title, illustration, caption, font, body text, subtitle, columns, text boxes, bold.*	Revise redrafting skills. Devise redrafting checklist for information writing.	Make short notes. Present information and explanations in the style of modern reference books using organizational devices.

ORGANIZATION (2 HOURS)

	INTRODUCTION	WHOLE-CLASS SKILLS WORK	DIFFERENTIATED GROUP ACTIVITIES	CONCLUSION
HOUR 1	Examine information texts and understand how features of layout help to access and convey information. Revise relevant terminology.	Revise note-taking by examining the kind of notes used on the 'Robot' resource sheet.	1–4*: Prepare first drafts of a double-page spread entitled 'Mechanical People', using the notes as the basis for work.	Share examples of the reference book pages.
HOUR 2	Use two examples of first drafts for discussion about redrafting.	Revise key redrafting skills. Devise redrafting checklist for information writing.	1–4*: Redraft work and write out neat versions.	Display and discuss the reference book pages.

RESOURCES

Photocopiable pages 108 (Robot Notes) and 109 (Writing Template) and, from previous unit, photocopiable pages 102 and 103 ('Body Framework') and, from 'Redrafting Simulation' unit, photocopiable page 98 (Redrafting Checklist), a selection of information and reference books that contain information about robots, OHP and acetate (optional), board or flip chart, writing materials.

PREPARATION

Prepare enough copies of photocopiable pages 108 (Robot Notes), 102 and 103 ('Body Framework') for one between two, and enough copies of page 109 (Writing Template) for two each (one for rough draft, one for revision). If possible, prepare OHTs of pages 108 (Robot Notes) and 102 and 103 ('Body Framework').

Introduction

If possible, display the OHTs of the 'Body Framework' spread from the previous unit. Alternatively, you can use enlarged A3 versions of the pages, or of any similar pages from an information book. Read the text and discuss it, concentrating on how the information is conveyed and the layout features of information texts that enable easy access to the information. Revise the terms: title, illustration, caption, font, body text, subtitle, columns, text boxes, bold. Ask the children to find examples in the text. Distribute the selection of information texts you have gathered and ask the children to open them randomly and find examples of the terms you have discussed. Can they find any other features in these books that you have not yet discussed?

Whole-class skills work

Explain to the children that during their group work session, they will work at producing an information book double-page spread similar to 'Body Framework' but based on bodies of a different sort – robots (that is, mechanical bodies!). Display the OHT of photocopiable page 108 and explain that this is a facsimile page of notes that someone has made when researching the subject of robots. Read the sheet and discuss it with the children, highlighting important note-taking skills and finding examples of each:

- illustrations are quickly sketched
- ideas are not written in full sentences
- some abbreviations are used
- not all the sketches and ideas have to be used in the final piece.

Discuss possible additions to each section, particularly the part on robots in the future.

Differentiated group activities

1–4*: All groups prepare first drafts of one or two pages for a reference book entitled 'Mechanical People'. They use the notes as the basis for their work. The first step is to design the page (where necessary) and to decide what information goes where. The next step is to write a rough draft. Children in Group 1 can design their page from scratch on a blank A3 sheet, and if appropriate could add to the notes using the collection of reference and information books available. Children in Groups 2 and 3 should be encouraged to produce a double-page spread, keeping their design fairly close to the template (although if they wish to adapt it, encourage their initiative) and writing from the notes provided, although they can adapt it as required. Children in Group 4 should write a single page straight onto the template, using it exactly as it is.

Conclusion

Share examples of the reference book pages. The rest of the class should evaluate them by discussing the following:

- How clear is the page layout?
- Do features such as titles, subtitles, captions, text boxes and bold help or confuse the reader?
- Have the notes been interpreted in the same way?

Introduction

Select two examples of first drafts for discussion about redrafting and (if available) display them on the OHP. Compare them with the 'Body Framework' spread and/or examples from other information texts. What possible improvements could be made? Make some suggestions yourself (for example, a diagram needs a caption or labels, some sentences are still in note form and need to be made into a complete sentence, and so on) and then invite the class (including those children whose work it is) to make their own suggestions. For each suggestion, determine what aspect of the work this involves – for example spelling, punctuation, layout, sentence construction.

Whole-class skills work

Use this session to devise with the children a 'redrafting checklist' for information text writing. You could use the checklist from the Redrafting unit, 'Kanda, the Fisherman', as a model, although this is primarily for fiction. Organize the list under headings as suggested above and write the checklist on the board or flip chart for the children to use as a reference. (Later on, this list could be written on A4 paper for photocopying and distributing; or children could make their own personal checklist from it.)

Differentiated group activities

1–4*: All children redraft their work and write out neat versions.

Conclusion

Display and discuss the reference book pages.

FURTHER IDEA

As soon as possible, use the ideas in this unit as a basis for writing up information in another curriculum area.

ROBOT NOTES

History

In ancient times – stories of 'mechanical monsters being brought to life'!
comes from Czech word 'robota' meaning 'forced labour'.
First used 1921 by Czech play writer Karel Capek. His robot a mechanical device that looked human but no thoughts or feelings. In play, robots destroy their makers!

Definition

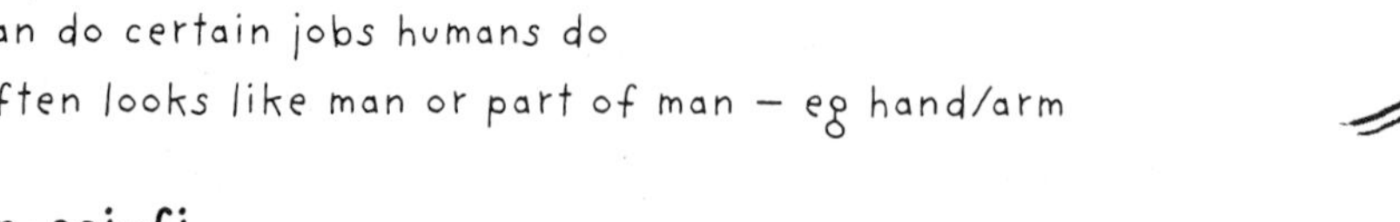

computer-controlled machine
can do certain jobs humans do
often looks like man or part of man – eg hand/arm

In sci-fi

Image of 'metal monsters' like in Karel's play
Examples: Isaac Asimov's stories

Sensors work in the same way as human nervous system in diagram

Robbie the robot in the 1956 film 'Forbidden Planet'

C3PO and R2D2 in 'Star Wars'

In real world

Used mainly in science research and industry
factories – assembly, paint spraying, welding.
They have sensors – touch sensors and laser vision, but do not look human.
Remote control R. are used for bomb disposal.

Advantages

Quicker, cheaper, more accurate than humans
can work in places and conditions humans can't – ocean, space, dangerous situations (bombs, germs).

Space exploration

The Viking landers had robot arms which dug and analysed samples of soil.

Future

Japan leads in robot technology.

WRITING TEMPLATE

Key Facts:

-
-
-
-

APPRAISING NON-FICTION TEXTS

OBJECTIVES

UNIT	SPELLING/VOCABULARY	GRAMMAR/PUNCTUATION	COMPREHENSION/ COMPOSITION
REFERENCE AND RESEARCH SKILLS Appraising Non-fiction Texts.	Understand and use the vocabulary related to features of non-fiction texts.	Identify features of non-fiction texts.	Appraise non-fiction books. Raise awareness of need to be critical when choosing and using information books.

ORGANIZATION (1 HOUR)

INTRODUCTION	WHOLE-CLASS SKILLS WORK	DIFFERENTIATED GROUP ACTIVITIES	CONCLUSION
HOUR 1 Use information books on a current topic of study and pupil-devised questions to model process of appraising suitable reference sources.	Distinguish the different features of information texts and establish their specific functions.	1–4: Audit and appraise a selection of information books. * Teacher works with Groups 1 & 4.	Share results of group work. Identify other criteria for appraisal.

RESOURCES

Photocopiable page 112 (Information Book Audit), several information books that are on a topic currently being studied in another curriculum area plus a large selection of other information books suitable for the various abilities in your class (these should include pairs of books on the same topic for children in Group 1), flip chart or board, writing materials.

PREPARATION

Make enough copies of photocopiable page 112 (Information Book Audit) for one between two children.

Introduction

Ask the children to think about a current topic of study and brainstorm some questions to which they would like to find answers. Write these questions on the board or flip chart. Show the children the books you have collected on the topic and, taking each question in turn, model how to find the answers. Determine which book might be the most likely 'first port of call' for the question. This might be suggested by the title, or even by a front cover illustration. (It may be that none of the books looks suitable – in which case what would they do?)

Having identified the most likely book, what book feature would they turn to next? Continue in this vein until at least a couple of the questions have been answered. Explain to the children that it is important for them to look critically at the books they use for information retrieval, so that when they are choosing books for research, they are aware of the various features that will help them find the information they need quickly.

In addition, because no book is perfect, they should be able to use a variety of strategies to find information in books that do not have all the features.

Whole-class skills work

Write the following words on the board or flip chart: *contents, index, glossary, caption, label, diagram, graph, photograph, illustration.* Discuss these as features of information books and establish that they all provide different kinds of information. Go through each of them, asking the children to tell you what they are and what kind of information they provide. Then probe a little further by asking questions such as: what is the difference between an index and a table of contents? If the information book you have chosen does not have an index, could you get by with just using the contents? What problems might arise? Can a glossary be used for the same purpose as an index? What is the difference between an illustration and a photograph? Between a label and a caption? What kind of information would a diagram give you that an illustration would not?

Differentiated group work

All children work in pairs in their ability groups to investigate and appraise information books using the 'audit' on photocopiable page 112.
1*: Identify the information retrieval features of any two information books *on the same topic*. Each child should then think of two questions to ask on the topic. Partners swap questions and try to find answers in the books. Evaluate their usefulness. Evaluate the questions.
2 & 3: Identify the information retrieval features of any two information books. Evaluate which is easier to find information from and why.
4*: Identify the information retrieval features of any two information books.

Conclusion

Ask selected pairs from each group to report back on their 'audits'. Are there some features that all books had? Are there any that none had? Ask children: If I wanted to find out information about the Internet, would I find it in a book published in 1975? Establish that there are also other criteria for judging the usefulness of an information book. Looking at when a book was published indicates whether the information might be out of date or not. Looking at who wrote the book might indicate bias.

INFORMATION BOOK AUDIT

Which of these features do your books have? Put a tick in the appropriate box.

Title of Book 1:

Title of Book 2:

Book feature	Book 1	Book 2
Clear title	☐	☐
Author	☐	☐
Cover picture	☐	☐
Book description on cover	☐	☐
Index	☐	☐
Contents page	☐	☐
Glossary	☐	☐
Introduction	☐	☐
Bibliography	☐	☐
Further reading list	☐	☐
Chapters	☐	☐
Illustrations	☐	☐
Photographs	☐	☐
Maps	☐	☐
Diagrams	☐	☐
Graphs	☐	☐
Captions	☐	☐
Labels	☐	☐
Page numbers	☐	☐
Guide words at top/ bottom of pages	☐	☐
Other:	☐	☐
Other:	☐	☐

Which book do you think is the better example of an information book? Why?

OLD PRAISE SONG OF THE CROCODILE

OBJECTIVES

UNIT	SPELLING/VOCABULARY	GRAMMAR/PUNCTUATION	COMPREHENSION/ COMPOSITION
READING POETRY Cultural variety: 'Old Praise Song of the Crocodile'.	Identify words and phrases which suggest poem is from a different culture. Collect and note new words from reading.	Mark up a text for reading aloud. Add own punctuation.	Focus on expressive and descriptive language. Respond orally and through drama.

ORGANIZATION (1 HOUR)

INTRODUCTION	WHOLE-CLASS SKILLS WORK	DIFFERENTIATED GROUP ACTIVITIES	CONCLUSION
HOUR 1 Shared reading of the song to the class.	Mark up a text for reading aloud.	1–4*: All groups plan a presentation of the song.	Two or three groups are chosen to present their versions to the class.

RESOURCES

Photocopiable page 115 ('Old Praise Song of the Crocodile'), a range of simple percussion instruments, a variety of dictionaries (some that are likely to contain the difficult words from the poem), OHP and acetate (optional), flip chart or board, writing materials.

PREPARATION

Make enough copies of photocopiable page 115 for one between two children. If possible, prepare the poem as an OHT. Move desks/tables aside to make room for drama or use a drama studio or hall if available.

Introduction

'Old Praise Song of the Crocodile' is a traditional song of the Sotho tribe (Northern Transvaal) which was chanted to the accompaniment of drums. Explain that songs like this were not written down until recently but were passed on by word of mouth for thousands of years. Give out the copies of the poem to the children (or use an OHP). Read it through once so that the children get a feel for the poem. Then re-read it through in short sections. Introduce each section with the explanation and follow up with a question. For example:

The first four lines describe the crocodile.
Q: How is he described? What is an invoker?

The next line is written from the crocodile's point of view.
Q: What does he call himself?

The next four lines are about the rain paying a tribute to the crocodile.
Q: What is a tribute? Who are the lords of the rivers? Why do you think the Sotho tribe call them this?

The next five lines are about the crocodile attacking a beast (probably a cow) and dragging it down into the pool.
Q: How does the crocodile do this?

The next four lines are about what the owners of the beast do.
Q: Where do the owners look for the beast? How do you think they feel?

The last section is about the crocodile again – Mmamolemana is a Sotho god.
Q: What does the crocodile do while he kills?

Finally, read the whole poem again without a break. The sections could be divided among the class.

Whole-class skills work

Ask children to identify difficult words in the poem. Write them down on the board or flip chart and then suggest that the children look up the meanings in the dictionary. First, look at each word in turn, and ask where in the dictionary they might be – would they find them in the beginning, middle or end of the dictionary? Ask the children to look them up and write their definitions by the words on the board or flip chart. Words they may offer are: *invoker, seeking, tribute, torrents.*

Check the pronunciation of *Mmamolemana* (pronounce phonetically).

Explain to the class how to mark up a text for reading aloud using a mixture of conventional and invented punctuation:

- Add full stops and commas where they might be helpful.
- Underline or highlight their own part.
- Double-underline words which must be emphasized.
- Add notes such as *loudly*, *angrily* and so on.

Differentiated group activities

All children should read through the poem in their groups, deciding how they would prepare it for a performance of the poem – for example they might all read it together in chorus or they might allocate specific sections to each child. They might use percussion instruments to try to re-create the style of the Sotho. They should then mark up their text for performance.

Each group should plan a follow-up to their reading, for example:
1: Make up a similar song for another animal. Use ideas from the Crocodile song.
2: Prepare a ceremony of praise for the 'lords of the river' – the hippo and the crocodile. Use some of the words and phrases from the song, such as 'O black one of the pool'.
3: Improvise a short scene in which someone is attacked by a crocodile.
4: Develop a mime or dance which is based on the events in the song.

* The teacher gives support to all groups as necessary.

Conclusion

Choose two or three groups to present their version of the poem and the follow-up to the class.

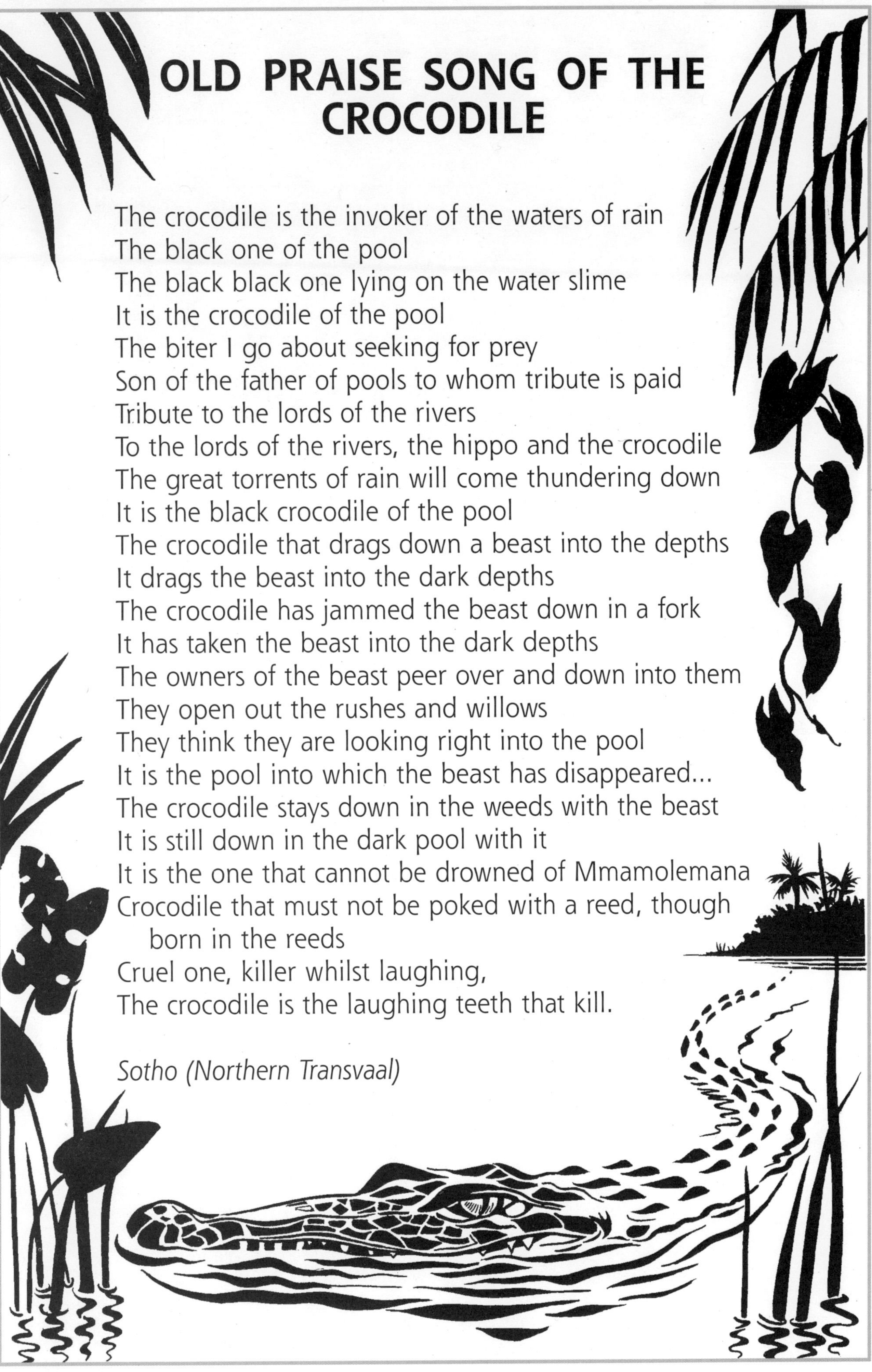

OLD PRAISE SONG OF THE CROCODILE

The crocodile is the invoker of the waters of rain
The black one of the pool
The black black one lying on the water slime
It is the crocodile of the pool
The biter I go about seeking for prey
Son of the father of pools to whom tribute is paid
Tribute to the lords of the rivers
To the lords of the rivers, the hippo and the crocodile
The great torrents of rain will come thundering down
It is the black crocodile of the pool
The crocodile that drags down a beast into the depths
It drags the beast into the dark depths
The crocodile has jammed the beast down in a fork
It has taken the beast into the dark depths
The owners of the beast peer over and down into them
They open out the rushes and willows
They think they are looking right into the pool
It is the pool into which the beast has disappeared...
The crocodile stays down in the weeds with the beast
It is still down in the dark pool with it
It is the one that cannot be drowned of Mmamolemana
Crocodile that must not be poked with a reed, though
born in the reeds
Cruel one, killer whilst laughing,
The crocodile is the laughing teeth that kill.

Sotho (Northern Transvaal)

LIMERICKS

OBJECTIVES

UNIT	SPELLING/VOCABULARY	GRAMMAR/PUNCTUATION	COMPREHENSION/ COMPOSITION
WRITING POETRY Limericks.	Identify stressed and unstressed syllables.	Revise capital letters for new lines of poetry.	Identify patterns of rhyme and rhythm in poetry. Write own poems based on structures of those read.

ORGANIZATION (1 HOUR)

INTRODUCTION	WHOLE-CLASS SKILLS WORK	DIFFERENTIATED GROUP ACTIVITIES	CONCLUSION
HOUR 1 Explain what a limerick is and read the examples to the class.	Revise the terms 'rhyme' and 'couplet'. Demonstrate how to mark stresses in lines of poetry. Analyse the rhythm and rhyme pattern of limericks.	1–4*: Take the whole class step by step through the limerick writing activity, then give support where necessary as they write their own.	Aim for each pupil to read out one limerick.

RESOURCES

Photocopiable pages 118 (Limericks) and 119 (Horrifying Limericks), enough dice for one between two children, a rhyming dictionary (optional), writing materials.

PREPARATION

Prepare enough copies of photocopiable page 119 (Horrifying Limericks) for the children to have one between two. Copy the sheet of limericks onto acetate for an OHP (or enlarge to A3 size).

Introduction

Read one of the limericks from photocopiable page 118 to the class. Ask if they know what kind of poem it is. Explain that the limerick is a well-known verse form which is named after the town in Ireland where it was invented about 100 years ago. A limerick is a short, funny poem that tells a little story. It has five lines. Lines 1, 2 and 5 rhyme and have three beats. Lines 3 and 4 rhyme and have two beats. The last line of a limerick is often like the punchline of a joke and is written to make the reader laugh. A limerick often resembles a mini-story with characters, setting and a plot (the events that take place).

Whole-class skills work

Briefly revise the terms 'rhyme' and 'couplet'. Display the page of limericks and ask individuals to read them out. Then pick one and together mark out the rhyme scheme using letters of the alphabet (a for the first rhyme, b for the second and so on). Do the same with a second one. What do the children notice? (That the rhyme scheme of a limerick is *a a b b a*.) Check by doing another one.

Now explore the concept of stressed and unstressed syllables. Ask children to read a line with great emphasis, clapping the stressed syllables. They should come to the conclusion that lines 1, 2 and 5 have three stressed syllables or beats, and lines 3 and 4 have two. They should then mark the syllables which receive most emphasis with a diagonal line. The following text shows an example of a limerick marked up in full.

/ / /
There once was a kangaroo
/ / /
Who hopped down the avenue
/ /
When he stopped to say,
/ /
'Have a fine day,'
/ / /
He caused quite a hullabaloo.

Differentiated group activities

Take the class step by step through the limerick-writing activity. Children should work in pairs and each pair will need a die and a copy of photocopiable page 119 (Horrifying Limericks).

- Child 1 shakes the die and looks up the number he or she has thrown in the first group of six lines. He or she then copies this down while child 2 takes a turn.
- Child 1 then does the same but this time looks up the number he or she has thrown in the *second* group of six lines. He or she copies this while child 2 takes a turn.
- The process is repeated until both children have written down a line from all five groups. They have now written a randomly generated limerick.

Children could then customize the sheet as follows:

- Think of different kinds of rooms and write a new set of first lines.
- Adapt the set of second lines by changing creatures, but keeping the same rhymes at the end.
- Mix in more reactions (ending with 'oo' rhymes) to sections 3 and 4.

Children now repeat the dice-throwing activity and create a whole new set of limericks.

Differentiation can be provided as follows:

1: Write their own limericks from scratch.
2 & 3: Try all the changes listed above.
4: Concentrate on adapting the set of first lines only, and if time allows, the set of second lines.

* The teacher gives support where necessary.

Conclusion

Encourage every child to read out one limerick. Discuss ways of 'publishing' the limericks as a class book and ensure there is time to do this outside the Literacy Hour.

LIMERICKS

There once was a kangaroo
Who hopped down the avenue
When he stopped to say,
'Have a fine day,'
He caused quite a hullabaloo.

There was a young lady from Crete,
Who was so exceedingly neat,
When she got out of bed
She stood on her head
To make sure of not soiling her feet.

There was a small maiden named Maggie,
Whose dog was enormous and shaggy;
The front end of him
Looked vicious and grim
But the tail end was friendly and waggy.

A diner was dining at Crew
Found a rather large mouse in his stew.
Said the waiter, 'Don't shout
And wave it about,
Or the rest will be wanting one, too.'

A glutton who came from the Rhine
Was asked at what hour he'd dine.
He replied, 'At eleven,
At three, five and seven,
And eight and a quarter to nine.'

A sea-serpent saw a big tanker,
Bit a hole in her side and then sank 'er.
It swallowed the crew
In a minute or two
And then picked its teeth with the anchor.

There was a young lady of Riga
Who went for a ride on a tiger.
They returned from the ride
With the lady inside
And a smile on the face of the tiger.

HORRIFYING LIMERICKS

Do you like limericks? If so, look no further. Using this page, you can create lots of your very own horror limericks! Just roll a die for each section, and read off the lines!

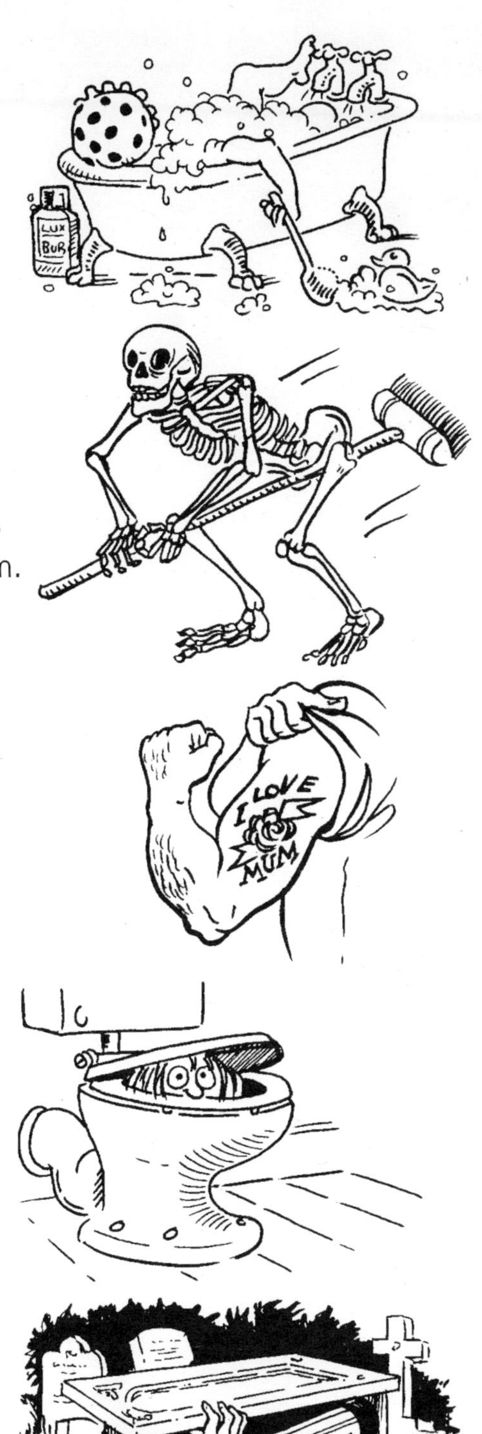

1. I was wallowing in my bathroom,
2. I was teaching in the old schoolroom,
3. I was on duty in the guardroom,
4. I was dancing in the duke's ballroom,
5. I was drunk in the landlord's taproom,
6. I was searching my grandad's storeroom,

1. When a vampire appeared in the gloom.
2. When a zombie arrived from Khartoum.
3. When a skeleton rode in on a broom.
4. When a ghost offered me some perfume.
5. When a werewolf charged in with a boom.
6. When I spotted a spooky bridegroom.

1. So I shouted out, 'Boo!'
2. So I squirted shampoo
3. So I showed my tattoo
4. So I said to him, 'Shoo!'
5. So I phoned up the zoo
6. So I said, 'Who are you?'

1. And showered him with glue
2. And the creature withdrew
3. And painted him blue
4. And swore in Hindu
5. And hid in the loo
6. What else could I do?

1. And today he is back in his tomb.
2. So he took off his spooky costume.
3. And he scurried away from the room.
4. But he dragged me away to my doom.
5. But he took me to his catacomb.
6. But he couldn't have been real, I presume.

The Snow Queen

OBJECTIVES

UNIT	SPELLING/VOCABULARY	GRAMMAR/PUNCTUATION	COMPREHENSION/ COMPOSITION
READING FICTION Long-established fiction – fantasy adventure story: *The Snow Queen* by Hans Christian Andersen.	Learn the archaic terms and other new vocabulary in the text. Spell *ou* and *ough* words.	Revise and identify adjectives. Develop knowledge of similes. Recognize prepositions. Recognize conjunctions.	Understand how writers create imaginary worlds. Identify clues to when story was written. Study plot, character, setting. Appreciate descriptive language. Literal and inferential comprehension.

ORGANIZATION (5 HOURS)

INTRODUCTION	WHOLE-CLASS SKILLS WORK	DIFFERENTIATED GROUP ACTIVITIES	CONCLUSION
HOUR 1 Preview the book and its illustrations. Predict genre. Shared reading of 'The Story of the Mirror and its Fragments' and 'The First Story', pages 5–14 (approx 12 minutes).	Identify archaic terms and other new vocabulary in the text.	1–3*: Play the 'Snow Queen Adventure Game'. 4*: Play the 'Snow Queen Board Game'.	Discuss the outcome of the different games and how they relate to the plot of the story.
HOUR 2 Shared reading of 'The Second Story', pages 15–20 (approx 12 minutes). Identify details that depict imaginary world.	Study selected descriptive passages and identify adjectives and similes.	1*: Guided reading and discussion of passage. 2 & 3: Cloze exercise. 4*: Guided reading and discussion of passage.	Groups 1 & 4 lead a discussion and summary of the day's passage.
HOUR 3 Shared reading of 'The Third Story', pages 21–26 (approx 12 minutes). Discuss the 'stories within a story' structure of the book.	Identify the use of prepositions.	1: Cloze exercise. 2 & 3*: Guided reading and discussion of passage. 4: Cloze exercise (first paragraph only).	Groups 2 & 3 lead a discussion of the day's passage.
HOUR 4 Shared reading of 'The Fourth Story', pages 27–33 (approx 10 minutes). Compare settings through illustrations.	Identify and understand the use of conjunctions.	1*: Guided reading and discussion of passage. 2 & 3: Character study (part 1). 4*: Guided reading and discussion of passage.	Sum up and review the story so far.
HOUR 5 Shared reading of 'The Fifth Story' and 'The Sixth Story', pages 34–48 (approx 18 minutes).	Spell *ou* and *ough* words.	1: Character study (part 1). 2 & 3*: Guided reading and discussion of passage. 4: Character study (part 2).	Discussion of the characters in the story.

RESOURCES

The Snow Queen by Hans Christian Andersen, illustrated by PJ Lynch (Red Fox, ISBN 0-09-948641-5) – if possible, enough copies for half the class, photocopiable pages 125 (The Snow Queen Adventure Game), 126 (The Snow Queen Board Game), 127 (Descriptions), 128 (The Story of the Mirror and its Fragments) and 129 (Character Study – Kay), dictionaries, board or flip chart, writing materials, enough coins for Groups 1–3, enough dice for Group 4.

PREPARATION

Make enough copies of photocopiable page 125 (The Snow Queen Adventure Game) for one between four children in Groups 1–3, and of photocopiable page 126 (The Snow Queen Board Game) for one between four children in Group 4. If possible, prepare an OHT of photocopiable page 127 (Descriptions), otherwise enlarge it to at least A3 or make enough A4 copies for one between two children. Make enough copies of photocopiable page 128 (The Story of the Mirror and its Fragments) and 129 (Character Study – Kay) for each child.

SYNOPSIS

This is Hans Christian Andersen's classic tale of how a young boy, Kay, is perversely affected by splinters of glass in his eye and heart which make him cold and unfeeling and cause him to see beauty in ugliness and vice versa. He is abducted by the Snow Queen and taken to her frozen palace, where he soon forgets his close friend, Gerda. But she does not forget him. She travels far and wide to find him and, after a series of adventures, eventually rescues him.

Introduction

Distribute the group set of books so that there is at least one per table and begin the shared reading session by previewing the book. Look at the front cover. What is the title of the book? What kind of story does the title suggest it is? Why? Who is the author? What do the children know about him? What other stories have they read or heard by him? Who is the illustrator? Examine the illustration and elicit children's responses to the style and image. Does the illustration help them to predict what the story may be about? Flick through the book. Ask the children to suggest what relationship the words and pictures have in a book like this. Read the 'blurb' and the quotes on the back cover. Read 'The Story of the Mirror and its Fragments' and 'The First Story' on pages 5–14.

Whole-class skills work

The language of Hans Christian Andersen is rich, even in translation, and children will benefit from collecting and learning the archaic terms and other new vocabulary in the text. This session should focus on the vocabulary in the day's passage. There will not be time to look at vocabulary in such detail every day but this session should demonstrate to children how to deal with new vocabulary themselves. Important new words should be discussed in the guided reading sessions.

Ask the children to suggest some difficult or unusual words from the book so far and write these up on the board or flip chart. There are many (for example: *odious, distorted, inhabitants, fragments* – page 5, *entwined, swarm* – page 6, *particles* – page 7), so limit your list to ten or twelve. Then ask the children to work in pairs to look up the words in a dictionary. Give each pair two or three of the words and perhaps only one to less able children. Ensure that the dictionaries used contain the words needed. Ask pairs to give their definitions and write these next to the appropriate words, as many as time allows.

Differentiated group activities

1–4*: All groups play one of the versions of the Snow Queen game. The purpose of this is to explore the 'linear' plot type and alternative plots, as well as to become familiar with key characters and settings. Playing groups should consist of two to four players.
1–3: Play the 'Snow Queen Adventure Game'. Give each group a copy (enlarged if possible) of photocopiable page 125 and a coin. Explain that they should take turns to make their way from Grandma's house in Nordheim to the Snow Queen's palace to rescue Kay. At each turn they must toss the coin and follow the instructions.

4: Play the 'Snow Queen Board Game'. This is simpler than the adventure game but achieves the same purposes. Give each group a copy (enlarged if possible) of photocopiable page 126 and a die. Explain that they should take it in turns to make their way from Grandma's house in Nordheim to the Snow Queen's palace to find Kay. First one there, wins!

Conclusion

Begin by pointing out that all the events, characters and settings are taken from the story, but because of the way the game was played, they would have happened in a different order in each game. Discuss the outcome of the different games and how they relate to the plot of the story. The key question is: Did Gerda save Kay in your version of the game? What obstacles did she face? What do you think will happen in Hans Christian Andersen's version of the story?

Introduction

Read 'The Second Story' on page 15–20 (approximately 12 minutes) and discuss briefly how the illustrations both support and extend the text. Ask the class what details from the text and illustrations help to create the imaginary world of the story (for example talking animals, an enchantress and an enchanted garden, Gerda's tears making the rose bush grow again, the time lapse from summer to late autumn).

Whole-class skills work

Give out copies of photocopiable page 127 (Descriptions) or display it on an OHP. Read the first description (of the magic mirror) and revise the term 'simile'. Ask the children to find the simile in the description (*the loveliest landscapes looked like boiled spinach*) and then to comment on why it is so effective. Read the second description (of the Snow Queen) and point out how the details the author uses makes this description so vivid. Ask the children to find another simile. Finally, ask them to find the adjectives.

Read through the other descriptions together, looking for:

- descriptive details
- adjectives
- similes and/or other examples of figurative language.

Differentiated group activities

1*: Guided reading and discussion of the passage. Ask the children to be prepared to lead a brief discussion about the description in the passage at the end of the hour. The following questions can be used as a starting point:

- What persuaded Gerda to look for Kay?
- Why did the old woman want Gerda to stay with her?
- What did she do to try to make her stay?
- What was it that reminded Gerda of Kay? Why?
- Discuss the description in the last paragraph.

2 & 3: Cloze exercise (photocopiable page 128). Explain that the purpose of the exercise is to fill in the gaps in any way that makes sense, *not* to try to reproduce from memory what the author wrote.

4*: Guided reading and discussion of the passage (see above).

Conclusion

Select children from Groups 1 and 4 to lead a discussion of the day's passage. They should summarize the story and point out some of the effective descriptions in the passage they read and relate it to the whole-class skills work on description.

Introduction

Read 'The Third Story' on page 21–26 (approximately 12 minutes). Discuss briefly the structure of *The Snow Queen,* how each 'adventure' is a story within a story. Summarize this third story in terms of beginning, middle and end.

Whole-class skills work

Introduce the concept of prepositions. Write some or all of the following list of words on the board or flip chart. Ask children to look for examples in 'The Third Story'. Explore their use and explain that these short words are important in sentences because they describe the relationship between things and/or people in terms of time and space. The purpose of the exercise is to help children have a feeling for what a preposition does in a sentence.

about	across	after	at
before	behind	by	down
for	from	in	inside
of	off	on	onto
out	over	round	through
to	under	up	upon

Differentiated group activities

1: Cloze exercise (see above).
2 & 3*: Guided reading and discussion of the passage. The following questions can be used as a starting point. Ask the children to be prepared to lead a discussion about the last point.

- What did the raven tell Gerda about Kay?
- Pick out some prepositions on page 21.
- What details of Kay's appearance and possessions do the raven and Kay describe when they are trying to decide if they are talking about the same person?
- How does Gerda get into the palace?
- Look carefully at the description on page 24. Pick out the adjectives and the descriptive details.
- What did the princess do when Gerda told her story?
- What things in the story give it a dreamlike quality?

4: Cloze exercise (first paragraph only).

Conclusion

Select children from Groups 2 and 3 to lead a discussion of the day's passage. They should point out some of the things (such as a raven speaking) that give the story a dreamlike quality.

Introduction

Read 'The Fourth Story' on pages 27–33 (approximately 10 minutes). Look at the illustration on page 28 and ask children to compare it with the setting of the enchanted garden on pages 18 and 19.

Whole-class skills work

Identify the use of conjunctions. Teach this simple definition: *a conjunction is a connecting word that joins words or parts of a sentence.* Write some or all of the list below on the board or flip chart and ask the children to look for examples in 'The Fourth Story'. The purpose of the exercise is to help children have a feeling for what a conjunction does in a sentence.

after	although	and	as
because	before	but	for
if	while	since	though
unless	until	when	where

Differentiated group activities

1*: Guided reading and discussion of the passage. The following questions can be used as a starting point:

- What happens to Gerda at the beginning of 'The Fourth Story'?
- In your own words, describe the character of the little robber-maiden. How does she compare to Gerda?
- Find examples of conjunctions on page 27.
- What did the wood-pigeons tell Gerda?
- How does the robber-maiden help Gerda?

2 & 3: Character Study – Kay (photocopiable page 129, part A). For those sections dealing with the parts of the story the children have not yet read, they should predict what happens to Kay's character. More able children can read on independently in order to finish the description.
4*: Guided reading and discussion of the passage (see above).

Conclusion
Sum up the story so far. Refer back to the board games and discuss how the characters and settings are now better known. Ask the children if anyone's game took a similar course to the story.

HOUR 5

Introduction
Read 'The Fifth Story' and 'The Sixth Story' on pages 34–48 (approximately 18 minutes).

Whole-class skills work
Investigate words with *ou*. First, write the following list of words from the story on the board or flip chart and ask the children to say what sound each *ou* makes. You could make a chart like the one below:

WORD	SOUND
touched	u (as in *such*)
ground	ow (as in *now*)
could	oo (as in *wood*)
you	u (as in blue)

Ask the children to give other examples, either from the story or ones they think of themselves.

Next, write out this list of problematic *ough* words, and determine the sound the letter string makes in each case. Ask the children to write them in their wordbooks and to learn them for homework.

bough	cough	dough	enough
plough	rough	thorough	though
through	tough	trough	

Differentiated group activities
1: Character study (part A) They should be encouraged to expand on the framework given and bring in evidence from other chapters.
2 & 3*: Guided reading and discussion of the passage. The following questions can be used as a starting point:
■ Study the description of the Lapland woman's hut. Look at the use of adjectives and the descriptive details.
■ Find more examples of the *ou* and *ough* letter strings.
■ How does the Finland woman help Gerda?
■ How does Gerda help Kay to get back to normal?
■ What happens at the end of the story?
4: Character study (part B).

Conclusion
Discuss the characters in the story. Begin asking the children to report back from their character studies on Kay, then discuss other characters in the same way: What are they like? What part did they play in the story?

FURTHER IDEA

Make OHTs of some of the illustrations showing settings. Use them to project backdrops for dramatic improvisations based on the story.

See the unit in Term 3 that focuses on the biography of Hans Christian Andersen (page 175).

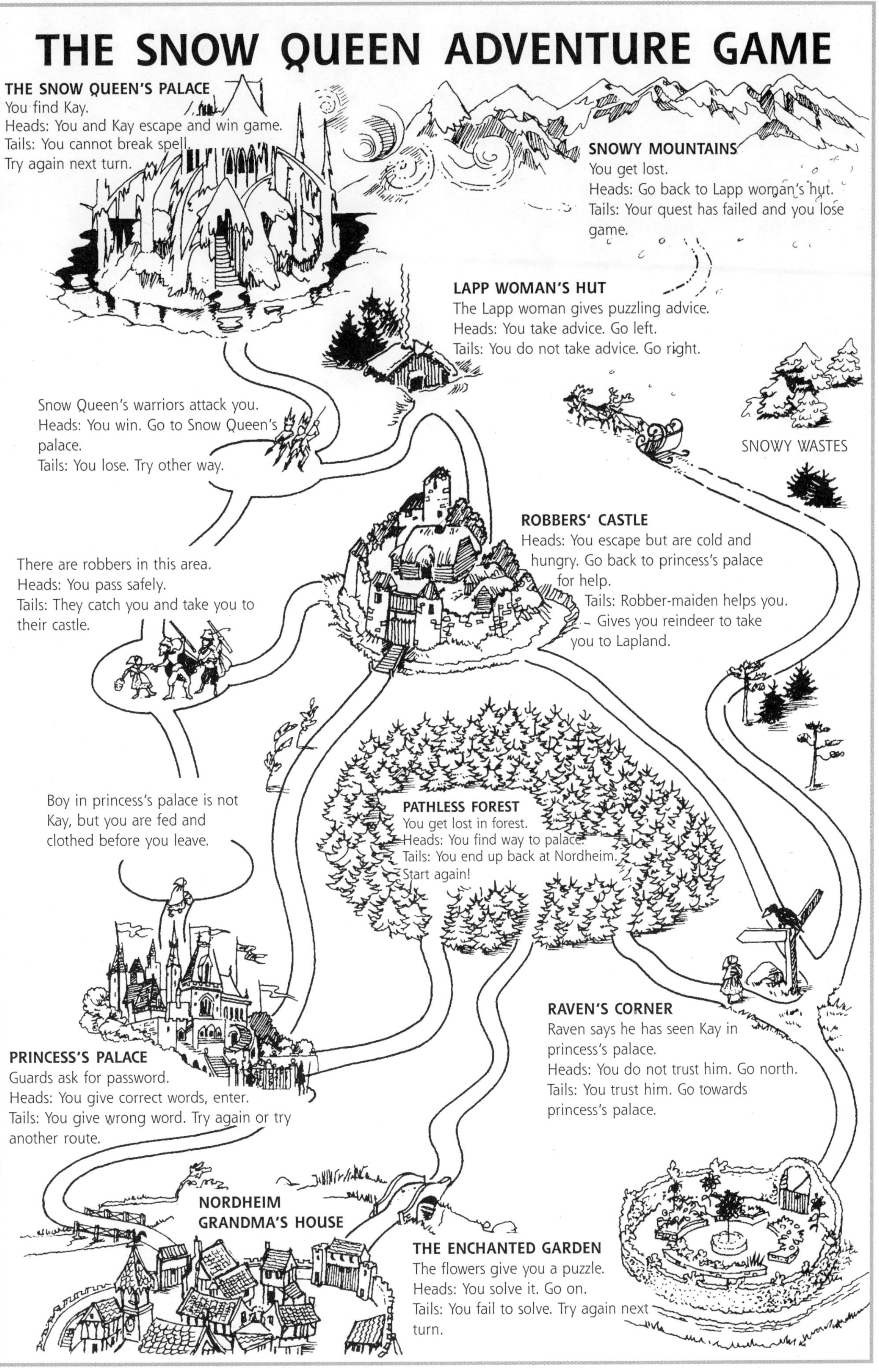
THE SNOW QUEEN ADVENTURE GAME
THE SNOW QUEEN'S PALACE
You find Kay.
Heads: You and Kay escape and win game.
Tails: You cannot break spell.
Try again next turn.
SNOWY MOUNTAINS
You get lost.
Heads: Go back to Lapp woman's hut.
Tails: Your quest has failed and you lose game.
LAPP WOMAN'S HUT
The Lapp woman gives puzzling advice.
Heads: You take advice. Go left.
Tails: You do not take advice. Go right.
Snow Queen's warriors attack you.
Heads: You win. Go to Snow Queen's palace.
Tails: You lose. Try other way.
SNOWY WASTES
ROBBERS' CASTLE
Heads: You escape but are cold and hungry. Go back to princess's palace for help.
Tails: Robber-maiden helps you. Gives you reindeer to take you to Lapland.
There are robbers in this area.
Heads: You pass safely.
Tails: They catch you and take you to their castle.
Boy in princess's palace is not Kay, but you are fed and clothed before you leave.
PATHLESS FOREST
You get lost in forest.
Heads: You find way to palace.
Tails: You end up back at Nordheim.
Start again!
RAVEN'S CORNER
Raven says he has seen Kay in princess's palace.
Heads: You do not trust him. Go north.
Tails: You trust him. Go towards princess's palace.
PRINCESS'S PALACE
Guards ask for password.
Heads: You give correct words, enter.
Tails: You give wrong word. Try again or try another route.
NORDHEIM
GRANDMA'S HOUSE
THE ENCHANTED GARDEN
The flowers give you a puzzle.
Heads: You solve it. Go on.
Tails: You fail to solve. Try again next turn.

THE SNOW QUEEN BOARD GAME

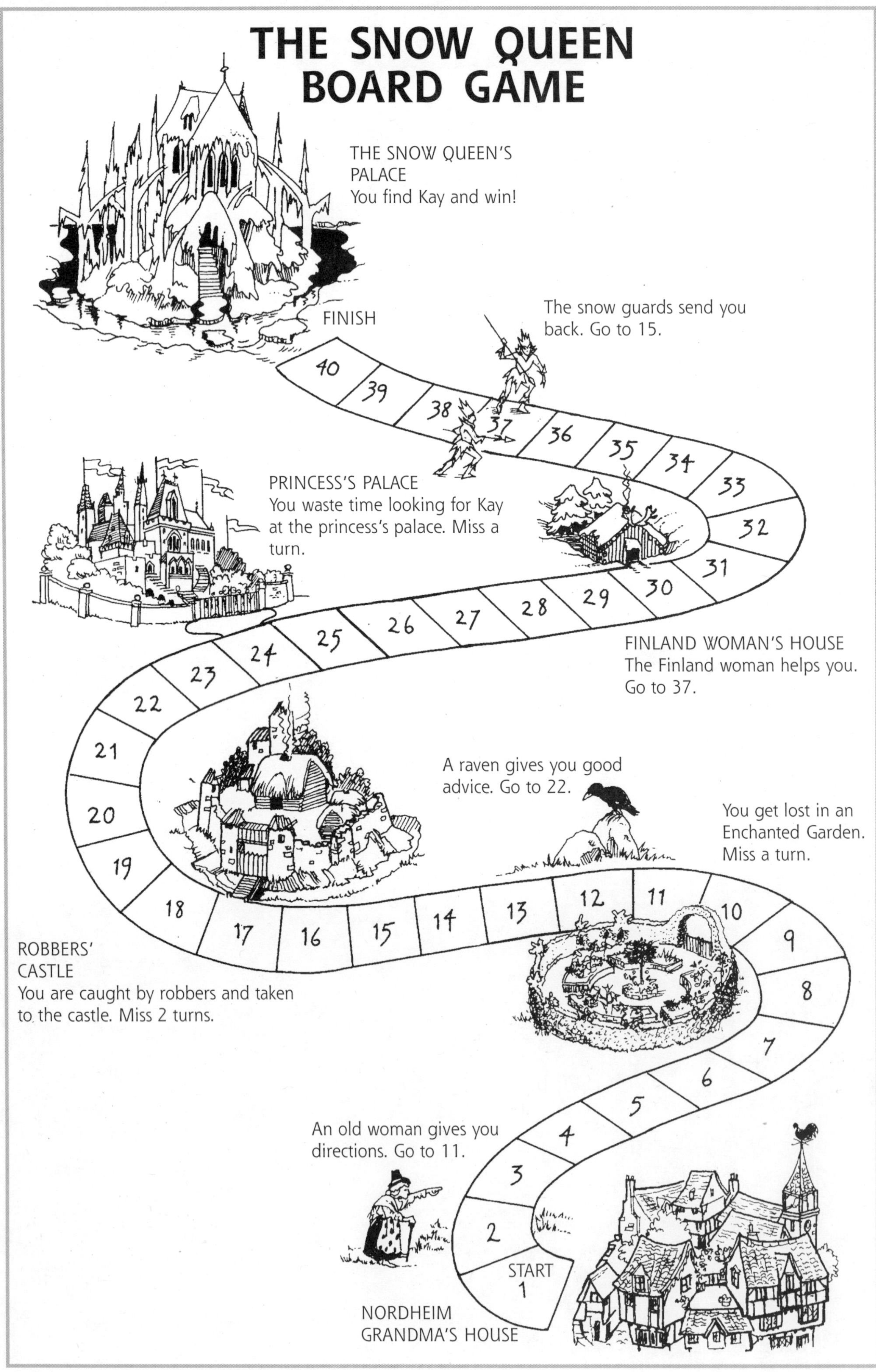
THE SNOW QUEEN'S
PALACE
You find Kay and win!
FINISH
The snow guards send you
back. Go to 15.
40
39
38
37
36
35
34
33
32
31
PRINCESS'S PALACE
You waste time looking for Kay
at the princess's palace. Miss a
turn.
30
29
28
27
26
25
24
23
22
FINLAND WOMAN'S HOUSE
The Finland woman helps you.
Go to 37.
21
20
19
A raven gives you good
advice. Go to 22.
You get lost in an
Enchanted Garden.
Miss a turn.
18
17
16
15
14
13
12
11
10
9
8
ROBBERS'
CASTLE
You are caught by robbers and taken
to the castle. Miss 2 turns.
7
6
5
4
An old woman gives you
directions. Go to 11.
3
2
START
1
NORDHEIM
GRANDMA'S HOUSE

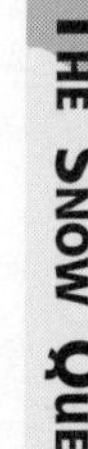

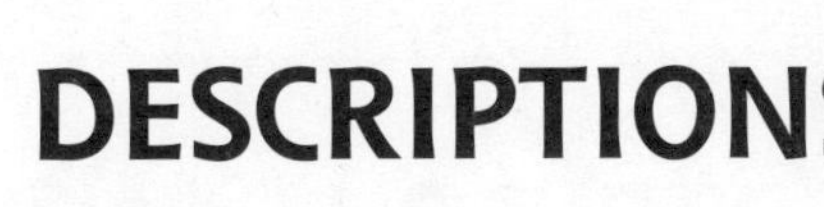

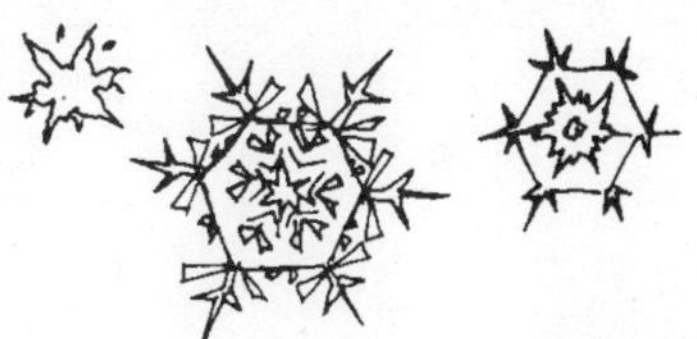

DESCRIPTIONS

Here are some short descriptions taken from different parts of the story. Read them carefully and study how Hans Christian Andersen made them so vivid and effective. Look for and underline similes, adjectives and descriptive details.

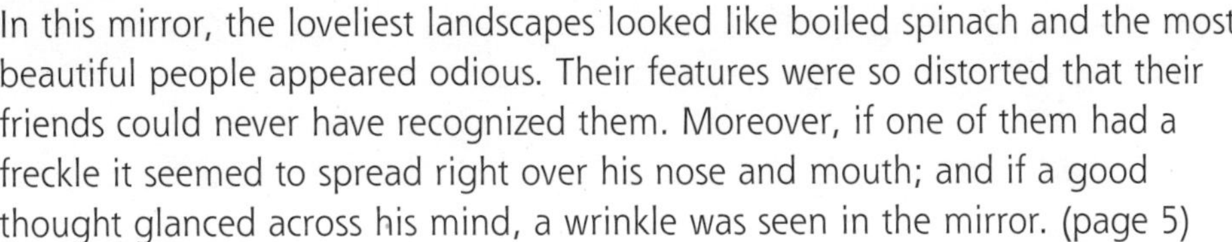

The mirror
In this mirror, the loveliest landscapes looked like boiled spinach and the most beautiful people appeared odious. Their features were so distorted that their friends could never have recognized them. Moreover, if one of them had a freckle it seemed to spread right over his nose and mouth; and if a good thought glanced across his mind, a wrinkle was seen in the mirror. (page 5)

The Snow Queen
The snow-flakes seemed to be getting larger and larger, till at last they looked like great white birds. All at once they parted, the large sledge stopped, and the person who drove it rose from the seat. Kay saw that the cap and coat were entirely made of snow, and that the driver was a lady, tall and slender, and dazzlingly white. It was the Snow Queen! (page 12)

The robber-maiden
The little robber-maiden was about as tall as Gerda, but much stronger. She had broad shoulders and very dark skin; her eyes were quite black, and had an almost melancholy expression. (page 27)

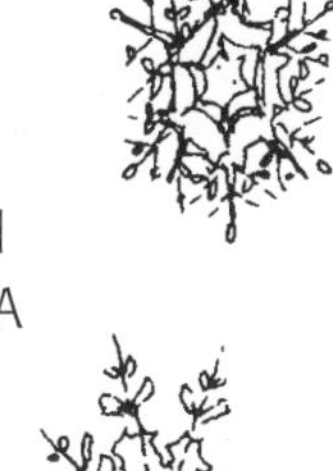

The robbers' castle
This castle was half ruined. Crows and ravens flew out of the openings and some fearfully large bulldogs, looking as if they could devour a man in a moment, jumped round the carriage... Gerda and the robber-maiden entered a large, smoky hall, where a tremendous fire was blazing on the stone floor. A huge cauldron full of soup was boiling on the fire, while hares and rabbits were roasting on the spit. (pages 27–29)

The Lapland woman's hut
They stopped at a little hut. It was a miserable building. The roof very nearly touched the ground and the door was so low that anyone who wanted to go in or out had to crawl on hands and knees. No one was at home except an old Lapland woman who was busy boiling fish over an oil lamp. (page 34)

The Snow Queen's palace
The walls of the palace were made of the driven snow, its doors and windows of the cutting winds. There were a hundred halls, the largest of which was many miles long, all illuminated by the Northern Lights. They were all alike: vast, empty, icily cold, and dazzlingly white. (page 40)

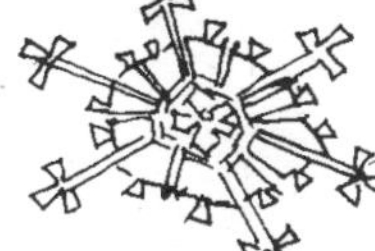

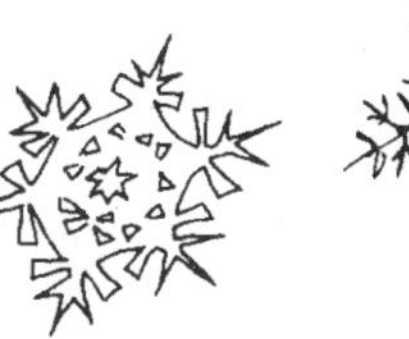

THE STORY OF THE MIRROR AND ITS FRAGMENTS

There was once a __________ troll who was more wicked than anybody else. One day he was in a very happy frame of mind for he had just __________ a mirror which made everything good and __________ shrink up to nothing when it was reflected in it, but all those things that were ugly and __________ were magnified and made to appear __________ worse than before. In this mirror, the loveliest landscapes looked like ____________________ and the most beautiful people appeared __________. Their features were so __________ that their friends could never have ____________________. Moreover, if one of them had a freckle it seemed to ______________________________; and if a good thought glanced across his mind, a __________ was seen in the mirror. The troll thought all this was ____________________, and he __________ at his clever work.

The goblins who studied at the school of magic where he taught, spread the fame of this __________ mirror, and said that for the first time the world and its inhabitants could be seen as they really were. They carried the mirror from place to place, until at last there was no country or person that had not been __________ in it. Then they ________________ with it, to see if they could carry on their fun there. But the higher they flew the more __________ the mirror became; they could scarcely hold it together. They flew on and on, higher and __________ , until at last the mirror __________ so much that it escaped from their hands and fell to the earth, breaking into a ____________________ pieces. And then it caused __________ unhappiness than before for __________ of it scarcely as large as a ____________________ flew about in the air, and got into people's eyes, making them see everything the wrong way and have eyes only for what was ____________________. For each little __________ retained the peculiar properties of the whole mirror. Some people were unfortunate enough to get a little splinter into their hearts and that was __________ for their heart became cold and hard, like a ____________________. The wicked troll was greatly amused with all this and he __________ till his sides ached.

CHARACTER STUDY – KAY

PART A
Use the sentence starters and notes to help you write a character study of Kay. Note that each sentence starter is the beginning of a new paragraph.

The Snow Queen was written by Hans Christian Andersen. It is a story about

(Briefly write what the story is about.)

At the beginning of the book, Kay

(Describe briefly what Kay is like and how he likes to spend his time. You will find information on page 7.)

In 'The First Story', Kay gets a splinter from the Magic Mirror in his heart and this changes him.

(Describe how Kay is changed. You will find the information on pages 10–11.)

The Snow Queen takes Kay to her palace. Here, Kay spends his time

(Describe briefly how Kay spends his time. See page 42.)

He returned to normal when he

(Describe how he gets back to normal. See page 42.)

At the end of the story

(Briefly describe the ending on page 46.)

PART B
Imagine that Gerda designed a poster to help her find Kay. What information would she write on the poster?

- Think of an eye-catching title for the poster.
- Sketch a picture of Kay (see page 6 or page 43).
- Write a paragraph of basic information. You will find information about Kay on page 7. There are some useful extra clues to help someone identify him on page 22.
- Finish by offering a reward, and by giving an address where the information can be sent.

HILDEBRAND'S DUNGEONS

OBJECTIVES

UNIT	SPELLING/VOCABULARY	GRAMMAR/PUNCTUATION	COMPREHENSION/ COMPOSITION
WRITING FICTION Adventure game story: 'Hildebrand's Dungeons'.	Check own spellings.	Learn the present continuous tense. Compare with simple present tense. Revise first, second and third person.	Investigate features of the 'adventure game' genre. Write an adventure story in the adventure game format. Plan story carefully using a decision tree.

ORGANIZATION (2 HOURS)

INTRODUCTION	WHOLE-CLASS SKILLS WORK	DIFFERENTIATED GROUP ACTIVITIES	CONCLUSION
HOUR 1 Introduce adventure game genre and read 'Hildebrand's Dungeons' interactively with pupils making choices.	Investigate features of the adventure game genre. Learn the present continuous tense.	1–4*: Plan adventure game stories.	Share ideas for adventure game stories.
HOUR 2 Shared re-reading of 'Hildebrand's Dungeons' making different choices.	Compare with simple present tense. Revise first, second and third person.	1–4*: Guided writing of adventure game stories.	Select one or two adventure game stories to play as a class. Make critical responses to genre.

RESOURCES

Photocopiable page 133 ('Hildebrand's Dungeons'), board or flip chart, writing materials, OHP and acetate (optional), postcards (optional).

PREPARATION

If possible, prepare photocopiable page 133 ('Hildebrand's Dungeons') as an OHT.

Introduction

Begin by giving the children the following background information:

The first adventure game, called 'Adventure', was written by two computer programmers called Crowther and Woods for a mainframe computer at Stanford University (USA) in 1976. The game (sometimes called 'Colossal Cave') is now freely available on the Internet. Since then, the adventure game has become a popular format for computer games. The adventure game format is also used in novels.

Read the adventure game story 'Hildebrand's Dungeons' provided on photocopiable page 133. Whenever there is a choice, ask the children what choice they would make, and go with the majority decision. When you have finished the story, ask the children if they can deduce answers to the following questions:

- What was Hildebrand making?
- Why do you think he kidnapped Madeline?

Whole-class skills work

Investigate the features of the adventure game genre. Ask the children to say how stories like 'Hildebrand's Dungeons' are different from ordinary adventure stories. The following list gives some ideas, and can be used to sum up the discussion:

- They are written (unusually) in the *second* person (you), which makes the reader the hero of the story.
- They are written in present continuous tense (as though they were happening *now*). Explain that the present continuous tense uses the auxiliary verb 'to be': *You are* walking. (The present continuous will be examined in more detail in the following hour.)
- The reader can make choices (as in real life).
- The plot is not fixed, but can be varied by the reader's choices.

Explain that the main challenge in writing an adventure game story is planning. Unlike a normal story, it has to be planned out *in every detail* before writing starts. The best way to plan it is to follow these steps:

- Brainstorm ideas for the story and work out roughly what the plot will be.
- Map out the choices (and puzzles, if any) and where they lead using a decision tree diagram (demonstrate on the board using the first few cards of Hildebrand's dungeons).

Differentiated group activities

All children, working in pairs within groups, plan their adventure game stories:
1*: Children in this group should attempt a fairly complex structure for their adventure games. 'The Snow Queen Adventure Game' (photocopiable page 125 from 'The Snow Queen' unit) will give some additional ideas for structure as it includes the concept of puzzles to solve as well as choices to be made.
2 & 3*: Children in these groups should keep to the eight-card structure modelled closely on the example.
4*: Children should attempt a simpler structure. Ask them to plan a story which leads to a choice. The reader makes a choice and is directed to one of two endings. Encourage them to try writing in the second person, but if this proves too difficult to sustain, they can write in the third person.

If children are stuck for ideas, the following may help:

- Write own version of 'Hildebrand's Dungeons' with different dungeons containing different problems.
- Use the characters and setting from *The Snow Queen* (see previous unit). One of the board games (photocopiable pages 125 and 126) will provide visual support.
- Take a well-known folk tale and turn it into an adventure game, for example 'Little Red Riding Hood'.

Conclusion

Select children to share their ideas for adventure game stories. Identify the choices, decisions and puzzles that send the story in different directions.

Introduction

Re-read the adventure game story 'Hildebrand's Dungeons', encouraging the children to try out different choices this time. When the reading is over, emphasize the characteristics of the form, particularly the use of the second person.

Whole-class skills work

Investigate the present continuous tense by asking children to help you complete the following table. This shows the present tense of auxiliary the verb 'to be' + present participle (*-ing* ending):

	SINGULAR	PLURAL
1st person	I am walking	We are walking
2nd person	You are walking	You are walking
3rd person	He/she/it is walking	They are walking

Compare with the simple present tense, which would be *I walk, You walk, He/she/it walks* in the singular, and *We walk, You walk, They walk* in the plural. Take the opportunity to revise first, second and third person. Focus particularly on second person, as this will be used in writing the adventure game stories.

Differentiated group activities

All groups write their adventure game stories.
1*: Children can write in any format they like (see note on using a computer, below), with the sections of the story of any length. However, they must ensure that 'navigation' through the different sections is easy for the reader. The postcard format suggested for Groups 2 and 3 may also be attractive to this group, though they can use as many cards as they can manage.
2 & 3*: A good format is to write on eight postcards. This makes the story easy to write and easy to follow. Also, if a mistake is made, it is easy to rewrite one card.
4*: Children should write on ordinary paper with the main story on one side and the two different endings on the other.

Using a computer: It is quite easy to write simple adventure games on the computer without the need for programming skills. There are two ways to do this:

- Use a hypercard-type program, such as Powerpoint which is part of the Microsoft Office '97 program or Illuminatus (Digital Workshop).
- Use an ordinary word processor. Any word processor will do as long as it has a 'find' facility. Write all the separate sections of text well spaced out so that only one can be seen on screen at a time. Each text should be given a unique word as its heading. When the person playing the game reads a section of text he or she will make a choice, type into the 'find' requestor the unique word for that choice, and be taken straight to it by the computer. It is even possible to pep up the game with graphics!

Conclusion

Select one or two children to read their adventure stories with the class, making decisions about how to proceed through the story. Ask the children to discuss their responses to this kind of story in comparison to conventional stories. Ensure that all children have time to play each other's adventure games outside the hour.

HILDEBRAND'S DUNGEONS

1.
It is your wedding feast. Your beautiful bride, Madeline, stands happily beside you and your guests raise a toast to your health. Suddenly there is a cold draught from outside. A hunched figure wrapped in a black cloak is glimpsed. There is a shout, a scream and confusion. Someone yells, 'Madeline has been kidnapped!' You rush headlong into the night until you arrive at the gateway to Hildebrand's castle. There are two doors: the huge main entrance, and a small door to the right. Which will you take?

If you decide to take the main entrance, go to 6. If you decide to take the small door, go to 3.

2.
The huge pipe organ on the far wall tells you that you are in the music room. All around there are instruments of every kind and shape, but no sign of Madeline. After a few moments you hear the harpsichord playing. You go over to look – the keys are moving, but there is no one there. With a shudder you run from the room. You could go through an archway, or through a door.

If you decide to go through the archway, go to 5. If you decide to go through the door, go to 4.

3.
You find yourself in a huge kitchen. Enormous pots and pans hang from hooks on the walls. They do not bother you, but the vast array of knives makes you shudder. On the kitchen table there are some red spots. Could it be – no – that would be too horrible! You decide to look elsewhere. You notice that a staircase leads from the kitchen and you can go either way, up or down.

If you decide to go up, go to 4. If you decide to go down, go to 7.

4.
You are in some sort of a laboratory. All around you, bizarrely shaped bottles and test tubes glug and bubble. Some of them contain objects that look like arms, legs and other body parts. Your heart thumps with terror and you decide to get out quickly. A staircase leads down from the laboratory, and a door leads to another room.

If you decide to take the staircase, go to 3. If you decide to take the door go to 2.

5.
You see a wall lined with books – you are in the library. You notice that somebody has left a book on the table. You see that it is by Mary Shelley and pick it up to look at the title. It is *Frankenstein* – shivers run down your spine! There is no sign of Madeline, so you decide to try somewhere else. You see a half-open door which seems to lead to a corridor. The only other door is a small trapdoor in the floor.

If you decide to take the door to the corridor, go to 6. If you decide to try the trapdoor, go to 8.

6.
This room is the main part of the house, but it looks like an operating theatre! In the centre is an operating table and on it something that looks a bit like Frankenstein's monster! You wonder if Hildebrand does the same sort of thing – makes monsters out of spare human parts. Suddenly you notice that the monster is moving! It's coming towards you. You try to run – but it is too late!

Game over.

7.
You come to a door. You open it and step into the darkness. Suddenly you are falling. You hit the floor with an uncomfortable thump, but luckily nothing is broken. You pick yourself up and look around. It is very gloomy; the only light comes from a tiny barred window high above. You realize that you are in some kind of a crypt and that there is no way out - you are doomed!

Game over.

8.
You find yourself in a dark dungeon. You hear a scurrying noise which sounds like rats. As your eyes get used to the dim light you see a ghostly figure huddled in the corner. But it's not a ghost, it is Madeline, still in her white wedding dress. She sees you and cries out with joy. Quickly, you lead her out of the castle and back home. You report the matter to the authorities. Hildebrand is imprisoned and you live happily ever after with the beautiful Madeline. You have won the game!

PIGGY BANK

OBJECTIVES

UNIT	SPELLING/VOCABULARY	GRAMMAR/PUNCTUATION	COMPREHENSION/ COMPOSITION
READING NON-FICTION Explanation genre: 'Piggy Bank'.	Develop vocabulary from text. Understand the terms 'summary' and 'abridgement'.	Identify and understand how certain words and phrases are used to indicate sequence in texts.	Investigate features of explanatory text. Experiment with re-sequencing text in different ways. Abridge and summarize text.

ORGANIZATION (2 HOURS)

	INTRODUCTION	WHOLE-CLASS SKILLS WORK	DIFFERENTIATED GROUP ACTIVITIES	CONCLUSION
HOUR 1	Discuss concept of piggy banks. Shared reading of 'Piggy Bank' text on photocopiable sheet.	Investigate the features of explanation genre.	1–4*: Re-sequencing exercise.	Discuss results of re-sequencing exercise and summarize what has been learned.
HOUR 2	Shared re-reading of article and discussion of how a simple fact has been presented in an interesting way.	Model processes of abridging and summarizing texts.	1*: Abridge and summarize text. 2 & 3: Abridge text only. 4*: Abridge text only.	Compare different approaches to abridgement and summary. Summarize features of explanatory texts.

RESOURCES

Photocopiable page 137 ('Piggy Bank'), a collection of piggy banks (optional), OHP and acetate (optional), board or flip chart, writing materials, scissors.

PREPARATION

If possible, prepare photocopiable page 137 ('Piggy Bank') as an OHT. Make enough copies of the sheet for one between two children. If possible, make a collection of piggy banks and have them on display. Write the list of features given below under 'Whole-class skills work' in Hour 1 onto the board or flip chart.

Introduction

If you have a display of piggy banks, draw the children's attention to it. Ask them:

- Do you have a place or container for saving money?
- Have you ever owned a piggy bank?
- Does anyone own one now?
- Why do you think the shape of a pig is used to save money?

Then read the explanation of this last question given in the 'Piggy Bank' text on the photocopiable sheet.

Whole-class skills work

Investigate the features of explanation genre. Begin by showing the class the following list of features on the board or flip chart.

Explanation genre
Purpose – *explains a process or answers a question.*
Structure – *usually begins with an introductory statement or paragraph to introduce topic, followed by sequential explanation organized into paragraphs.*
Language – *usually uses simple present tense; use of connectives to indicate sequence of time or cause and effect.*
Presentation – *often makes use of illustrations, maps, charts and diagrams.*

Ask the children to investigate these features in the 'Piggy Bank' text. This is what they will find:
■ The article answers a question.
■ They will find three statements, a question and three more statements to introduce the article.
■ The historical answer to the question is given in chronological order (the sequential nature of the piece is explored in the group activity that follows).
■ The first seven lines and the last two lines are written in the simple present tense. (Question: Why is the middle section of the article written in the past tense? *Because the explanation needs to refer to something that happened in the past. This would not be the case with most explanations, for example how a CD player works or how the water cycle works.*)
■ There are connectives to do with time sequence (*whenever, when*) and with cause and effect (*so, because*).
■ There is an illustration and a diagram.

Differentiated group activities
Ask the children to work in pairs in their groups. Give out a copy of the photocopiable sheet to each pair. Tell them to cut up their text as follows:
■ Cut away the borders to remove the illustrations.
■ Cut across the text below line 8 (after '...Because someone made a mistake.')
■ Cut across the text above the second line from the end ('Pigs are still one of the most popular forms of coin...')

They should then try these sections in different orders, read them, and see if the text still makes sense. Ask them to number the sections and make a note of the different orders they tried followed by a comment on whether the text was still understandable. Next, they should try cutting the middle section of text at the paragraph divisions and try reordering these. Again, they should number the sections and make notes on the results of their experiments. More able children could experiment with further subdivisions.

Conclusion
Discuss the results of the exercise. They should have concluded that the main part of the text – the middle section which contained the actual explanation – is sequential. In this case it is sequential over a long period of time, but most explanations are sequential in that one event or operation is explained before another as part of a continuous process.

Introduction
Re-read the article and explain that a simple fact has been presented in an interesting way. Ask the children to pick out the words and phrases used to make it interesting (the whole first section is a good example of this!)
Explain to children that they are going to produce an abridgement and/or a summary of the text. Explain the terms as follows:
■ An abridgement is where all non-essential words and phrases are cut, but no other words or phrases are altered. Explain that many long classic novels are abridged. Ask the children to look out for examples.
■ A summary expresses the content of the text in a shortened and altered form. This involves rewriting the whole text. Explain that many long classic novels are 'retold' for younger children. The text is rewritten in a shortened form with simpler words. Often blurbs on the back cover of novels offer a very short summary of the book.

Whole-class skills work
Model how to abridge a text by working on the first paragraph with the children. Ask them what is essential information and what can be cut. Note that this will depend

partly on how short you wish the final text to be. Two possible solutions are:

- Three examples are given in the first three sentences. Delete two of them.
- Delete all the examples. This would leave the following: 'So why do we save our coins in a piggy bank?' The answer: 'Because someone made a mistake.'

A summary of the passage would read: 'We save our coins in a piggy bank because someone made a mistake.'

Differentiated group activities

1*: Children in this group should do the abridgement and the summary. Writing a summary is a challenging exercise and is only appropriate for the more able children at this stage.
2–4: Write the abridgement of 'Piggy Bank'. Teacher supports Group 4*.

Conclusion

Compare the different approaches to abridgement and summary. Revise the characteristic features of explanatory texts.

FURTHER IDEA

Choose a classic novel, and ask children to abridge a selected passage. Less able children could do the same with an easier modern children's novel.

PIGGY BANK

Dogs bury bones.

Squirrels gather nuts to last through the winter.

Camels store food and water so they can travel many days across deserts.

But do pigs save anything? No! Pigs save nothing. They bury nothing. They store nothing.

So why do we save our coins in a piggy bank? The answer: Because someone made a mistake.

During the Middle Ages, in about the fifteenth century, metal was expensive and seldom used for household wares. Instead, dishes and pots were made of an economical clay called pygg.

Whenever housewives could save an extra coin, they dropped it into one of their clay jars. They called this their pygg bank or their pyggy bank.

Over the next two hundred to three hundred years, people forgot that "pygg" referred to the earthenware material. In the nineteenth century when English potters received requests for pyggy banks, they produced banks shaped like a pig. Of course, the pigs appealed to the customers and delighted children.

Pigs are still one of the most popular forms of coin banks sold in gift shops today.

WACKY MOUSETRAP

OBJECTIVES

UNIT	SPELLING/VOCABULARY	GRAMMAR/PUNCTUATION	COMPREHENSION/ COMPOSITION
WRITING NON-FICTION Explanation genre: 'Wacky Mousetrap'.	Use prefixes and suffixes to generate a name for the invention.	Use appropriate connectives.	Write an explanatory text.

ORGANIZATION (2 HOURS)

	INTRODUCTION	WHOLE-CLASS SKILLS WORK	DIFFERENTIATED GROUP ACTIVITIES	CONCLUSION
HOUR 1	Display the Wacky Mousetrap (with text covered up) and explain verbally how it works.	Revise or introduce the term 'connective'.	1–4*: All pupils devise and sketch a Wacky Invention.	Selected pupils display and explain their Wacky Inventions.
HOUR 2	Display the Wacky Mousetrap, this time revealing the text. Discuss the text.	Devise a name for the Wacky Inventions using the prefixes and suffixes in the Wacky Invention Name Bank.	1–4*: Guided writing of an explanation of the Wacky Invention to go with the diagram.	Pupils share and discuss their explanations while others evaluate how clear they are.

RESOURCES

Photocopiable pages 140 (Wacky Mousetrap) and 141 (Wacky Invention Name Bank), OHP and acetate (optional), board or flip chart, writing materials.

PREPARATION

If possible, prepare an OHT of photocopiable pages 140 (Wacky Mousetrap) and 141 (Wacky Invention Name Bank), otherwise enlarge them to at least A3 size. Make enough copies of photocopiable page 141 (Wacky Invention Name Bank) for each child.

Introduction

Display the Wacky Mousetrap on the OHP (with the text covered up) and explain verbally to the class how it works. Tell them that the purpose of this is to give them ideas for their own Wacky Invention, for which they will have to write an explanation of how it works. Stress that they must *explain* how it works, *not give instructions*. Make sure that you make the distinction clear during your explanation of the Wacky Mousetrap.

Whole-class skills work

Explain or revise the term 'connective'. It is a 'blanket' term referring to words which 'connect' groups of words. The following examples will be particularly useful in writing the explanation of the Wacky Invention (they are called 'temporal connectives' because they refer to relationships of time). Write them on the board or flip chart for children to use as an aide-mémoire when writing.

after that	at first	until	before
eventually	finally	in the end	later
meanwhile	next	then	to begin with

Differentiated group activities

1–4*: All children devise and sketch their Wacky Invention. When they have done this they should explain how it works to a partner. More able children should take this opportunity to listen for connectives. Help children in Group 4 to draw a clear diagram in which all the processes are shown. This will help them later to write a clear explanation of how it works. Note that any children who cannot think of an idea for a Wacky Invention could invent their own Wacky Mousetrap.

Conclusion

Select children to display their Wacky Invention sketches and explain orally how they work. Jot down any additional connectives used by the children and ask the rest of the class to add them to their lists.

Introduction

Display the OHP (or enlargement) of the Wacky Mousetrap and reveal the text. Read out the text as an example and revise the features of the explanatory genre (see 'Piggy Bank' unit, page 134). Ask children to identify connectives.

Whole-class skills work

Talk about prefixes and suffixes and ask the children to give examples. Display an OHT (or enlargement) of photocopiable page 141 (Wacky Invention Name Bank) and explain how to use it. Jot down some appropriate nouns in the middle column and then look for an effective prefix and suffix. Model the process with the Wacky Mousetrap as follows:

- In the middle column write *mouse* and *trap*.
- Choose a prefix. *Super-* is good because this is better than any other trap.
- Choose a suffix. What about *-zapper*? No, this is supposed to be a kind mousetrap! -*omatic* might do.
- Now let's look at what we've got: *Super Mouseomatic*, or *Super Trapomatic* – perhaps a bit long.
- Final result – *Mouse-o-matic*.

Differentiated group activities

1–4*: Write the explanation to go with their own diagram. Children in Group 4 should work from one end to the other of their diagram. If this has been drawn clearly and simply it will help them to write a clear explanation.

Conclusion

Select children to share and discuss their explanations. The rest of the class should evaluate them by commenting on how easy the explanations were to understand.

FURTHER IDEA

Apply the skills learned to an explanation required in another area of the curriculum, for example an explanation of how a steam engine works, or how the water cycle works.

WACKY MOUSETRAP

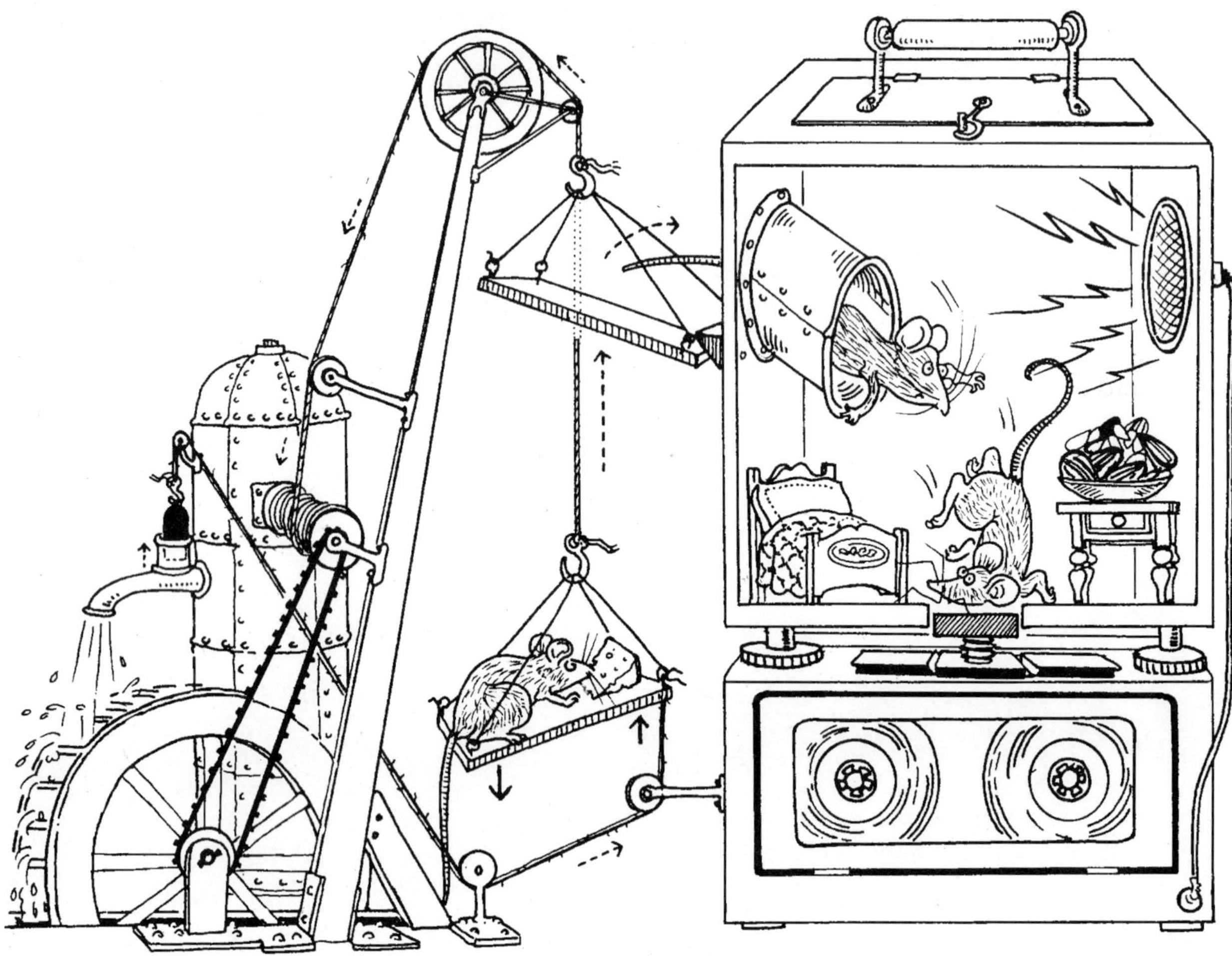

This mousetrap is designed to catch the mouse every time, but in a kind way. The householder will get rid of the mouse, and the mouse will think he has had a free holiday in a five star hotel! Here's how it works: The mouse is attracted onto the lift by a piece of cheese. The weight of the mouse opens the valve of a water tank. The water flows over a waterwheel which provides power to lift the mouse to the next level. The mouse is tipped into a tube and slides down into a little room.

As this is a 'kind' mousetrap, the room is comfortably equipped with everything a mouse would need. There is a supply of food and water, a comfortable bed, and some toys to play with. However, to make sure that other mice do not come along just for a pleasant stay, something else happens at the same time that the mouse enters the room. The mouse's weight triggers an electrical switch which turns on a cassette recorder. This plays the sounds of crashing, banging and instruments of torture at work. Worst of all is the sound of a mouse screaming (note that the mouse's room is soundproofed as we do not wish to upset him). The sounds make sure that other mice are frightened away. The same switch sets an alarm bell ringing in the kitchen, so that the householder can take the mouse back into the wild before the food and drink run out.

One word of warning! It is important to take the mouse a long way away before setting him free (Europe or America are recommended) because otherwise he might want to come back for another stay – and next time he might bring his friends and relatives!

WACKY INVENTION NAME BANK

How to use the Wacky Invention Name Bank

- Write some nouns to do with your invention in the centre column.
- Choose some prefixes and suffixes that make sense and sound good.
- Experiment until you get a name you like – it does not have to have a prefix and a suffix.

PREFIX	NOUN	SUFFIX
astro		blaster
auto		otron
bio		ation
compu		ator
designer		ene
desktop		fizz
dyna		gram
electro		graph
euro		izer
hyper		ite
mega		ix
micro		ine
midi		ion
mini		matic
mono		max
multi		meter
photo		rite
post		tech
techno		tone
tele		trak
trans		tred
super		trek
syn		trex
un		tric
uni		zapper
vege		zon

Preparing for Research

OBJECTIVES

UNIT	SPELLING/VOCABULARY	GRAMMAR/PUNCTUATION	COMPREHENSION/ COMPOSITION
REFERENCE AND RESEARCH SKILLS: Preparing for Research.	Understand the term 'research' and investigate other words from the root word.	Formulate questions.	Prepare for research by reviewing what is known, what is needed, what is available, and where to search.

ORGANIZATION (1 HOUR)

	INTRODUCTION	WHOLE-CLASS SKILLS WORK	DIFFERENTIATED GROUP ACTIVITIES	CONCLUSION
HOUR 1	Use current topic to brainstorm what is already known and what pupils would like to find out. Demonstrate how to use KWLW chart.	Investigate the meaning of the term 'research' and explore other words from the word *search*.	1–4*: Practise using KWLW Chart according to ability levels.	Selected pupils from each group share questions and answers. Summarize KWLW method and suggest alternative strategies.

RESOURCES

A collection of information books on a current topic of study in another curriculum area (this can be on one topic or on several different ones, but ensure that you have an adequate range to provide for the reading abilities in the class), photocopiable page 144 (KWLW Chart), dictionary, OHP and acetate (optional), board or flip chart, writing materials.

PREPARATION

If possible, prepare an OHT of photocopiable page 144 (KWLW Chart), otherwise enlarge it to at least A3 size. Make enough A4 copies for one between two children. Ensure that you have enough information books so that pairs of children have access to at least two on the topic.

Introduction

Choose a topic you are currently studying (or are about to study) in another curriculum area, write the topic on the board or flip chart and ask the children to brainstorm all the facts they already know about the topic. Write them down in note form. Then ask the children for suggestions of things they would like to find out about the topic – and to formulate these as questions. (It may be useful to list appropriate question words to help them: *Who? Where? What? Why? When? How?*) Again, write these down in note form.

Display the KWLW chart (either on the OHP or as an enlarged photocopy) and explain to the class that it is a useful tool to use at the beginning of a new topic to list what they already know (K), what they would like to know (W), what they learned from their research (L) and where they found their information (W). Demonstrate how to use it by picking out four or five of the facts already known and four or five questions they would like answered from those on the board or flip chart – and write them onto the chart.

Discuss how they should go about filling in the L and second W columns. They should look at the resources they have available (remind them these may not always be book-based resources – they could also be other people, visual resources, computer information), and determine which source is most appropriate for each question. They should find the answer, note it down and then note down where they found the answer. Explain that it is important to complete this last column as they may need to check their information later or find further related information.

Whole-class skills work

Write the word *research* on the board or flip chart. Ask the children what they think the word means. Write down their suggestions and, as a class, agree on a definition (for example *detailed investigation to discover facts*). Establish that the word can be both a noun and a verb. Confirm this and the definition by checking in a dictionary. What is the root word from which *research* comes? Write the word *search* on the board or flip chart and challenge them to find as many other words as possible from this root (for example *searched, searches, searching, searcher*).

Differentiated group activities

Give copies of the KWLW to pairs of children working within their ability groups and with information books suited to their reading abilities.
1*: Provide up to three texts on the same topic so that the children have to make choices about which text is most suited to each question. Suggest that they limit themselves to six items in each of the first two columns. Explain that they might not have the texts to answer all their questions but should try to answer as many as they can. They should also try rephrasing questions which may help to find the answer.
2 & 3*: Provide two texts on the same topic. Suggest the children think of four or five items for each of the first two columns.
4*: Provide one text and encourage the children to find the answers to two questions. Help them to devise questions which you know can be answered by the text provided.

Conclusion

Select children from each group to show their charts and to share with the others one or two of their questions and the answers they found. Discuss: Were they able to find answers to all their questions? If not, what other strategies could they use? (Looking for different sources, rephrasing questions.)

KWLW CHART

TOPIC:

K	W	L	W
List what you already know about the topic.	List questions about the topic that you want to find out more about.	Using your questions as a guide, write what you have learned.	Write where you found the answers to your questions (book, title, page number).

FIGURATIVE LANGUAGE

OBJECTIVES

UNIT	SPELLING/VOCABULARY	GRAMMAR/PUNCTUATION	COMPREHENSION/ COMPOSITION
WORD PLAY Figurative language: 'The Spring Wind ' by Charlotte Zolotow.	Use appropriate language in adjectival phrases in poetry.	Extend skills in using adjectives. Punctuate own poetry.	Understand the use of figurative language in poetry.

ORGANIZATION (1 HOUR)

	INTRODUCTION	WHOLE-CLASS SKILLS WORK	DIFFERENTIATED GROUP ACTIVITIES	CONCLUSION
HOUR 1	Share the poem.	Examine adjectives used in poem. Brainstorm ideas for further poetry.	1–4*: Guided writing of individual poems on season of own choice, supported according to ability.	Share poems and discuss format for 'publishing'.

RESOURCES

Photocopiable page 146 ('The Spring Wind'), flip chart or board, writing materials, paper, OHP and acetate (optional).

PREPARATION

Prepare enough photocopies of photocopiable page 146 ('The Spring Wind') for one between two children. If possible, prepare it also as an OHT or enlarge to at least A3 size.

Introduction

Read the poem aloud with expression. Ask the children what type of writing it is. How can they tell? Have the words been used in a particular way? Display the poem. Why are some lines long and some lines short?

Whole-class skills work

Re-read the poem carefully and ask the children to listen for words or phrases which appeal to them. Can they give reasons for their choices? Remind them about the use of adjectives to make writing more interesting. Explain that they are going to work with a partner, using a highlighter pen to identify the adjectives in the poem. Suggest that they re-read the whole poem together slowly, before discussing which words they will highlight. Discuss their findings, as a class, commenting on particular words and phrases and exploring why they are effective.

Using the flip chart or board, follow with a brief brainstorming session to come up with adjectives for a poem on autumn, winter or summer wind.

Differentiated group activities

1–4*: Ask the children to choose a season and incorporate adjectives from the brainstorming session into a poem, starting with: *The _____ wind/is...* Tell them to think carefully about the sense of their poem and to keep reading it back to themselves. Remind them to think carefully about their punctuation.

Conclusion

Invite children to share their poems with the class. Discuss similarities and differences, then 'publish' them as a class book, wall display or personal anthology.

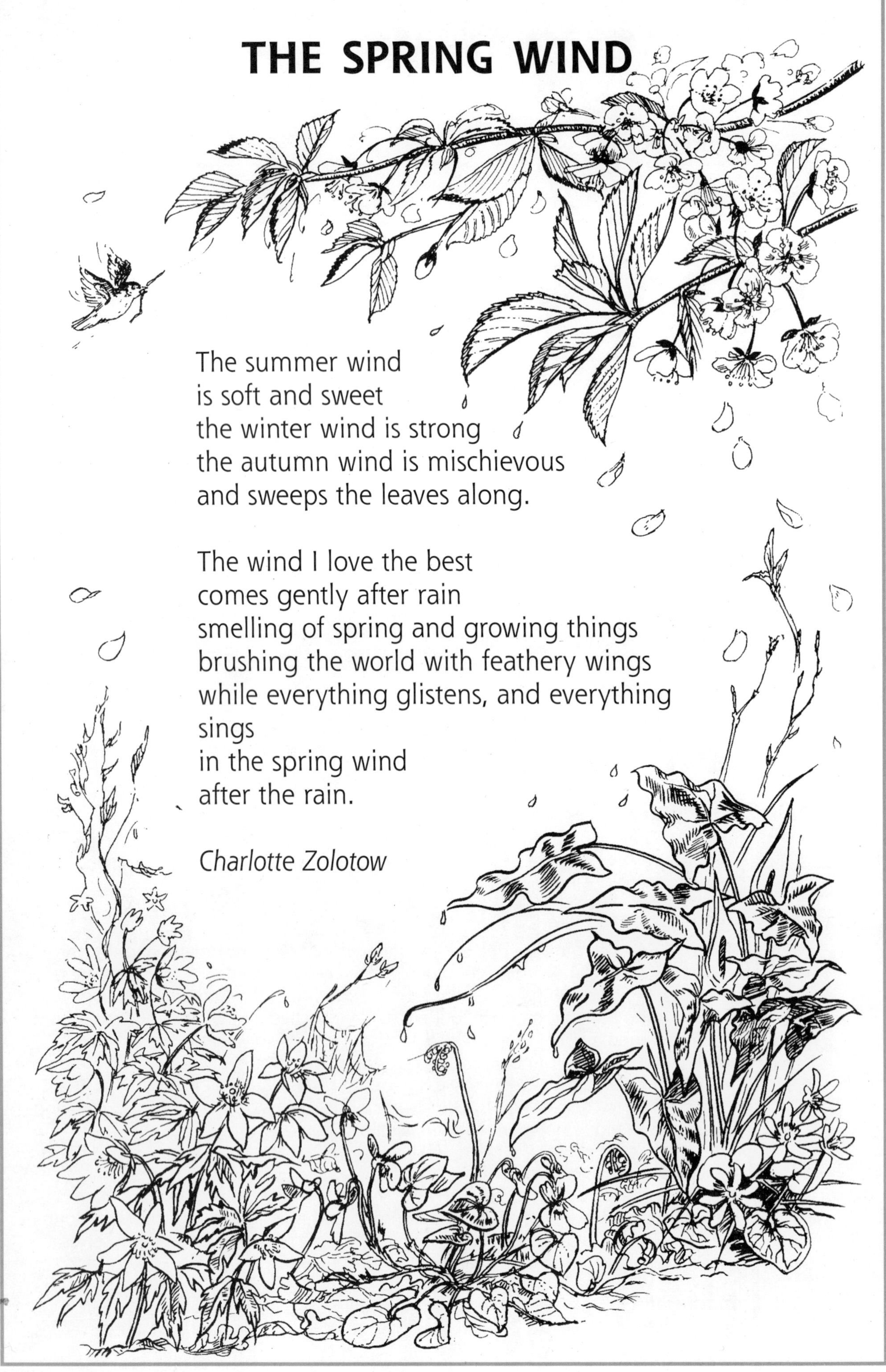

THE SPRING WIND

The summer wind
is soft and sweet
the winter wind is strong
the autumn wind is mischievous
and sweeps the leaves along.

The wind I love the best
comes gently after rain
smelling of spring and growing things
brushing the world with feathery wings
while everything glistens, and everything
sings
in the spring wind
after the rain.

Charlotte Zolotow

Term 3

BIG FEARS

OBJECTIVES

UNIT	SPELLING/VOCABULARY	GRAMMAR/PUNCTUATION	COMPREHENSION/ COMPOSITION
READING POETRY Modern free verse: 'Big Fears' by John Rice.	Investigate building words with similar patterns and meanings.	Investigate features of free verse. Revise third person narrative structure.	Read a poem with enjoyment. Respond by comparing own experiences. Explore pattern in free-verse poetry.

ORGANIZATION (1 HOUR)

	INTRODUCTION	WHOLE-CLASS SKILLS WORK	DIFFERENTIATED GROUP ACTIVITIES	CONCLUSION
HOUR 1	Shared reading of the poem.	Establish meanings of and distinctions between poetry, prose, verse and free verse.	1*: Guided reading of the poem and discussion of it. 2 & 3: Write another section for the poem. 4*: Guided reading of the poem and discussion of it.	Discussion on own big fears.
HOUR 2	Shared re-reading of the poem. Investigate third person narrative voice.	Investigate pattern in poem. Investigate building words with similar patterns and meanings.	1: Add another verse to the poem. 2 & 3*: Guided reading of the poem and discussion of it. 4: Add another verse to the poem.	Selected pupils read out their extra verses, followed by evaluation.

RESOURCES

Photocopiable page 151 ('Big Fears'), OHP and acetate (optional), board or flip chart, writing materials.

PREPARATION

Prepare enough copies of photocopiable page 151 ('Big Fears') for one between two for the group work. If possible, prepare an OHT of the poem, or enlarge to at least A3 size.

Introduction

Begin by reading the poem aloud to the class. Ask the children what kind of writing they think it is and to give reasons for their answers. Because it is written in free verse and in the present tense, and is largely about real environmental dangers, the children may well suggest poetry, fiction and non-fiction!

Display the poem to establish it as poetry. How can the children tell? Now re-read the poem.

Whole-class skills work

Write the following terms on the board or flip chart: *poetry, verse, prose, free verse.* Through discussion and suggestion, establish their meanings, for example:

Poetry: an arrangement of words using patterned language to convey an important idea or strongly felt emotion in a short space. Traditional poems often use a pattern of rhythm and rhyme.

Verse: another word for poetry; a section of a poem.

Prose: ordinary writing in sentences that does not have a poetic or dramatic format.

Free verse: poetry without rhyme (and usually without rhythm). The 'pattern' that makes it poetry is usually a pattern of lines or format and/or a pattern of ideas. Note that modern free verse often starts lines of poetry without capital letters.

Look at the poem again to help the children see a pattern: the first section describes the reality of the electrical cable outside Sian's house; the second section describes what Sian thinks might happen; the third states that this is her fear. Does this pattern apply to the next three sections? Why do they think the poet chose to leave out 'This is Karen's Big Fear'?

Differentiated group activities

1*: Guided re-reading and discussion of the poem with the teacher. The following questions can be used as a starting point for discussion:

- In your own words, describe what each child is frightened of.
- Which of these 'big fears' is the most sensible, in others words, could actually happen?
- Which of these 'big fears' is the least sensible, in other words, is all in the mind?
- Read Matthew's fear very carefully. What does he say about his cat that tells us he does not really understand the danger of a falling tree?
- What is the 'metallic scarecrow' the poet talks about in the first section?
- Do you remember what a simile is? Can you find a simile in the section about Matthew?
- What are your 'big fears'. Are they based on something that could actually happen, or are they mostly in the mind?

2 & 3: Write another section about their own fears for the poem. They should write in the third person, using their own name and writing about themselves as though they were somebody else. They should model their writing on that of the poem – free verse with one section describing the reality and the other describing what might happen.

4*: As Group 1. The teacher should begin by working with this group and should give particular attention to their re-reading of the poem. The first three questions and the last one are most suitable for discussion with this group.

Conclusion

Talk about children's 'big fears' with the whole class. Are the fears based on sensible reasons, or are they just in their imagination? Did the poem give a good description of children's fears?

Introduction

Shared re-reading of the poem. Ask the children whose fears are described in the poem. Is it Sian, Matthew and Karen who are describing their own fears? If not, who is describing them and how do the children know? Establish that the poet is describing them 'from a third person point of view'. Ensure that children understand the concept of third person narrative by writing the following diagram on the board or flip chart. Remind them of work done on verbs, and explain that this is the singular of the verb *to worry*, and that a person's name from the poem has been added to the third person.

1st person:	I worry
2nd person:	You worry
3rd person:	He/she/it/Matthew worries

Explain that when children write their continuation verses in the group work, they should be writing about themselves but using the third person, in other words, using their own name instead of 'I'. The reason for this is that it fits in stylistically with the other verses of the poem. Encourage the children who wrote their continuations in the previous hour to check that they have done this correctly.

Whole-class skills work

Investigate building words with similar patterns and meanings. Begin with an example from the poem:

electric	electricity
electrical	electrocute

Next, give children the words in italic from the list below and ask them if they can think of any other words with similar patterns and meanings:

metal	*country*	*dentist*
metallic	countryside	dental
medical	*crime*	
medicine	criminal	

Differentiated group activities

1: Add another verse to the poem (see above).
2 & 3*: Guided reading and discussion of the poem. All the discussion questions suggested above for Group 1 are suitable for these groups, though they made need help to answer the fourth and fifth questions.
4: Add another verse to the poem (see above).

Conclusion

Select children to read out their extra verses and follow this with a constructive evaluation. Ask the class to listen carefully and comment on how well the extra verse blends with the rest of the poem.

BIG FEARS

Twenty-five feet above Sian's house
hangs a thick wire cable
that droops and sags between two
electricity pylons.
A notice says it carries 40,000 volts
from one metallic scarecrow to the next,
then on to the next and the next
right across the countryside to the city.
The cable sways above Sian's council house
making her radio crackle and sometimes
making her television go on the blink.

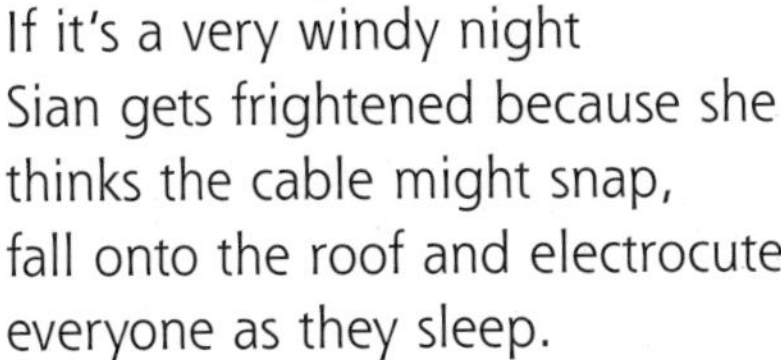

If it's a very windy night
Sian gets frightened because she
thinks the cable might snap,
fall onto the roof and electrocute
everyone as they sleep.

This is Sian's Big Fear.

Outside Matthew's bedroom there
is a tall tree. Taller than the house.
In summer it is heavy with huge leaves.
In winter it stands lonely as a morning moon.

On a windy night, Matthew worries
that the tree might be blown down
and crash through his bedroom window.
It would certainly kill him and his cat
if it wasn't in its own cardboard box.

This is Matthew's Big Fear.

Outside Karen's bedroom there's nothing
but a pleasant view, meadows, hedges, sheep
and some distant gentle hills.
There's nothing sinister, nothing to worry about.

But in the dark, Karen thinks
the darting shapes on the ceiling
are really the shadows of a ghost's
great cold hands and that the night noises
made by the water pipes are the
screeches and groans of attic skeletons.

John Rice

MOTHER SHIPTON'S PROPHECIES

OBJECTIVES

UNIT	SPELLING/VOCABULARY	GRAMMAR/PUNCTUATION	COMPREHENSION/ COMPOSITION
WRITING POETRY 'The Prophecies of Mother Shipton'.	Investigate vocabulary in text.	Investigate the future tense.	Write a poem using rhyming couplets, based on model read.

ORGANIZATION (2 HOURS)

	INTRODUCTION	WHOLE-CLASS SKILLS WORK	DIFFERENTIATED GROUP ACTIVITIES	CONCLUSION
HOUR 1	Shared reading of 'The Prophecies of Mother Shipton'.	Investigate vocabulary in text.	1–4*: Guided reading and discussion of the poem.	Selected pupils read out a few lines containing *one* of their prophecies.
HOUR 2	Shared re-reading of 'The Prophecies of Mother Shipton'.	Study the rhythm and rhyme. Investigate the future tense.	1–4*: Guided writing of notes on own prophecies for the future. Rewrite them in poetry: free verse, rhyming verse, or mixed, according to ability.	Compare: are any the same?

RESOURCES

Photocopiable page 155 ('The Prophecies of Mother Shipton'), OHP and acetate (optional), dictionary, board or flip chart, writing materials.

PREPARATION

If possible, prepare an OHT of photocopiable page 155 ('The Prophecies of Mother Shipton'). Alternatively, enlarge it to at least A3 size. Make enough A4 copies for one between two children. Write the following questions on the board or flip chart for the children to refer to during group work:

- Which of the prophecies seem to have come true?
- Are there any prophecies which seem vague, or little more than guesses?
- What does Mother Shipton prophesy will happen just before the end of the world?
- Do you think that Mother Shipton really had the ability to see into the future?

Introduction

Give the following background information to the class before reading the extract from 'The Prophecies of Mother Shipton':

Mother Shipton, whose real name was Ursula Sonthiel, was born in 1488. She was a local 'wise' woman (some people would have called her a witch) who lived in Knaresborough, Yorkshire. She performed simple cures and made love potions but she was most famous for her prophecies which were written in rhyming couplets and which filled many, many pages.

Establish the meaning of the word *prophecy*, and then check its meaning using a dictionary. Read the extract.

Whole-class skills work

Give out copies of the poem. Write the following words or terms on the board or flip chart and ask the children if they know what they mean. Ask them to find them in the poem. Can they establish their meanings from the context? If not, either tell them or ask them to look them up in the dictionary.

Bishop's See – an area in which a bishop has authority over all the churches
dynasty – a family of rulers
strife – an archaic (old) word for 'war'
vales – an archaic word for 'valleys'

Revise the term 'couplet' and write the following example on the board:

/ / / /		
The British Olive next shall twine	(a)	(8 syllables)
/ / / /		
In marriage with the German vine.	(a)	(8 syllables)

Revise previous work on counting syllables in lines of poetry (see 'Haiku' unit, Term 1, page 51) and on stress in lines of poetry (see 'Limericks' unit, Term 2, page 116).

Emphasize that this is the basic pattern of the poem but a great deal of flexibility is allowed, for example:

- the numbers of stresses in a line will sometimes vary
- the number of syllables in a line will sometimes vary
- the rhyme scheme is sometimes broken altogether.

Ask the children to work briefly in pairs to examine the poem to try to find examples of all the above. Then discuss these as a class.

Differentiated group activities

1–4*: All children re-read and discuss the poem in their groups, using the questions on the board or flip chart (see above under 'Preparation') as a guide to discussion. The teacher gives support where needed.

Conclusion

All children share and discuss their ideas on whether Mother Shipton really could see into the future.

Introduction

Shared re-reading of 'Mother Shipton's prophecies'.

Whole-class skills work

These prophecies provide an ideal opportunity for children to investigate the future tense. The future tense is formed in a number of ways. One of the commonest is by using the auxiliary verbs *will* or *shall*, for example:

	SINGULAR	PLURAL
1st person	I will go	They will go
2nd person	You will go	You will go
3rd person	He/she/it will go	They will go

Ask the children to investigate the use of the future tense in the poem by underlining all the verbs in the future tense. Emphasize that they should underline both the auxiliary *will* or *shall* and the main verb that follows.

Differentiated group activities

1–4*: All the children write their own prophecies for the future in note form. They can work in small groups, in pairs or individually. They should then rewrite them in poetry using different forms according to their ability. Emphasize that whichever form they are writing in, they should try to use the future tense, and that it is what they say and how well they say it that is important. Group 1 should aim to write rhyming couplets. Groups 2 & 3 should aim to write rhyming couplets where they can but when they are stuck to write couplets without rhyme. Group 4 should write mainly in free verse (see photocopiable page 151 as a model) but should use the occasional couplet where it comes naturally.

Conclusion

Select children to read out a few lines containing *one* of their prophecies. Ask if other children included the same prophecy. If time allows, outside the hour, these could be collated into a long class poem.

FURTHER IDEA

Experiment with tenses by rewriting the first ten lines of the poem in the *past* tense. Rewrite them again in the *present* tense. Then discuss the results:

- Does it make sense?
- Can the flow of the sentences be improved by changing the word order a little?

THE PROPHECIES OF MOTHER SHIPTON

Carriages without horses will go,
And accidents fill the world with woe.
Primrose Hill in London shall be
And in its centre a Bishop's See.
Around the world thoughts shall fly
In the twinkling of an eye.
Water shall yet more wonders do,
How strange, yet shall be true.
The world upside down shall be,
And gold found at the root of a tree.
Through hills men shall ride
And no horse or ass by their side,
Under water men shall walk
Shall ride, shall sleep and talk;
In the air men shall be seen,
In white, in black, and in green.
A great man shall come and go–
Three times shall lovely France
Be led to play a bloody dance
Before her people shall be free.
Three tyrant Rulers shall she see,
Three times the people's hope is gone,
Three Rulers in succession see,
Each springing from different dynasty.
Then shall the worser fight be done,
England and France shall be as one.
The British Olive next shall twine
In marriage with the German vine.
Men shall walk over rivers and under rivers,
Iron in the water shall float,
As easy as a wooden boat;
Gold shall be found, and found
In a land that's not now known.
Fire and water shall more wonders do
England shall at last admit a Jew:
The Jew that was held in scorn
Shall of a Christian be born and born.
A house of glass shall come to pass
In England, but alas!
War will follow with the work,
In the land of Pagan and Turk,
And State and State in fierce strife,
Will seek each other's life.
But when the North shall divide the South
An eagle shall build in the lion's mouth.
Taxes for blood and for war,
Will come to every door.
All England's sons that plough the land,
Shall be seen, book in hand:
Learning shall so ebb and flow,
The poor shall most learning know.
Waters shall flow where corn shall grow,
Corn shall grow where waters doth flow,
Houses shall appear in the vales below,
And covered by hail and snow;
The world then to an end shall come
In the year two thousand and one.

SCARECROW

OBJECTIVES

UNIT	SPELLING/VOCABULARY	GRAMMAR/PUNCTUATION	COMPREHENSION/ COMPOSITION
READING NON-FICTION Discussion text: '"I Feel Like a Scarecrow," Says Vicky'.	Investigate abbreviations.	Identify and understand use of discursive connectives.	Read and evaluate an article. Understand how it presents arguments to discuss issues.

ORGANIZATION (2 HOURS)

	INTRODUCTION	WHOLE-CLASS SKILLS WORK	DIFFERENTIATED GROUP ACTIVITIES	CONCLUSION
HOUR 1	Shared reading of the article. Establish what sort of text it is.	Explain discursive connectives and ask pupils to find examples in the article.	1*: Guided reading and discussion of Reading Comprehension – parts A & B. 2 & 3: Discussion of Reading Comprehension – part C. 4*: Guided reading and discussion of Reading Comprehension – parts A & B.	Selected pupils from Groups 2 & 3 share their opinions arising from their discussion with the rest of the class.
HOUR 2	Shared re-reading of the article.	Explore abbreviations beginning with those used in the article.	1: Discussion of Reading Comprehension – part C. 2 & 3*: Guided reading and discussion of Reading Comprehension – parts A & B. 4: Discussion of Reading Comprehension – part C.	Discuss answers to Reading Comprehension – parts A & B.

RESOURCES

Photocopiable pages 158 ('"I Feel Like a Scarecrow," Says Vicky') and 159 (Reading Comprehension), OHP and acetate (optional), board or flip chart, writing materials.

PREPARATION

If possible, prepare an OHT of photocopiable page 158 ('"I Feel Like a Scarecrow," Says Vicky'), otherwise enlarge it to at least A3 size. Make enough copies of photocopiable pages 158 ('"I Feel Like a Scarecrow," Says Vicky') and 159 (Reading Comprehension) for one between two children.

Introduction

Display photocopiable page 158 ('"I Feel Like a Scarecrow," Says Vicky') and read the article to the class. Discuss what type of writing it is – fiction or non-fiction, explanation, report, discussion? Lead them to see that it is a discussion in which the writer puts forward both sides of an argument, based on interviews. Where would they find writing of this sort? Check the children's understanding by asking them what each of the different people interviewed think about school uniform.

Whole-class skills work

Point out that one of the features of discussion writing is the use of connectives to present the arguments. Write the following list on the board or flip chart.

because	however	next	therefore
but	instead	so	these
finally	on the other hand	that	this
for	nevertheless	then	yet

Ask the children which ones they can find in the article. In each case, analyse how the connective functions are used. For example: 'I think that's unfair *because* boys can!' 'Because' is used to justify Karen's argument; '*On the other hand*, all the children...' 'On the other hand' is used for balance, to present the other side of the argument.

Differentiated group activities

1*: Guided reading of the article. Use the questions on the Reading Comprehension sheet (page 159), as a basis for discussion. Note that part A consists of basic-level questions and part B of higher-level questions. The final question in part B requires children to make careful inferences from the text. In fact, the writer presents both sides of the argument through the opinions of the people interviewed.
2 & 3: Discuss questions in part C of the comprehension. These are open-ended questions which invite children to develop the debate begun by the article.
4*: Guided reading of the article. Re-read the article with the children, supporting basic reading skills, then use questions in part A as a basis for discussion. Some questions in part B could also be used.

Conclusion

Children in Groups 2 and 3 share the results of their discussion with the class.

Introduction

Re-read the article, or ask selected children to read it.

Whole-class skills work

Write the following on the board or flip chart and ask the children what they are – *St, Ms, Mrs, Mr, Dr*. Establish that an abbreviation is a shortened form of a word or phrase. What words do these abbreviations stand for? (St = Saint or Street, Mr = Mister, Ms = Miss or Mistress, Dr = Doctor, Mrs = Mistress.)

Note that many abbreviations are indicated by a full stop but common abbreviations (like those above) often are not. It is usually the case (though not always!) that if the abbreviation ends with the last letter of the word, no full stop is needed.

Write some more words or phrases and their abbreviated forms on the board, sometimes writing the full word or phrase and sometimes the abbreviation, and asking the children for the other form. For example:

Rd = Road
k.p.h. = kilometres per hour
am = before noon
(from the Latin *ante meridiem*)
pm = after noon
(from the Latin *post meridiem*)
PO = Post Office
BC = Before Christ

Ave = Avenue
DIY = do-it-yourself
Co. = Company
Dept = Department
HM = Her Majesty
p. = page
FC = Football Club
BBC = British Broadcasting Corporation

If dictionaries with an abbreviations index are available, encourage children to use these to find abbreviations and quiz the rest of the class.

Differentiated group activities

1 & 4: Discuss questions in part C of the Reading Comprehension sheet.
2 & 3*: Guided reading of the article: use questions from parts A and B of the Reading Comprehension sheet as a basis for discussion.

Conclusion

Now that the whole class has done all of the Reading Comprehension, use it as the basis of a plenary discussion. The final question to ask the class could be: do you agree with the opinion expressed by the writer at the end of the article?

"I FEEL LIKE A SCARECROW,"

SAYS VICKY

I went to St Marks Junior School to find out about their school uniform. Ms Sharp, head teacher, is a great fan of uniform. "It makes the school look neat and tidy," she said. "Children behave better and work harder."

Mrs Tennant, a parent, said, "The girls' last school didn't have a uniform and they were always arguing about what to wear. You'd think they were going to a fashion show instead of school. St Marks has a uniform, so there are no arguments."

Vicky Tennant, 9, has a different view. "I feel like a scarecrow in this uniform. It's dead old-fashioned."

Her sister, Karen, 10, agrees. "Girls can't wear trousers at this school. I think that's unfair because boys can! Trousers are warmer in winter!"

'What uniform?'

'I feel like a scarecrow!'

I asked two of the Y6 boys what they thought about uniform. "I want to wear an earring", said Dean, but it's against the rules."

"What uniform?" said Wayne.

I asked them if they thought uniform made them behave better and work harder. "Wearing this stuff makes me grumpy," said Vicky.

"I'd work better if I was comfortable," said Karen.

"I'm always in trouble," grumbled Wayne.

So, what do these interviews tell us about the school uniform? Adults prefer it. On the other hand, all the children I spoke to disliked it, though for different reasons. There is no evidence that children work better in uniform – as Ms Sharp suggests – or that they work better without it – as Karen believes. However, I think none of us would want to see schoolchildren looking like Wayne, so perhaps Ms Sharp is right after all!

READING COMPREHENSION

PART A

- What does Ms Sharp think about school uniform?
- What does Vicky Tennant think about uniform?
- Look at Vicky's picture – how do *you* think she looks?
- What does Dean say about uniform?

PART B

- Do you agree with Ms Sharp that uniform makes children behave better and work harder?
- Do you agree with Karen that girls should be allowed to wear trousers?
- Why does Wayne say, "What uniform?"
- Would a uniform help Wayne to behave better?
- What does the writer of the article think about school uniform?

PART C

- What is your opinion about school uniform?
- What would a school uniform for the year 2000 be like?

LETTER TO THE EDITOR

OBJECTIVES

UNIT	SPELLING/VOCABULARY	GRAMMAR/PUNCTUATION	COMPREHENSION/ COMPOSITION
WRITING NON-FICTION Discursive/persuasive writing: 'Letter to the Editor'.	Explore abbreviations used in address.	Use discursive connectives.	Read and evaluate an article. Use a letter-writing frame to structure presentation of arguments and personal point of view.

ORGANIZATION (2 HOURS)

	INTRODUCTION	WHOLE-CLASS SKILLS WORK	DIFFERENTIATED GROUP ACTIVITIES	CONCLUSION
HOUR 1	Shared re-reading of '"I Feel Like a Scarecrow," Says Vicky'. Discuss the issues raised and how the arguments are presented. (If following on from previous unit, recap concentrating on the structure of the writing).	Explain how to use discursive letter-writing frame.	1*: Guided writing using the writing frame as a basis. 2 & 3: Write answers for parts A & B of the 'Scarecrow' Reading Comprehension. 4*: Guided writing on the writing frame.	Selected pupils from Groups 1 & 4 read out examples of effectively supported arguments.
HOUR 2	Read out a good example of a pupil's letter from Hour 1 as an example.	Revise the list of discursive connectives.	1 & 4: Write answers to the 'Scarecrow' Reading Comprehension sheet questions. (Group 4, part A.) 2 & 3*: Guided writing with the letter frame (see above).	Selected pupils from groups 2 & 3 share their letters to the editor. The class, in role as an editorial committee, evaluates the letters for publication.

RESOURCES

Photocopiable pages 158 ('"I Feel Like a Scarecrow," Says Vicky') and 159 (Reading Comprehension) from the previous unit, 162 (Letter to the Editor), OHP and acetate (optional), examples of letters to editors from magazines and newspapers which put forward opposing arguments and express a personal view (optional), writing materials.

PREPARATION

If possible, prepare OHTs of photocopiable pages 158 ('"I Feel Like a Scarecrow," Says Vicky') from the previous unit and 162 (Letter to the Editor), or enlarge them to at least A3 size. Make enough copies of photocopiable pages 158 ('"I Feel Like a Scarecrow," Says Vicky') and 159 (Reading Comprehension), from the previous unit, for one between two, and enough copies of photocopiable page 162 (Letter to the Editor) for one each.

Introduction

Read '"I Feel Like a Scarecrow," Says Vicky' to the class and discuss the issues raised. If this unit is following on immediately from the 'Scarecrow' unit, it is not necessary to read the article again. However, children should be reminded of the key issues, as they will be writing a letter to the editor of a magazine, prompted by the article.

Whole-class skills work

Display a copy of photocopiable page 162, which is a letter-writing frame for discursive writing. Explain to the class that, in their group work, they will be writing a letter to the editor in response to the Scarecrow article. Tell the children that the basic structure of the letter that they write will be:

Paragraph 1:
Introduction which states the subject of the letter.
Paragraphs 2–4:
Each paragraph states an argument supported by one or more reasons.
Paragraph 5:
Conclusion in which the writer states his or her opinion or point of view.

Revise the list of discursive connectives introduced in the 'Scarecrow' unit (see page 156) and encourage the children to make use of them in their persuasive writing.

Practise the skills of making a point and supporting it with reasons by recapping on the uniform debate. Ask the children to:

- state their point of view
- give a reason to support it.

Differentiated group activities

1*: Guided writing based on the writing frame. Give each child a copy of photocopiable page 162 (Letter to the Editor). Encourage children in this group to go beyond the basic structure by making more points and supporting them more fully.
2 & 3: Give each pair of children a copy of photocopiable page 159 (Reading Comprehension) from the 'Scarecrow' unit, and ask them to write answers to parts A and B. This should be fairly straightforward if children have done the 'Scarecrow' unit and answered the questions orally.
4*: Guided writing based on the writing frame. Children in this group should write on the frame itself for the maximum level of support.

Conclusion

Select some children from Groups 1 and 4 to read out good examples of paragraphs which make a point and support it with reasons. Select some examples of whole letters and discuss their effectiveness.

Introduction

Read out two or three examples of children's letters that you feel are particularly good to refresh their memories of the issues, and to act as a model for those who will be writing their letters in this hour. If available, you could also read out similar examples from real magazines or newspapers.

Whole-class skills work

As children are writing letters, this is a good opportunity to look at the formatting conventions of letter writing and to continue work on abbreviations by looking at abbreviations used in addresses. The following abbreviations are often used in addresses. Ask children to say what they are short for:

Cres. (Crescent)	Sq. (Square)
St (Street)	Pl. (Place)
Rd (Road)	Oxon (Oxfordshire)
Ave (Avenue)	Hants (Hampshire)
Bldgs. (Buildings)	Cambs (Cambridgeshire)

Differentiated group activities

1: Write answers to the 'Scarecrow' Reading Comprehension sheet questions.
2 & 3*: Guided writing based on the letter-writing frame (see above).
4: Write answers to the 'Scarecrow' Reading Comprehension sheet, part A.

Conclusion

Read selected letters from those written by Groups 2 and 3. Ask the class to imagine that they are the editorial committee of the magazine. Which letters would they publish? Explain that there will be room for four letters which should be well written and give a balance of points of view.

LETTER TO THE EDITOR

[YOUR ADDRESS]

[THE DATE]

The Editor
Current Issues Magazine
High St
NEWTOWN
Warks

Dear Editor

I am writing in response to the article in your magazine about

Those in favour of school uniform argue that

They also say that

However, an important argument put forward by those who are against school uniforms is

They also argue that

Having read both points of view, my opinion is

because

Yours faithfully

[YOUR NAME]

CRIC CRAC

OBJECTIVES

UNIT	SPELLING/VOCABULARY	GRAMMAR/PUNCTUATION	COMPREHENSION/ COMPOSITION
READING FICTION *Cric Crac: A Collection of West Indian Stories* by Grace Hallworth.	Develop vocabulary from text. Spell words that are from common letter strings but have different pronunciations – *ea* and *ou* words. Practise *-tion*, *-sion* suffixes.	Understand how nouns, verbs and adjectives can be changed by adding endings. Compare dialect with standard English. Explore concept of abstract nouns.	Read folk stories from other cultures. Identify morals, common themes, characters. Write own episode in the style of a story read.

ORGANIZATION (5 HOURS)

	INTRODUCTION	WHOLE-CLASS SKILLS WORK	DIFFERENTIATED GROUP ACTIVITIES	CONCLUSION
HOUR 1	Establish format and genre of book. Locate West Indies. Shared reading of 'The Magic Pot', pages 11–18 (approximately 7 minutes).	Revise sentence types. Investigate changes to sentence types.	1*: Guided reading and discussion. 2 & 3: Draft own short story with a moral. 4*: Guided reading and discussion.	Selected pupils from Groups 2 & 3 read out their stories. Other pupils evaluate how effectively the moral has been put across.
HOUR 2	Shared reading of 'How Tacooma Found Trouble', pages 33–40 (approximately 7 minutes). Discuss similarities and differences with 'The Magic Pot'.	Investigate word changes: verb endings and noun endings.	1: Draft another episode for the story. 2 & 3*: Guided reading and discussion. 4: Draft another episode for the story.	Selected pupils from Groups 1 & 4 read out their stories. Other pupils evaluate how well they fit into the rest of the story.
HOUR 3	Shared reading of 'The Greedy Brother', pages 41–46 (approximately 5 minutes).	Investigate word changes: noun endings.	1*: Guided reading and discussion. 2 & 3: Exercise on *ea* and *ou* words. 4*: Guided reading and discussion.	One or two pupils read out their versions of the ending of the story.
HOUR 4	Shared reading of 'How the Stars Came Into the Sky', pages 55–64 (approximately 8 minutes).	Investigate word changes: adjectival endings (comparatives).	1: Exercise on comparative adjectives. 2 & 3*: Guided reading and discussion. 4: Exercise on comparative adjectives (Q1 only).	Discuss: What was the puzzle and what was the answer?
HOUR 5	Read the introduction and discuss the key ideas and vocabulary related to oral storytelling.	Identify and spell words with *-tion*, *-sion* suffixes.	1–4*: All groups experiment with oral storytelling.	One pupil chosen by fellow pupils from each group tells an oral story to the class.

RESOURCES

Cric Crac: A Collection of West Indian Stories by Grace Hallworth (Mammoth, ISBN 0-7497-1717-3) – if possible, enough copies for one between two children, board or flip chart, world map or globe, photocopiable pages 168 (Sounds Alike) and 169 (Comparing Adjectives), dictionaries, writing materials.

PREPARATION

Make enough copies of photocopiable page 168 (Sounds Alike) for one between two children in Groups 2 and 3 (for Hour 3) and page 169 (Comparing Adjectives) for one each in Group 1 and one between two in Group 4 (for Hour 4).

SYNOPSIS

This book offers a rich collection of eight traditional tales from the West Indies, some of which will be familiar, others of which are less well-known. Grace Hallworth is a superb storyteller and the language in these beautifully reflects the oral tradition from which they arise.

Introduction

Distribute copies of the book. Ask the children to spend a few minutes examining the cover and leafing through the pages to get an idea of what sort of book it is. Then ask them how it differs from a story such as *It's Too Frightening For Me!* (see Term 1, page 20). Establish that:

- it is a *collection* of short stories
- the stories are *traditional tales.*

Discuss briefly whether the stories are related in any way (Yes; they are all traditional tales from the West Indies) and make sure the children understand what is meant by 'traditional tale'. Locate the West Indies on a map or globe.

Read 'The Magic Pot' (pages 11–18). Ask the children for their opinions on the little rhyme on the last page. Establish that it is the 'moral' of the tale – that is, what the story teaches about right and wrong and how to behave.

Whole-class skills work

Revise sentence types. Ask the children to find examples of a statement, a question, an exclamation and an order in the story. For example, from page 12:

- One morning Anansi took a walk along a path... (statement)
- "...How often do you perform?" he enquired. (question)
- "Ye gods and little fishes!" (exclamation)
- "Fill the pot," said the pot. (order)

Now experiment with transformations. Take the first sentence in the story (*Anansi was troubled*) and write it on the board. Then turn it into a question. Ask children what you did to turn it into a question (transposed subject and verb, and replaced the full stop with a question mark). Use arrows to show them what you did. Ask them to choose four statements and turn them into questions.

Next, ask children to find an order, and to turn it first into a question, then into a statement. What changes did they have to make to do this?

Differentiated group activities

1*: Guided reading and discussion. The following questions can be used as a basis for discussion:

- Why was Anansi troubled?
- What did he do that was wrong?
- How did his wife find out?
- How did she punish him?

Remind children of what a simile is. Ask them to find the two similes on page 12 and explain them.

Look at the wife's saying on page 15. Discuss its dialect features and what the saying means.

2 & 3: Draft a short story with a moral. This should be approximately one side in length. Advise children to think of the moral they wish to write about first and then plan backwards from the ending before beginning to write.

4*: Guided reading and discussion (see above).

Conclusion

Select one or two children from groups 2 and 3 to read out their stories with morals. Ask the rest of the class to evaluate how effectively the moral has been conveyed.

Introduction

Read 'How Tacooma Found Trouble' (pages 33–40). Ask the children what this story has in common with 'The Magic Pot' (both Anansi stories; both about trick-playing). How is it different? (Anansi is successful at playing a trick; involves animals.)

Whole-class skills work

Investigate word changes: verb endings. Begin by revising the term 'verb' – a verb is a doing word. Ask the children to choose a verb from the story and write out the simple (regular), past and present tense on the board. Ask one of the children to come up and underline all the verb endings.

Next, ask the children to choose a noun from the text and then to try adding the verb endings. They will note that the *-ed* endings do not make sense (though the '-s' endings do – due to the historical simplification of the English language, the letter 's' is used for three different types of inflectional ending; this in itself is a cause of confusion for children). Establish that word endings can be clues when trying to identify what part of speech a word is. Reinforce the concept using other examples.

Differentiated group activities

1: Draft another episode for the story in which Anansi plays more tricks on Tacooma to teach him the meaning of trouble. This should be about a side in length and should fit in to the original story between page 34 ('Just do whatever you see me do, Tacooma, and you will find Trouble') and the final paragraph on pages 39–40.
2 & 3*: Guided reading and discussion. The following questions can be used as a starting point:

- How does Anansi get Tacooma into trouble and out of it again?
- Discuss the dialect forms in the verses. How do they differ from standard English?
- How do we know that Tacooma has learned about trouble at the end of the story?
- What class of word is *trouble*? Discuss the concept of abstract nouns (things that cannot be perceived by the senses). What are other examples? (*Love, hate, truth, power.*)

4: Draft another episode for the story (see above).

Conclusion

Select one or two children from Groups 1 and 4 to read out their episodes. Ask the rest of the class to evaluate how effectively they fit into the beginning and ending of the story.

Introduction

Read the introduction to 'The Greedy Brother' on page 41. Discuss why some people might think there is a man in the moon. Locate Guyana on a map or globe. Then read the story, pausing briefly at page 44 ('...I shall set a trap for him this night.') to ask the children to predict who the thief is.

Whole-class skills work

Investigate word changes by looking at noun endings. One of the distinguishing features of common nouns is that they can be made plural, whereas proper nouns, which are names for specific things, cannot. For example:

SINGULAR	PLURAL
boy	boys
bus	buses

In contrast, there is only one Grace Hallworth (the author of this collection of stories) and one Guyana (the place where this particular story comes from). What has been added to the nouns to make them plural?

Can the children add s and es to other classes of words to make new words? Write the following verbs on the board or flip chart and ask them to add s and es: *live, carry, have, pass, catch.* Lead them to see that the endings we add to nouns to make them plural can be added to some verbs to make new words (but, of course, this does not make them nouns!). Try it with these adjectives: *little, dead, wicked, greedy.* Does it work?

Differentiated group activities

1*: Guided reading and discussion. The following questions can be used as a starting point:

- What happens when the sister finds the honey?
- How does her brother deceive her?
- How does she catch him out?
- What happens to him in the end?
- Explain what the opening phrase means: 'Long, long ago when time was not...'
- What kind of words are *bee-hive* (page 42) and *fireplace* (page 43)? Can they think of other compound words?

2 & 3: Exercise on *ea* words – photocopiable page 168.
4*: Guided reading and discussion (see above, questions as appropriate).

Conclusion

Ask children to share their answers to the discussion questions. Include children from Groups 2 and 3 who will have heard the story in the introductory session. Recap on the purpose of the story – to explain how the man in the moon got there.

Introduction

Read 'How the Stars Came into the Sky' (pages 55–64). Discuss the fact that this is an Anansi story but it is not a 'trickster' tale like many of the Anansi stories. What sort of story is it? Explain that this is a 'pourquoi' story – an imaginative tale that tells why or how something in nature came to be that way (*pourquoi* is the French word for 'why'). 'The Greedy Brother' is also a pourquoi story.

Whole-class skills work

Investigate word changes resulting from adding adjectival endings (comparatives). Explain that we often need to compare things and use different adjectival endings to do this. The degrees of comparison are: absolute, comparative (comparing two things) and superlative (comparing more than two things). Write this table on the board or flip chart:

ABSOLUTE	COMPARATIVE	SUPERLATIVE
no additional ending	*-er ending*	*-est ending*
bright	brighter	brightest

Ask the children to find more adjectives from the story and add them to the table. Note that many two-syllable and all three-syllable adjectives use *more* for comparative and *most* for superlative. An example is *beautiful* (page 58).

beautiful	more beautiful	most beautiful

Ask the children to suggest other examples and write them on the board or chart. Then ask them to make up sentences for each of the three forms of one or two of the adjectives listed.

Differentiated group activities

1: Exercise on comparative adjectives – photocopiable page 169.
2 & 3*: Guided reading and discussion. The following questions can be used as a starting point:

- What are the differences between the four sons?
- Why does Anansi take a trip?
- What offer did the chief make to Anansi?
- How did the ball end up as the stars and planets?

4: As for Group 1, first part of sheet only.

Conclusion

Re-read the small section on page 57 in which Anansi announces he needs to find the answer to a puzzle. Discuss: What was the puzzle and what was the answer to it?

Introduction

Read the introduction. Discuss the ideas it presents, ensuring that the key vocabulary which is relevant to the oral tradition is identified and explained. For example:

The Caribbean is a *melting pot* of many *cultures* which are *interactive*.
The majority of people in the Caribbean are of African *origins* and have therefore kept alive African *folklore*.
Oral storytelling is part of all people's *roots* and *traditions*.
When people tell stories they *change* them so that we get *variations* and different *versions* of the same story which the *storytellers* have made their *own*.
Anybody can be a storyteller.

Whole-class skills work

Use the Introduction to focus on the spelling of words with *-tion* and *-sion* suffixes. Write the headings *-tion* and *-sion* on the board or flip chart. Ask the children to look through the introduction for words that have those endings and list them under the appropriate heading. Ask the children to pronounce them. Establish that *-tion* and *-sion* are both pronounced 'shun'. Ask them to think of other words with a 'shun' sound at the end and add them to the appropriate list. Some other suggestions are:

-tion	**-sion**
introduction	version
variation	collision
distraction	decision
tradition	discussion
satisfaction	division
ambition	mansion
communication	confusion
creation	impression

Differentiated group activities

1–4*: Children should work in groups of two to four to make their own oral version of a well-known story, myth or legend. One way to do this is to take one of the *Cric Crac* stories, or any other well-known story, and to place it in a modern, local setting. For example, a modern Little Red Riding Hood might walk through city streets rather than a forest and the villain might be a mugger rather than a wolf.

Conclusion

One child from each group (or as many as time allows) chosen by fellow children tells their oral story to the class.

FOLLOW-UP (3 HOURS)

See page 208 which provides a grid plan for a 3-hour follow-up unit focusing on three of the other stories in *Cric Crac*. Note that the remaining story is read as the basis for writing in the following unit ('Pourquoi Stories').

SOUNDS ALIKE

The **ea** words below can be found in the story 'The Greedy Brother'. In each case the **ea** is pronounced differently. Say each word and listen for the different **ea** sound. Then look through the story and find as many other **ea** words as you can. Say each one aloud and then write it in the column under the word with the same **ea** sound.

hearth	weaving	bread	heard

Read each of the **ou** words below and write it in the column with the header word that has the same **ou** sound. Then try to think of some other **ou** words to put in the columns.

house	court	found	enough	shouted	gourd
our	amount	could	thought	soup	route

cloud	ought	young	group	would

COMPARING ADJECTIVES

1. Complete the chart below.

ABSOLUTE no additional ending	COMPARATIVE **-er** ending or **more**	SUPERLATIVE **-est** ending or **most**
bright	brighter	brightest
	taller	
long		
		steepest
	darker	
round		
		dearest
		fattest
brave		
	happier	
	more important	
enormous		

2. Did you notice that some words need to change their spelling before adding **-er** and **-est**? Finish these sentences to say what you did.

When I added **-er** and **-est** to **fat**, I had to ________________________________.

When I added **-er** and **-est** to **happy**, I had to ____________________________.

When I added **-er** and **-est** to **brave**, I had to ____________________________.

3. Find the adjective **industrious** (page 56) in the story. Add it to the chart above, filling in all three columns.

Write down what you think it means.

Look it up in a dictionary and write down the dictionary definition. Were you right?

Write a sentence using **more industrious**.

Pourquoi Stories

OBJECTIVES

UNIT	SPELLING/VOCABULARY	GRAMMAR/PUNCTUATION	COMPREHENSION/ COMPOSITION
WRITING FICTION Pourquoi Stories.	Check spellings.	Revise items on the redrafting checklist.	Write a short 'pourquoi' story using one read as a model.

ORGANIZATION (2 HOURS)

	INTRODUCTION	WHOLE-CLASS SKILLS WORK	DIFFERENTIATED GROUP ACTIVITIES	CONCLUSION
HOUR 1	Shared reading of 'How Turtle Got a Cracked Back' from *Cric Crac*, pages 27–32, (approx 5 minutes). Discuss what a 'pourquoi' story is and discuss examples of others read previously.	Revise paragraphing and story structure using the Story Planner (from 'School Cards' unit, Term 2).	1–4*: Begin writing individual story.	Selected pupils from Groups 1 & 4 share the ideas for their stories and read their beginnings.
HOUR 2	Selected pupils from Groups 2 & 3 share the ideas for their stories and read their beginnings.	Talk about changes to the ending of the plan needed for a 'pourquoi' story. Revise the items on the Redrafting Checklist (from 'Redrafting Simulation' unit, Term 2).	1–4*: Finish off story and redraft with a partner.	Selected pupils read out their whole stories.

RESOURCES

Cric Crac: A Collection of West Indian Stories by Grace Hallworth (Mammoth, ISBN 0-7497-1717-3) – if possible enough copies for one between two children, photocopiable pages 93 (Story Planner) from 'School Cards' unit, Term 2) and 98 (Redrafting Checklist) from 'Redrafting Simulation' unit, Term 2), OHP and acetate (optional).

PREPARATION

Make enough copies of photocopiable pages 93 (Story Planner) and 98 (Redrafting Checklist) for one between two children. If possible, prepare these two sheets also as OHTs for use in the whole-class skills sessions.

Introduction

Read 'How Turtle Got a Cracked Back' from *Cric Crac* (pages 27–32), pausing first after the introduction to discuss what a 'pourquoi' story is – an imaginative tale that tells why or how something in nature came to be that way (*pourquoi* is the French word for 'why'). If you have done the previous unit, 'Cric Crac', ask the children if they can remember any other 'pourquoi' stories they have read.

Pause after reading the first paragraph of the story. Point out that this story beginning contains a moral, 'pride goes before a fall', so this tale is a fable as well as a 'pourquoi' story. Explain that this combining of different story types within folk literature is quite common. Make sure the children understand the saying 'pride goes before a fall' and the word *vanity*. After reading, ask the children to explain how vanity was Turtle's downfall.

Whole-class skills work

Revise paragraphing conventions and story structure using the Story Planner (photocopiable page 93 from the 'School Cards' unit, Term 2). If possible, display the Planner on an OHP and, as a class, use it to outline the structure of 'How Turtle Got a Cracked Back'. Discuss whether the Planner needs to be adjusted for a 'pourquoi' story. Lead the children to understand that the ending of a 'pourquoi' story is neither 'problems solved' nor 'a twist in the tale', but a statement which summarizes what the story has just explained. In fact, a 'pourquoi' story is best planned *backwards*. This gives the story a really effective ending that grows out of the rest of the story. To help children understand this, talk them through an example with the story planner displayed on an OHP. The following example can be used:

How the Beetle got its shape:
This 'pourquoi' story is going to be about the car of that name. My last line will be: 'And that's how the Beetle got its shape.' Next I need to think of a good explanation. One explanation could be that they bent the nose down to save metal. Why should they want to save metal? Because they wanted to keep the price down. What was the original design? The original design was a big bonnet with a high grill like all the other 1930s cars.
(Explain that, now that we have the outline, it needs to be brought to life.)
I will invent an eccentric engineer called Dr Bodge who will have all these ideas and a sales manager who thinks his ideas are silly because nobody will buy such a car. I am now ready to begin my story.

Differentiated group activities

1–4*: All children draft a 'pourquoi' story, using the Story Planner to support their writing and beginning with the ending. Some suggestions are given below:

Traditional: How the elephant got its trunk.
Why the sea lion has 'lion' in its name.
How the double bass got so much bigger than the rest of its family.

Modern: Why skyscrapers are so tall.
Why the helicopter has no wings.
How the computer 'mouse' got its name.

Children in Group 4, and any others who find it difficult to generate their own ideas, could use one of the above or develop the Beetle idea.

Conclusion

Select children from Groups 1 and 4 to share the ideas for their stories (the endings) and read their beginnings.

Introduction

Select children from Groups 2 and 3 to share the ideas for their stories (the endings) and read their beginnings.

Whole-class skills work

Use the Redrafting Checklist (from the 'Redrafting Simulation' unit, Term 2) to revise the main aspects of content, spelling, grammar, punctuation and layout that should be the focus of their redrafting in this unit.

Differentiated group activities

1–4*: All groups finish off their stories and redraft with a partner.

Conclusion

Select children to read out their whole stories. The rest of the class discuss and evaluate them as follows:

- Was the story based on a good idea?
- Was there a good explanation of how something came to be?

Discuss as a class how the stories might be 'published' (wall display, class anthology, library anthology) and ensure that time is allocated outside the hour to produce them.

Using a Dictionary: Guide Words

OBJECTIVES

UNIT	SPELLING/VOCABULARY	GRAMMAR/PUNCTUATION	COMPREHENSION/ COMPOSITION
REFERENCE AND RESEARCH SKILLS Using a Dictionary: Guide Words.	Use guide words in dictionaries to find more easily words needed for developing vocabulary.	Recognize and identify the guide words on a dictionary page.	Understand that guide words in a dictionary can help to find a word.

ORGANIZATION (1 HOUR)

INTRODUCTION	WHOLE-CLASS SKILLS WORK	DIFFERENTIATED GROUP ACTIVITIES	CONCLUSION
HOUR 1 Investigate pages from class dictionaries to recognize and identify words and to understand their purpose. Look for variations among dictionaries.	Practise exercise using photocopiable sheet (Guide Words).	1–4*: Pupils work at own level, choosing words from own reading books at random to find in dictionary and to identify the guide words on the page.	Give children guide words. They have to list words that would be on that page and then put them into alphabetical order.

RESOURCES

Photocopiable page 174 (Guide Words), enough dictionaries for at least one between two children (these should be at differentiated levels to cater for the range of ability in the class), current reading book for each child, OHP and acetate (optional), board or flip chart, writing materials.

PREPARATION

Choose a page from each of the dictionaries you will be expecting the children to use. Ideally, prepare them as OHTs, otherwise make enlarged photocopies.

Introduction

Display an OHT or enlarged copy of one of the dictionary pages. Establish in the first instance that all children know that it is a dictionary page! Draw their attention to the two words at the top of the page. Explain that these words are called 'guide words' because they help to guide you to the page you want to find. The guide word on the left is the first word on the page and the guide word on the right is the last word on that page. The words listed on each page will be those words that come alphabetically between the guide words. Show pages from the other dictionaries and ask the children to identify the guide words. Point out that the layout may vary slightly from dictionary to dictionary.

Whole-class skills work

Display photocopiable page 174 (Guide Words) and work through it as a class exercise. You may wish to give pairs of children a copy of the sheet, do the first part with the whole class and then let pairs of children put the words in alphabetical order before coming back together to confirm the alphabetical order task.

Differentiated group activities

Each group works with a dictionary appropriate for its level of ability. Children can work in pairs or individually.
1*: Open reading book at random. Close eyes. Place finger on page. Write word down. Choose ten words in this manner. Look up each word in the dictionary and write down the two guide words that appear on that page. Children should then look up the same words in another dictionary, write down the guide words and compare. If there are different guide words, why might this be?
2 & 3*: As above for the first part of the task but limit the choice of words to six. They should then choose two or three more words and see if they can find them more quickly using their knowledge of how to use guide words.
4*: As for Groups 2 and 3, first part only.

Conclusion

End the session by writing two or three sets of guide words on the board or flip chart and asking children to give you six to eight words that would appear on each page. Write their suggestions down and then ask them to put each set into alphabetical order.

GUIDE WORDS

Here is a list of words. They belong on one of the three dictionary pages below. Next to each word write the page number on which the word belongs, using the guide words to help you. Then write the words in alphabetical order on the lines for each dictionary page.

erase	edge	bath	empty	fair	egg
bear	skeleton	face	fact	send	sink
shave	exit	bet	blind	birth	blank
blood	selfish	spoon	skate	bicycle	sleep

bat	blow
1	

echo	fairy
2	

sea	sport
3	

HANS CHRISTIAN ANDERSEN

OBJECTIVES

UNIT	SPELLING/VOCABULARY	GRAMMAR/PUNCTUATION	COMPREHENSION/ COMPOSITION
READING NON-FICTION Recount (biography): *Hans Christian Andersen* by Andrew Langley.	Investigate the *wa* letter string. Practise extending words by adding prefixes and suffixes.	Identify dashes and hyphens and respond to them when reading. Investigate the past perfect tense.	Read non-fiction related to history. Identify problems faced by a subject and discuss how resolved. Understand features of biography. Summarize ideas in shortened form (postcard).

ORGANIZATION (5 HOURS)

	INTRODUCTION	WHOLE-CLASS SKILLS WORK	DIFFERENTIATED GROUP ACTIVITIES	CONCLUSION
HOUR 1	Introduce characteristics of biography. Find out what pupils already know about Andersen. Shared reading of pages 4–9 (approx 4 minutes).	Investigate the *wa* letter string.	1–4*: Write a school report for Hans Christian Andersen.	Compare and discuss reports.
HOUR 2	Establish problems faced by Andersen and how he dealt with them. Shared reading of pages 10–15 (approx 4 minutes).	Examine purpose and skill of postcard writing – summarizing ideas; shortened form of writing.	1*: Guided re-reading and discussion. 2 & 3: Write postcards. 4*: Guided re-reading and discussion.	Compare and discuss postcards.
HOUR 3	Shared reading of pages 16–21 (approx 4 minutes). Examine Andersen's character.	Practise extending words by adding parts.	1: Write postcards. 2 & 3*: Guided re-reading and discussion. 4: Write postcards.	Compare and discuss postcards. Discuss comprehension questions.
HOUR 4	Shared reading of pages 22–27 (approx 4 minutes). Identify main idea in each paragraph.	Identify dashes and hyphens and understand their uses and purpose.	1*: Guided re-reading and discussion. 2 & 3: Character sketch activity. 4*: Guided re-reading and discussion.	Discuss passage and paragraphs. How has Andersen's life changed?
HOUR 5	Shared reading of pages 28 to end (approx 3 minutes).	Investigate the perfect tense.	1: Character sketch activity. 2 & 3*: Guided re-reading and discussion. 4: Character sketch activity.	Share character sketches. Recap on characteristics of biography and relate to *Hans Christian Andersen*.

RESOURCES

Hans Christian Andersen by Andrew Langley (*What's Their Story?* series, Oxford Reading Tree, ISBN 0-19-910443-3) – ideally enough copies for one between two children, photocopiable pages 180 (School Report) and 181 (Character Sketch), a large pack of postcards (or photocopied sheets with three postcard outlines per sheet), board or flip chart, writing materials, OHP and acetate (optional), world map or globe.

PREPARATION

Prepare sufficient copies of the photocopiable pages 180 (School Report) and 181 (Character Sketch) for the children to have one each. Prepare postcard sheets (if real postcards are not available). Write on the OHT, board or flip chart the following list of biography characteristics:

- tells about a real person
- usually written in chronological order
- demonstrates that the writer knows a lot about the person
- describes the person's environment
- relates anecdotes or gives details that show the person in action
- shows how the person affected other people's lives or influenced them
- says or implies what the writer thinks about the person.

Introduction

Begin by looking at the cover of the book and establishing that the class is going to study a biography of Hans Christian Andersen. Explain that *biography* means 'life story'. Briefly brainstorm other words beginning with or including *bio*:

biology
biodegradable
biologist
antibiotic
autobiography

Show the children the prepared list of characteristics of biography and read it through with them. Ask them to look out for these features as they read the Hans Andersen biography.

Establish what the children already know about Hans Christian Andersen and the stories he wrote. If you did the 'Snow Queen' unit in Term 2, review the story with the children.

Read pages 4–9. Locate Denmark, Odense and Copenhagen on a map or globe. Talk about the descriptions of Hans. How is he different from other children? What clues are there in the text about Hans growing up to become a storyteller? What does the text say about Hans' teacher? Did Hans like him?

Whole-class skills work

Explore the *wa* letter string. Here is a list to investigate:

afterwards	dwarf	swamp
always	sewage	swat
awake	water	wash
aware	swallow	
beware	swam	

Ask the children to:

- add more examples to the list from the day's passage (page 4: *was, washerwoman;* page 6: *way, wanted;* page 7: *watched)*
- investigate how many different sounds (phonemes) can be represented by the *wa* letter string.

Differentiated group activities

1–4*: Children in all groups work in pairs or individually to complete photocopiable page 180 (School Report) for Hans Christian Andersen. They should use information from the passage where possible, make inferences about other aspects of his work, and make up the rest to fit in. For less able children, you might adapt the photocopiable sheet so that it contains only those subjects mentioned in the biography. Higher-ability groups should be expected to write in more detail and make more accurate inferences.

Conclusion

Share the school reports and discuss them. Are the children generally in agreement about Hans' performance at school? If not, how do they differ? Invite the children to identify the parts of the text that gave them clues about Hans.

Introduction

Recap on the previous section read, establishing what problems Andersen faced and how he dealt with them. Then read pages 10–15. Look at the illustrations in this section. Ask children what they think Andersen is thinking and feeling in each section. What does his expression in the illustration on page 14 tell us? As a class, write the thought bubbles that might appear above Andersen's head on pages 11–14.

Look at the list of important dates on the last page of the book and establish the dates covered by the reading (up to 1835). What other date is given in the biography that could be added? (1829. Made a tour of Denmark and met Riborg Voigt.)

Whole-class skills work

Talk about the different places in Europe that Hans visited and locate them on a map or globe. Discuss the different things he did and how he might have told someone else about them by writing postcards. When do we send postcards? What sort of things do we write in them? How do we write them? Do we always use full sentences? Make a list of the events Hans might have written postcards about.

Differentiated group activities

1*: Guided re-reading and discussion of the passage. The following questions can be used as a basis for discussion:
- Do you remember, from yesterday's reading, what Hans wanted to be when he grew up?
- What did he do to prepare himself for this?
- Why was he not successful?
- What other idea did he have about what he would do when he grew up?
- What was his life at school like?
- What happened in the summer of 1829?
- Which countries did Hans visit, and what did he think of them?

2 & 3: Write a series of postcards from abroad (ideally on real postcards). The children should refer back to the text to find out which countries Andersen visited and what he thought of them. They should then use their imagination to fill in additional details and write in the style of a postcard home.

4*: Guided re-reading and discussion of the passage, placing particular emphasis on monitoring basic reading skills during re-reading. Use the same questions as for Group 1 as discussion prompts.

Conclusion

Ask children from Groups 2 and 3 to share their postcards. Read examples aloud and discuss the style and content: Do they sound like real postcards? Do they fit in with the information we are given in the book?

Introduction

Read pages 16–21. Talk about how Hans has changed since the beginning of the book. In what ways is he the same?

Whole-class skills work

Write the following words from today's passage on the board or flip chart:

wonderful	magical	badly	carefully
beautiful	invisible	lonely	dangerous

Draw the children's attention to the fact these are all words that have been made by adding a suffix or a prefix. Ask them to identify the prefix or suffix in each case (*invisible* is the only one with a prefix; *carefully* has two suffixes.) Discuss how the endings have changed the words (from nouns to adjectives, from adjectives to adverbs and, in the case of *invisible* to the opposite). Write *-ful, -al, in-, -ly, -fully,* and *-ous* as headings and write the words above under the correct heading. Brainstorm others words for each list.

Differentiated group activities

1: Write postcards from Hans to his family and friends, using information from today's and yesterday's readings.
2 & 3*: Guided re-reading and discussion of the passage. The following questions can be used as a starting point:

- Some of Hans Christian Andersen's characters are listed in the passage. Which ones are they? Have you read the stories about them?
- What did he do to make his storytelling sessions interesting?
- Which other places did he visit? What did he think of them?

4: Write postcards from Hans to his family and friends, using information from both today's and yesterday's readings.

Conclusion

Select some children to share their postcards. Discuss the children's answers to the comprehension questions.

Introduction

Read pages 22–27. Talk about what happens and discuss how each paragraph presents a new idea or event. Look at each paragraph in turn and, together, pick out the main idea in each, summing it up in one sentence.

Whole-class skills work

Introduce the dash and the hyphen as punctuation marks:
A dash is often used to mean 'namely', 'that is', 'in other words', 'for example' as in:
'I wanted to meet one person above all – the inventor of the bass guitar, Leo Fender'.
A hyphen links two or more words or parts of words to show they should be read as one. Examples are:

twenty-one	fifty-three	do-it-yourself
blue-eyed	home-made	anti-aircraft

Hyphens are also used to show when words have to be split up at the end of a line of print.

Ask children to look through the passage for the day and find two examples of dashes and one example of a hyphen. How can they tell which is which? (Dashes are usually longer and have a space before and after them.)

Differentiated group activities

1*: Guided re-reading and discussion of the passage. Talk about how Hans Christian Andersen's life had become 'a fairy tale come true', the kings, queens, princes and princesses he met, and the places he visited.
2 & 3: Complete parts A and B of photocopiable page 181 (Character Sketch) which provides a format for summarizing the key facts about Hans Christian Andersen's life.
4*: Guided re-reading and discussion of the passage.

Conclusion

With the whole class, discuss the passage. What events in the text show how Hans' life has changed since the beginning of the book? Ask individual children to summarize each paragraph.

Introduction

Read pages 28 to the end.

Whole-class skills work

Re-read pages 28 and 29. Draw the children's attention to the use of different tenses. How do you know that Hans had met the old woman a long time ago? (he *had* thought; she *had* said)

Explain that *had* is an auxiliary or 'helper' verb which is used to create the perfect tense (which describes completed or 'perfected' actions). Write out this example of the perfect tense for children to study:

	SINGULAR	PLURAL
1st person	I had thought	We had thought
2nd person	You had thought	You had thought
3rd person	He/she/it had thought	They had thought

Ask the children to find two more examples of verbs in the perfect tense in the first paragraph, and choose one to write out in full, as above.

Differentiated group activities

1: Completes all parts of the Character Sketch photocopiable sheet (see above).
2 & 3*: Guided re-read and discussion of the passage. Use the following ideas as a basis for discussion:

- What kinds of things did Hans use as ideas for stories?
- How did Odense honour its famous citizen?
- What did Hans feel about it?
- When did he die and how is he remembered today?

4: Complete part A only of the Character Sketch photocopiable sheet.

Conclusion

Discuss the character sketches. Brainstorm, as a class, ideas for filling in part C, then let the children work outside the hour individually to complete it. Return to the list of characteristics of biography discussed in Hour 1. Ask the children to find examples of each characteristic in the biography of Hans Christian Andersen.

FURTHER IDEA

Talk about the various stories by Hans Christian Andersen mentioned in the text. How many do the children know? Can they recount any of them?

SCHOOL REPORT

NAME AGE

NAME OF CLASS TEACHER

	EFFORT
ENGLISH	
HANDWRITING	
SPELLING	
MATHEMATICS	
SCIENCE	
HISTORY	
GEOGRAPHY	
MUSIC	
DRAMA	
PE	
HEAD TEACHER'S COMMENTS	

CHARACTER SKETCH

PART A: Key facts

Name

Date of Birth

Place of Birth: Town Country

Occupation of father

Occupation of mother

Hobbies and interests as a child

Early ambitions in life

Date and place of death

PART B: Further details

Date and title of first book

Date and titles of first fairy tales

Names of some of his story characters

Countries visited

Date of visit to England

What he did and who he met in England

PART C

What do you admire most about Hans Christian Andersen's life story?

AMY JOHNSON

OBJECTIVES

UNIT	SPELLING/VOCABULARY	GRAMMAR/PUNCTUATION	COMPREHENSION/ COMPOSITION
WRITING NON-FICTION Recount (biography): Amy Johnson.	Develop vocabulary from text.	Summarize key ideas. Write from notes. Explore links between paragraphing and structure.	Research and write non-fiction related to history (biography), using a short biography read as a model.

ORGANIZATION (3 HOURS)

INTRODUCTION	WHOLE-CLASS SKILLS WORK	DIFFERENTIATED GROUP ACTIVITIES	CONCLUSION
HOUR 1 Shared reading and discussion of the biography on the photocopiable sheet.	Revise previous work on paragraphs. Explore the features of recount genre.	1: Reading Comprehension: all parts. 2 & 3*: Reading Comprehension: parts A and B. 4: Reading Comprehension: part A.	Discussion of new vocabulary. Pupils from Groups 2 & 3 share responses to part B of the Reading Comprehension sheet.
HOUR 2 Display the biography sheet and remind pupils how different resources, such as text, pictures, maps, can give them ideas for writing. Discuss ideas for biography subjects.	Model note-taking strategies, using the biography sheet as a basis.	1–4: Research material for a biography using photocopiable page 187 (Biography Research Questions) to support research. *Teacher works with Group 4.	Think about suitable biography subjects. All groups share ideas on the subjects of their research and the resources found.
HOUR 3 Use examples of good notes from the previous hour to model the process of turning notes into text.	Explore links between paragraphing and structure.	1*: Write a biography. 2 & 3: Write a biography using the template as a guide. 4*: Write a biography using the template.	Selected biographies or extracts are read aloud. Recap on key skills learned.

RESOURCES

Photocopiable pages 185 (Amy Johnson), 186 (Reading Comprehension), 187 (Biography Research Questions) and 188 (Biography Template), OHP and acetate (optional), dictionaries, board or flip chart, writing materials, information and reference books containing information about famous people.

PREPARATION

Make enough copies of the photocopiable pages 185 (Amy Johnson), 186 (Reading Comprehension) and 187 (Biography Research Questions) to allow for one between two children. If possible, prepare the Amy Johnson biography also as an OHT (or enlarge it to A3 size). Children in Groups 2 and 3 will need one copy of photocopiable page 188 (Biography Template) between two, and children in Group 4 will need one each.

Introduction

Begin by asking the children if they know who Amy Johnson is. Write any prior knowledge they have on the board or flip chart. Display the biography of Amy Johnson and read it with the children. Do not forget to spend some time looking at the pictures, the map and the captions. These visual elements have an important part to play in reading non-fiction texts. Discuss whether any of their prior knowledge was supported by the text.

Whole-class skills work

Revise work on paragraphing. Ask the children: What is a paragraph? How do we know when a writer has started a new paragraph? Remind them of the terms 'indent' and 'indentation'. Ask them to point out where each new paragraph starts.

Explain that although biographies are a non-fiction genre, they take place over a period of time, like stories. The technical term for this type of non-fiction is 'recount genre'. Write this list of features of recount genre on the board or flip chart:

Recount genre uses:
- the past tense
- chronological order
- many 'action' verbs.

Ask the children to examine these features by finding examples in the text.

Differentiated group activities

All children work in groups using the Reading Comprehension sheet as a basis for their work. The parts suggested on the organization grid above should be treated flexibly so that children who complete the part set for their group should be encouraged to move on to the next part.
1: All parts.
2 & 3*: parts A and B
4: part A.
NB: There is some difficult vocabulary in this text and it might be valuable to go over this *before* children begin working on their own.

Conclusion

Begin this session by going over the vocabulary; both the listed words and any other words which children found difficult. Select children from Groups 2 and 3 to read aloud examples of their responses to part B of the Reading Comprehension sheet.

Explain to the children that they will be researching and writing a biography themselves. Between now and the next hour, they should think about who they would like to write about. Explain it needs to be someone about whom something has already been written so that they can carry out their research. Their choice will also be determined by what resources you have in the school library. You might suggest ideas yourself which incorporate differentiation:
1: Research a 'serious' historical figure using a wide range of sources, such as Shakespeare, Sir Francis Drake, Newton.
2 & 3: Research a recent or current figure from a limited range of sources, such as a modern children's author, a film star.
4: Research a recent or current figure from one source.

Introduction

Begin by asking the children to share their ideas about the person who is the subject of their biography. Ensure that the people whom they have chosen are suitable. Then discuss the research, which is a necessary preliminary to the writing of any biography. The Amy Johnson biography sheet contains examples of some of the different types of resource they may find: text, pictures, a map and captions. Display the sheet again and explain how each can be useful as a source of information.

Whole-class skills work

The key skill required for research is note-taking. Help children with these skills by taking them through the following process.

■ Ask them to find five of the most important facts in the passage (children in Group 4 will need help with this).
■ Explain that we cannot mark reference books, so we must write down the key facts in brief note form. Stress that the important phrases or sentences must not be copied out, but written in their own words.
■ Demonstrate how to do this by taking a key fact from the text and showing how to make a note on it. For example, sentence 1, paragraph 4, could be noted as: *take-off: 5/5/30.*

Differentiated group activities
Children now carry out the research they need for their biographies. Explain that they can do the research in pairs or small groups but must write their own version of the biography. Give out copies of photocopiable page 187 (Biography Research Questions) for the children to use as a guide for their research, and support Group 4.

Conclusion
Discuss together the subjects chosen and the resources the children have found. Examples of good notes could be read out.

Introduction
Ask the children with examples of good notes from the previous hour to read them out. Others in the class should then suggest how to turn them into sentences and paragraphs with the teacher acting as guide and scribe.

Whole-class skills work
Revise paragraphing by analysing the paragraph structure of the Amy Johnson biography. Do this by asking the children to read each paragraph and think of a subheading for it. The subheading should reflect the main idea of the paragraph. Discuss different subheadings and write the most appropriate on the board, then use them to point out two things:
- Each paragraph deals with a separate idea.
- Each idea is a step forward in time.

Ask the children to try to paragraph their own biographies in a similar way.

Differentiated group activities
1*: Write their biographies from notes. Children in this group should write freely and present their material in any way they like as long as they write in sentences and paragraphs.
2 & 3: Children in these groups should use the template as a guide for paragraphing and layout only, that is, they should write on a different sheet of paper and adapt the suggested phraseology, structure and layout, as they wish.
4*: Children should write on the actual template. Two boxes are provided for illustrations.

Conclusion
Select children to read their biographies aloud to the class. Ask these children why they chose their particular subject. Discuss possible reasons why a biographer would choose to write about a particular person. Conclude the lesson with a recap of the key skills learned.

FURTHER IDEA

Apply the skills learned to another curriculum area, for example writing a biography of a historical character from a period currently being studied.

AMY JOHNSON (1903–1941)

Amy Johnson was a brave and daring female pilot. Although she broke many records in her short life, she is most famous for being the first woman to fly solo across the world.

Amy was the daughter of a Hull fish merchant. After she graduated from university, she became a secretary. But that was not what she really wanted to do. Her big ambition was to become a qualified pilot. So, even though she was very badly paid, she managed to save the money for flying lessons.

Amy Johnson in her flying gear.

In 1928 her determination was rewarded. She earned her pilot's licence and also qualified as a flight engineer. She then made an announcement: she intended to fly solo from England to Australia.

These are some of the things Amy had with her for her flight.

Amy took off from near London on 5 May 1930 in her Gipsy Moth plane, *Jason*, and flew over 16,000km (10,000 miles). She had to stop several times during the exhausting flight to refuel and also to make repairs to *Jason*. Although an unfortunate crash landing in Burma meant that she missed the time record by three days, when she touched down in Darwin, Australia, 19 days after take-off, she was a celebrity. She had achieved a different record. She was the first woman to have flown solo across the world.

In 1932 she married another pilot – and then proceeded to beat a record he had set. Their marriage lasted only six years, and when the Second World War broke out, Amy joined the Women's Auxiliary Air Force. In 1941 she was killed while flying in the service of her country.

Jason: The bottle-green Gypsy Moth plane in which Amy Johnson flew halfway round the world.

This map shows Amy Johnson's flight path and the places she landed on the way.

READING COMPREHENSION

PART A

- Read the biography aloud, taking paragraphs in turn.

- Do you know what these words mean? If not, use a dictionary to find out. Add any other words you don't know to the list.

ambition
qualified
announcement
intended
solo
determination
exhausting
celebrity

- Some of the things Amy took with her are illustrated. Say what you think each thing was needed for.

PART B

- Write a short description of *Jason* (Amy's aeroplane).

- How does *Jason* compare with a modern aeroplane?

- Write a short description of Amy's flying costume.

PART C

- How did Amy Johnson manage to go from secretary to pilot?

- How many kilometres did she fly on her record-breaking flight?

- What do you think made Amy's flight so exhausting?

- What prevented her from reaching Australia in record time?

- What other record *did* she achieve?

- When and how did Amy die?

BIOGRAPHY RESEARCH QUESTIONS

Name of person:

Date of birth:

Date of death:

What is he/she famous for?

Make a note about an important event in his/her life:

Make a note about another important event:

Anything else?

How did he/she die OR what is he/she doing now?

■ Sketch below any objects, maps or diagrams which are linked with the person. Label the objects.

BIOGRAPHY TEMPLATE

________________ was born on ________________.
(name)

When he/she was young ________________________

____

____

______________________________.

________________ is famous for
(name)

____

____

______________________________.

______________________________.

This is how he/she did it.________________________

____

____

____

____

____________ died __________
(name)

OR

Today________________ is
(name)

____

____

____

NINEVAH

OBJECTIVES

UNIT	SPELLING/VOCABULARY	GRAMMAR/PUNCTUATION	COMPREHENSION/ COMPOSITION
WRITING SIMULATION Ninevah.	Develop new vocabulary from text. Use dictionaries to investigate word origins. Extend work on synonyms.	Identify verb tenses. Identify common punctuation marks: colon semicolons. Reinforce verb work.	Read a newspaper article. Research information linked to other curricular area (history). Write labels/captions, descriptions, stories, articles and letters.

ORGANIZATION (5 HOURS)

	INTRODUCTION	WHOLE-CLASS SKILLS WORK	DIFFERENTIATED GROUP ACTIVITIES	CONCLUSION
HOUR 1	Read and discuss 'The Illustrated London News' article on the discovery of Ninevah. Use empathy to respond.	Use phonic knowledge to work out pronunciation of difficult words. Develop vocabulary. Identify paragraph structure. Identify verb tenses.	1–4*: Reconstruct the broken plate and write a description of the picture for 'The Illustrated London News'.	Different descriptions are read out and compared.
HOUR 2	Display and introduce the artefacts sheet. Model the process of preparing for factual research.	Dictionary work on word roots and origins.	1–4*: Discuss the possible uses of the artefacts and write a display card for each one.	Compare descriptions of some of the more enigmatic artefacts.
HOUR 3	Display and introduce the bas-reliefs Describe and interpret the scenes.	Work on synonyms and using a thesaurus.	1–4*: Discuss what they can see in the bas-reliefs and construct a story around one of them.	Selected pupils read out their stories.
HOUR 4	Read an encyclopaedia entry on an ancient civilization. Briefly discuss the language and style.	Revise conventions of setting out a letter. Investigate how persuasive points are organized.	1*: Write a chapter about Ninevah for a book on ancient civilizations. 2 & 3: Write a persuasive letter asking for more funding. 4*: Make a list of what has been found out about Ninevah.	Selected pupils read out their letters.
HOUR 5	Re-read 'The Illustrated London News' front page and display the artefacts and bas-reliefs pages.	Identify colon and semicolon.	1: Write a letter to the government requesting more funding. 2 & 3*: Write an encyclopaedia entry about ancient Ninevah. 4: Write a short letter.	Whole-class role-play based on what they have found out about Ninevah.

RESOURCES

Photocopiable pages 193 ('The Illustrated London News'), 194 (Ninevah Plate), 195 (Artefacts) and 196 (Bas-reliefs), OHP and acetate (optional), reference books that contain information on the ancient civilization of Ninevah, dictionaries, thesauruses, card.

PREPARATION

Photocopy enough resource sheets for one between two children. Group 4 will need one each of photocopiable page 195. If possible, make OHTs of the newspaper article, the artefacts and the bas-reliefs (or enlarge to at least A3 size).

Introduction

The purpose of this 'simulation' is to provide a context for a range of writing for different purposes and audiences. It also develops skills of inference and deduction. The newspaper article on photocopiable page 193 is used to set up the situation (note that it is adapted from a real article that appeared in 'The Illustrated London News' of June 26, 1847).

Display the article and read it with the class. Discuss what it is about, ensuring that the children have a firm grasp of the context which will form the basis for this unit's work. Establish what an archaeologist is and does. Ask the children to imagine that they are archaeologists in Sir Henry Layard's team. How would they feel about the discovery? Lead them to understand that the work of an archaeologist is often very painstaking and frequently involves careful piecing together of information, often from broken artefacts.

Whole-class skills work

Investigate unfamiliar vocabulary as necessary (for example *ruins, excavating, finds, bas-reliefs, chariot/charioteer*) and work with the children to come up with pronunciations of any difficult words or names. Encourage the children to break down long words into syllables to help with reading them.

Discuss how the text is separated into paragraphs, each containing a new piece of information, the main idea of which is summarized in the subheading.

Draw the children's attention to the various verb tenses used (news *has* reached; this *will* interest; it *was* the capital; the King *is* in; he *will* be able). Discuss why, in each case, the verb tense was used.

Differentiated group activities

1–4*: Children should work in groups of three or four to piece together the plate fragments on photocopiable page 194. Explain that the picture shows a broken plate and that the groups have to reassemble it. The plate shows a picture of Ninevah. Children should discuss what they can see in the picture and try to work out every detail in the same way that 'The Illustrated London News' article gave a detailed description of the lion hunt bas-relief. They should also use the newspaper article to help them with their speculation. The following questions can be used as prompts:

- What are the buildings for?
- What is on top of the nearest high building?
- What is the statue?
- Who are the armed men in the foreground? Describe their armour.

More able children can go a step further and be encouraged to draw broader inferences from the picture, for example that Ninevah was a civilized city where there were fine buildings, bridges, an army and an organized religion.

The conclusions should be written up in the form of an article for 'The Illustrated London News'. Children in Group 4 could be given this sentence to start them off: '*Sir Henry Layard's team of archaeologists recently found a plate which shows us what ancient Ninevah looked like...*'

Conclusion

Ask selected children to read out their articles. Discuss the different interpretations of the picture, making sure that children understand that their ideas and suppositions should be based on evidence.

Introduction

Re-establish the simulation by reminding children that they are archaeologists in Sir Henry Layard's team excavating ancient Ninevah. Display photocopiable page 195 which shows a range of artefacts. Explain to the children that they should imagine that these are what they have dug up in the previous week. Discuss: What are these items? What were they used for? How could we find out? Encourage the children to look for further information about the objects and about Assyrian civilization in encyclopaedias and other reference books. Model the process of preparing for research and finding information from books that you have available.

Whole-class skills work

What is an *artefact*? Look the word up in a dictionary and talk about the word root and origin. Ensure children understand how and where to find out this information from a dictionary entry. Practise using other relevant vocabulary from the unit, for example *archaeology, discover, historian, museum.*

Differentiated group activities

1–4*: Give each pair a copy of photocopiable page 195 (Artefacts). Children in all groups should write caption or description cards for each artefact to explain the object in a museum display. More able children should write in more detail on separate cards. Children in Group 4 should write in the boxes on the sheet.

Conclusion

Choose some of the objects for discussion. For example, what is the object at the top left? At the bottom right? Explain that any sensible interpretation supported by reasons is acceptable. Archaeologists often find themselves in the position of having to make intelligent guesses about the artefacts they find.

Introduction

Re-establish the simulation as in Hour 2. Display the bas-reliefs on an OHP if possible. Ask the children if they know what is meant by a *bas-relief* (a carved picture in which the shapes are raised slightly from the background giving a three-dimensional effect). Talk about what can be seen in the pictures. The following information can be given as a starting point:

- Bas-relief 1 shows the king crossing the river. Discuss where he might be going. Is there a clue in the things some of the men are carrying?
- Bas-relief 2 shows scenes from everyday life. What do they show?

Whole-class skills work

As the children describe and interpret the bas-reliefs, encourage them to think carefully about their choice of words. Is the word that they have chosen precise or descriptive enough? Pause children at points in their discussion when you think they could use a synonym that would be more effective. Identify the word or phrase and ask the others if they can think of a more appropriate one. Model using a thesaurus to find alternative words.

Differentiated group activities

1–4*: All groups should choose one of the bas-reliefs on the photocopiable sheet and discuss it. They should try to explain every detail in the relief. Then, as a group, they should make up a story based on the bas-relief. If there is time, each child in the group should write down their own version of it. The top bas-relief is recommended for Group 4 as it is easier to turn into a story.

Conclusion

Select children to tell or read out their stories. Compare versions of the story for the same bas-relief.

Introduction

Read an encyclopaedia entry about any ancient civilization. Briefly discuss the language and style.

Whole-class skills work

Revise the conventions of letter writing (how to set out addresses, introduce a letter and end a letter). Talk about how good organization of points can enhance a persuasive argument and draw attention to the use of: *if... then, on the other hand..., finally, so, because,* and so on.

Differentiated group activities

1*: Write a chapter on Ninevah for a book entitled 'Ancient Civilizations'. This chapter should piece together all the information. Present it to a readership of junior school age.
2 & 3: Write a persuasive letter to the government asking for more money to complete the excavations. Include at least three good reasons why the money should be given. Begin, 'Dear Prime Minister...'
4*: Make a list of the facts and information they have learned so far about Ninevah.

Conclusion

Select children from Groups 2 and 3 to read out their letters. Encourage the rest of the class to evaluate the reasons they gave for more money being given by the government. If they were the Prime Minister, would they be persuaded to give the money?

HOUR 5

Introduction

Re-read the article from 'The Illustrated London News' on photocopiable page 193 and display all the photocopiable sheets. Explain that all the 'discoveries' that have been investigated so far will now be looked at together to see what has been learned about Ninevah.

Whole-class skills work

Re-read the article, looking for colons and semicolons. Ask the children to highlight or underline them on their own copies. Then focus particularly on paragraph 2. This is a good example of one of the uses of colon and semicolon. The colon is used to *introduce the list*. Semicolons are used to *separate phrases in the list*. Note that one of the phrases is a short list which is in itself separated by commas.

Model the process in the following way. Say that you are going to write a list of things in a school bag. The list is introduced with a colon, like this:

In my bag you will find the following items:

Next, group the items in the bag into categories, for example:

two pens, three coloured pencils and one highlighter pen,
ten sheets of paper and two books
a mouldy sandwich, a half-eaten chocolate bar and a bag of crisps

Now put everything together using semicolons:

In my bag you will find the following items: two pens, three coloured pencils and one highlighter pen; ten sheets of paper and two books; a mouldy sandwich, a half-eaten chocolate bar and a bag of crisps.

Ask the children to write a list of what is in their bags, trays or pockets, following this pattern very closely.

Differentiated group activities

1: Write a letter to the government asking for more money to complete the excavations. Explain what has been achieved so far and give several persuasive reasons to support the request.
2 & 3*: Write an entry under Ninevah for a children's encyclopaedia. This is more concise (and therefore easier) than the book chapter written by Group 1 in the previous hour.
4: Write a short letter to the government asking for more money to complete the excavations. The main focus should be on correct use of conventions although a good reason should also be given.

Conclusion

Invite children to suggest roles for, and participate in, a role-play exercise. Roles could include the government minister in charge of finance for the dig, the archaeologists, local people involved in the dig, a journalist, the families of the archaeologists.

FURTHER IDEA

Ask children to research the work of other famous archaeologists such as Sir Arthur Evans who discovered Knossos, Shliemann, who discovered Troy.

NINEVAH DISCOVERED

Exciting news has reached this country of the discovery of the ruins of Ninevah. This will interest Christians as well as historians: Ninevah is mentioned in the Bible. It was the capital of the kingdom of Assyria whose king, Tiglath-Pileser (1115–1076BC), defeated the Israelites and took them into slavery.

A BRITISH FIRST

Two archeologists have been excavating Ninevah: a Frenchman, Monsieur Botta, and a Briton, Sir Henry Layard. Sir Henry was the first to discover the ruins and has sent back some interesting finds to the British Museum. These include two pieces of a huge statue; pottery, pieces of pottery and numerous small beads; several items of gold jewellery; and eleven bas-reliefs: stone carvings showing scenes from Assyrian life.

THE LION HUNT BAS-RELIEF

One of the bas-reliefs is shown below. It portrays a Lion Hunt. The King is in his chariot drawn by three horses; you can see the charioteer urging the horses forward to escape from the lion which has his claws on the back of the chariot. The King has already shot four arrows into the lion and is about to shoot a fifth. Behind the lion are two of the King's bodyguards in full uniform. In front of the chariot is another lion which seems to be badly wounded.

GOVERNMENT FUNDS

As a result of these interesting finds, Mr Layard has been awarded a sum of money by the British Government to continue his excavations. It is hoped he will be able to find out enough to give us an idea what the ancient city of Ninevah looked like and to tell us something about the everyday life of its people.

NINEVAH PLATE

Cut out the fragments of this broken plate and reassemble it. Then discuss what you can see in the completed picture.

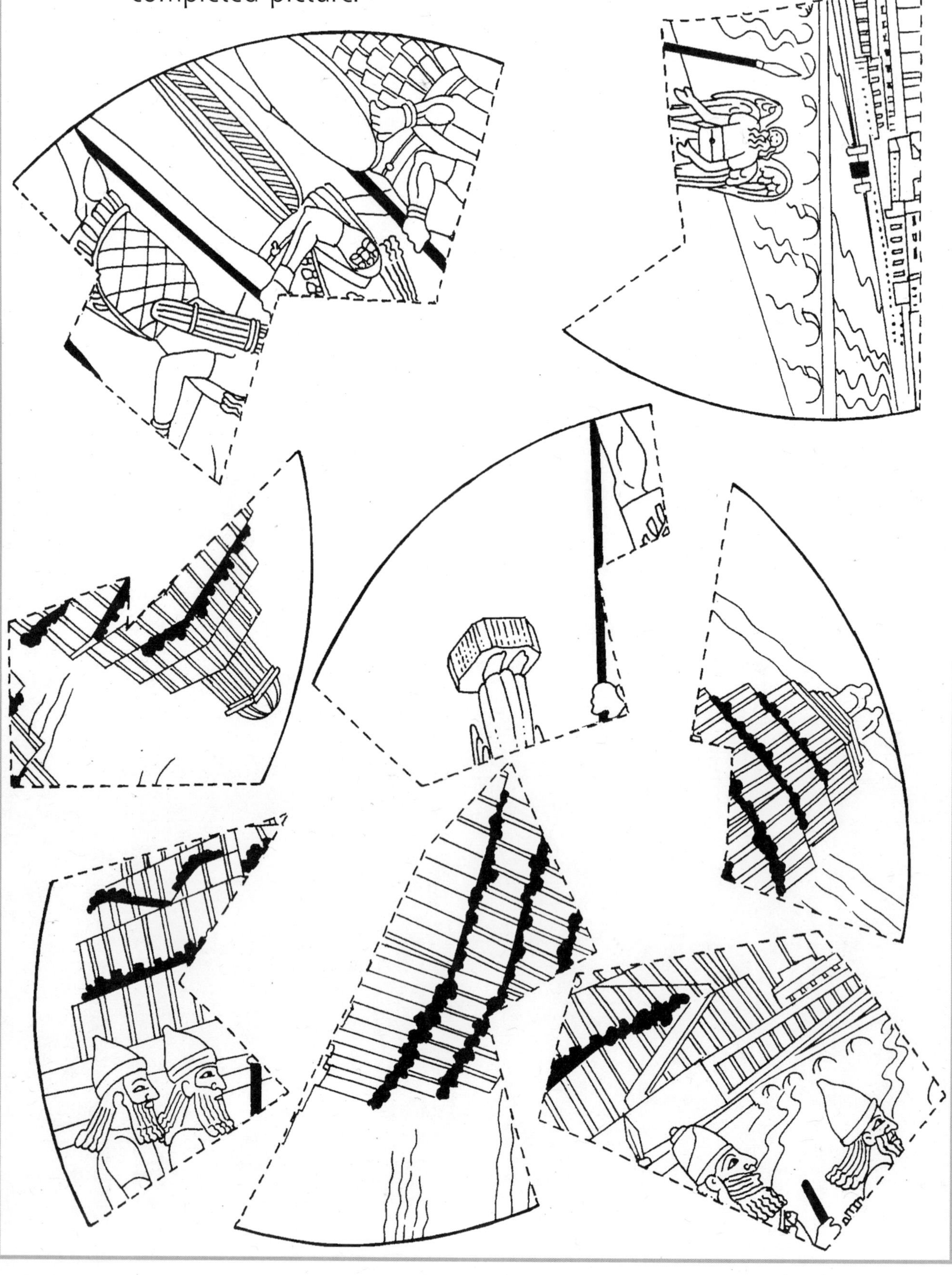

NINEVAH ARTEFACTS

Discuss the objects on this page.
What do you think they are?
What do you think they were used for?
Fill in the museum display card for each one.

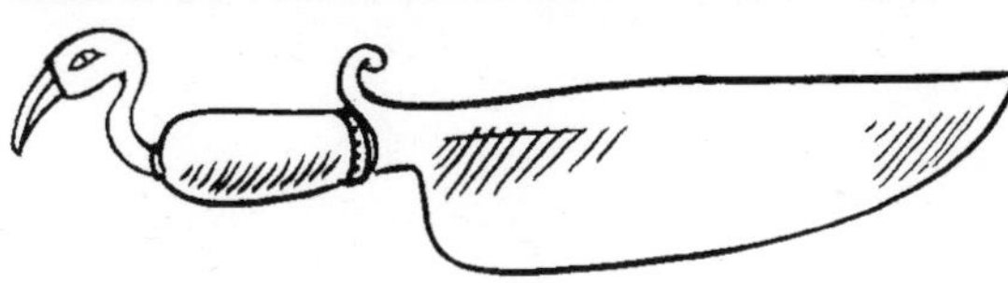

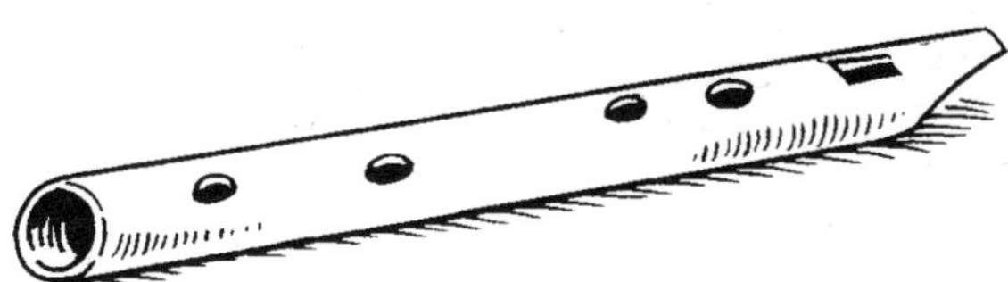

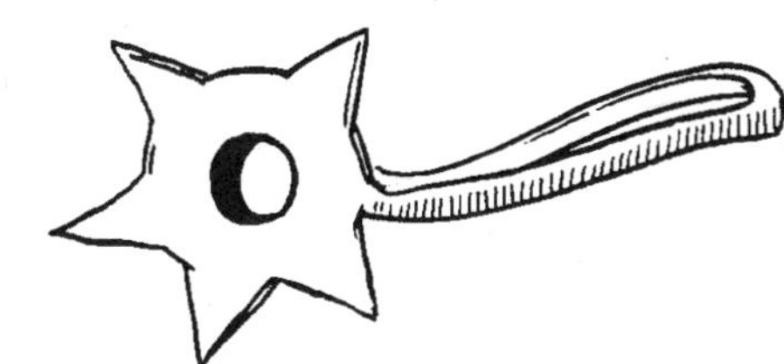

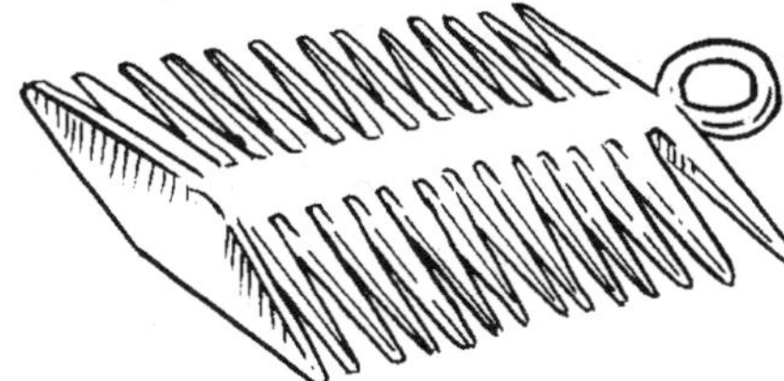

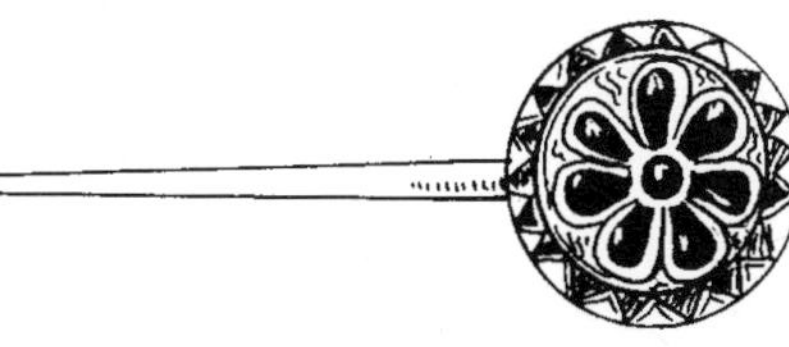

NINEVAH BAS-RELIEFS

Discuss the pictures on these bas-reliefs.
Try to explain every detail.
Make up stories based on these bas-reliefs.

SUMMARIZING

OBJECTIVES

UNIT	SPELLING/VOCABULARY	GRAMMAR/PUNCTUATION	COMPREHENSION/ COMPOSITION
REFERENCE AND RESEARCH SKILLS Summarizing: Spiders.	Develop subject specific vocabulary from text.	Revise use of present tense for information texts.	Summarize key ideas from text. Use note-making strategies. Write information clearly and concisely.

ORGANIZATION (1 HOUR)

INTRODUCTION	WHOLE-CLASS SKILLS WORK	DIFFERENTIATED GROUP ACTIVITIES	CONCLUSION
HOUR 1 Shared reading of non-fiction text 'Spiders' on photocopiable sheet. Identify unfamiliar subject specific vocabulary and find meanings.	Model summarizing key ideas in text.	1–4*: In pairs, read a page from a non-fiction book, pick out key ideas and summarize.	Selected pairs present their summaries, describing the process to the rest of the class.

RESOURCES

Photocopiable page 199 ('Spiders'), OHP and acetate (optional), a collection of information and reference texts appropriate to children's varying levels of reading ability and preferably related to topics currently being studied in other curricular areas, dictionaries, board or flip chart, writing materials.

PREPARATION

If possible, prepare an OHT of photocopiable page 199 ('Spiders'). Alternatively, enlarge the sheet to at least A3 size. Make enough copies for one between two children.

Introduction

Give out copies of the 'Spiders' text and display it on an OHP or as an enlarged version. Read it through with the class. Establish what type of text it is. Draw the children's attention to the use of the present tense as a characteristic feature of information texts. Ask them to identify any unfamiliar words or phrases and underline these in the text. Discuss and model different ways of finding out what they mean: from the context; from someone else who knows the meaning; by looking them up in a dictionary.

Whole-class skills work

Use the 'Spiders' text to model for the children how to look for key ideas in the text and write a summary in their own words using notes they have made. Begin by identifying the paragraphs and establishing that paragraphs chunk information into different sub-topics of the main topic. Read each paragraph in turn and establish the sub-topic. This could be written down as a subheading. Then go through each paragraph underlining the most important words or phrases. Delete the non-essential words. Go through it again and pare it down further if you can. Then write the words left on the board or flip chart to model the note-taking procedure. (An example is shown on page 198.)

Finally, turn off the OHP or take down the displayed text (and ask the children to turn over their copies). Then use the notes to make a class summary of the 'Spiders' text.

Differentiated group activities

1–4*: Children should work in pairs within their ability groups and with texts that are appropriate to their reading ability. Tell them to choose one page (or more for the more able children) from the range of non-fiction books and to read and make notes on the content, using key words and phrases, headings and diagrams. Ask the children to summarize information given on the page as briefly as possible.

Conclusion

Ask several pairs to present their summaries to the rest of the class, describing the process they went through to arrive at their summaries.

Example of procedure for note-taking

Spiders
Spiders live all over the world – on mountains, in forests, deserts, caves and even under the water. There are more than 30,000 different kinds of spiders. Spiders are not insects. They belong to a group of animals called **arachnids** (pronounced *a-rak-nids*) with only two body segments, which sometimes appear to be fused or stuck together.

Legs and Eyes
All spiders have eight legs. Some have delicate, slender legs, like a cobweb spider. Others, like the trap-door spider, have thick hairy legs. Most spiders have eight eyes, but others only have six or four – and some have none! The weirdest feature belongs to the midget spider, whose eyes are perched at the end of stalks.

Making Silk
All spiders can spin silk, which is made by special glands in their abdomens. Some spiders wrap their prey in silk, some spin cocoons for their eggs, some line tunnels with silk, others weave nets with it, and some, like the orb spiders, spin the webs that are most familiar to us.

Web-making
Web-spinning spiders hang lines of sticky silk in bushes, trees or fences. They add more and more threads until a net is formed. Insects get caught in the sticky net and are held like prisoners until the spider eats them.

Gender Differences
Male spiders are much smaller than females, which sometimes mistake the males for insects and eat them!

Notes
Spiders live all over the world
30,000 different kinds
Not insects – group of animals called arachnids – two body parts.

All have 8 legs
some slender – cobweb spider
some thick and hairy – trap-door spider
Most 8 eyes but some 4 or 6, some none
weirdest feature – midget spider – eyes on stalks.

All spin silk made in glands in abdomen
Some use silk to:
wrap prey in it, spin cocoons for eggs, line tunnels, weave nets, spin webs.

Web-making spiders hang lines, add threads to make web to catch insects.
Prey held until spider eats them.

Females bigger – can mistake males for insects and eat them.

SPIDERS

Spiders live all over the world – on mountains, in forests, deserts, caves and even under the water. There are more than 30,000 different kinds of spiders. Spiders are not insects. They belong to a group of animals called **arachnids** (pronounced *a-rak-nids*) with only two body segments, which sometimes appear to be fused or stuck together.

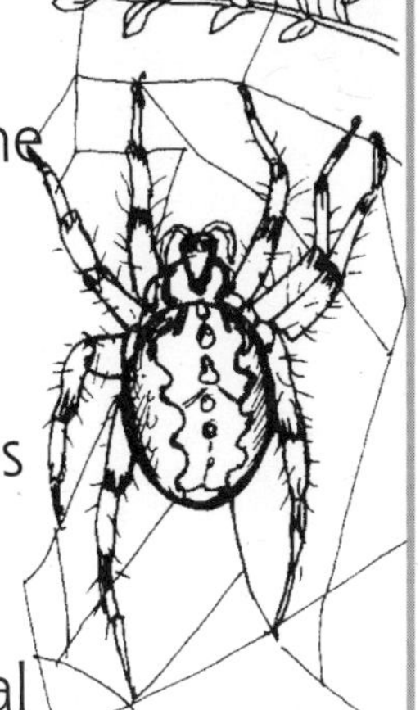

All spiders have eight legs. Some have delicate, slender legs, like a cobweb spider. Others, like the trap-door spider, have thick hairy legs. Most spiders have eight eyes, but others only have six or four – and some have none! The weirdest feature belongs to the midget spider, whose eyes are perched at the end of stalks.

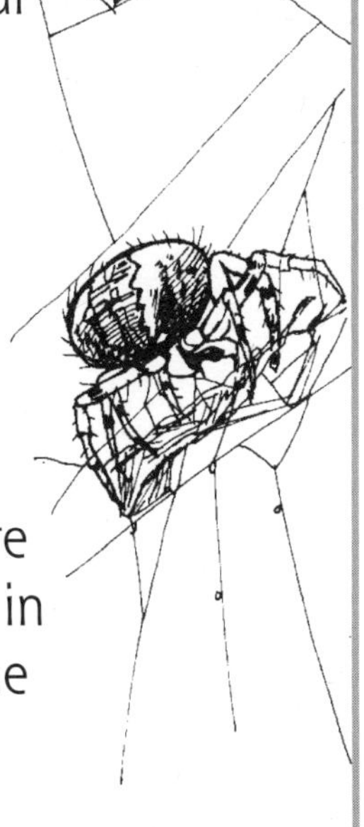

All spiders can spin silk, which is made by special glands in their abdomens. Some spiders wrap their prey in silk, some spin cocoons for their eggs, some line tunnels with silk, others weave nets with it, and some, like the orb spiders, spin the webs that are most familiar to us.

Web-spinning spiders hang lines of sticky silk in bushes, trees or fences. They add more and more threads until a net is formed. Insects get caught in the sticky net and are held like prisoners until the spider eats them.

Male spiders are much smaller than females, which sometimes mistake the males for insects and eat them!

SKIPPING AND ACTION RHYMES

OBJECTIVES

UNIT	SPELLING/VOCABULARY	GRAMMAR/PUNCTUATION	COMPREHENSION/ COMPOSITION
WORD PLAY Skipping and Action Rhymes.	Identify rhymes and syllables.	Exhibit knowledge of punctuation marks when reading.	Recognize simple forms of poetry and their uses. Investigate rhythm, rhyme and syllables.

ORGANIZATION (1 HOUR)

	INTRODUCTION	WHOLE-CLASS SKILLS WORK	DIFFERENTIATED GROUP ACTIVITIES	CONCLUSION
HOUR 1	Discuss skipping rhymes.	Recognize simple rhyme schemes.	1: Write new skipping/ action rhymes. 2 & 3: Identify rhyme schemes. 4: Clap rhymes.	Selected members of Groups 2–4 present their group work. Volunteers from Group 1 read their rhymes.

RESOURCES

Photocopiable page 202 (Skipping Rhymes), rhyming dictionaries (if available), writing materials, flip chart or board, writing materials, OHP and acetate (optional).

PREPARATION

Prepare enough copies of the poems for one between two children. If possible, also prepare the poems as an OHT – or enlarge to at least A3 size.

Introduction

Display the rhymes on the photocopiable sheet but block out the title 'Skipping Rhymes'. Read them aloud. Ask the children if they recognize any of them. Where might these rhymes be said? How many people would be saying them at one time? What would they be doing as they said the rhymes? Ask for volunteers to read each rhyme. Do the children know any others? If so, ask them to recite them.

Whole-class skills work

Ask the children to look for rhyming words in 'Not last night...' Make a list on the flip chart or board. Can they find a pattern? Demonstrate, by labelling, the first two rhyming words as A A, followed by B B and so on. Explain that this pattern is a simple rhyme scheme: two lines together are called a rhyming couplet.

Not last night but the night before,
Twenty four robbers came knocking at the door.
When I went down to let them in,
They hit me on the head with a rolling pin.
And this is what they said to me –
'Spanish ladies turn around

Spanish ladies touch the ground
Spanish ladies do the splits
Spanish ladies count to six.'
One – two – three – four – five – six!

Rhyming couplets help us to remember skipping rhymes. Ask the children if they can think of any other features which make the rhyme easy to remember, for example simple vocabulary, repetition, rhythm, counting words and actions. List these on the board or flip chart.

Refer to the word *rhythm* and tell the children that the class is going to clap the rhythm of the verse. They will clap each syllable of every word. Demonstrate this first by clapping the first two lines. Repeat this with the children. Ask for volunteers to demonstrate other lines.

Differentiated group activities

Explain that although these rhymes have always been spoken and remembered, it is important to have rhymes written down too.

* The teacher gives support where necessary.

1: Re-read all the rhymes and work with a partner to write a new rhyme. Establish that it should not be one that they already know. Can they include action?

2 & 3: Write out the rhyme scheme for the first two rhymes on photocopiable page 202. Write the rhyme scheme for another short poem they know.

4: Read through all three rhymes. Work with a partner, clapping all the syllables. What do they discover? Do their partners agree?

CONCLUSION

Selected members of Groups 2–4 present what they have done in their group work. Volunteers from Group 1 read their rhymes. Ask one child to teach his or her rhyme to the class.

SKIPPING RHYMES

One, two, three,
Mother caught a flea.
Put it in the teapot to make a cup of tea.
The flea jumped out!
Mother gave a shout!
In came father with his shirt hanging out!
In comes the Doctor
In comes the Nurse
In comes the lady
With the alligator purse.
'Dead!' said the Doctor.
'Dead!' said the Nurse.
'Dead!' said the lady with the alligator purse.

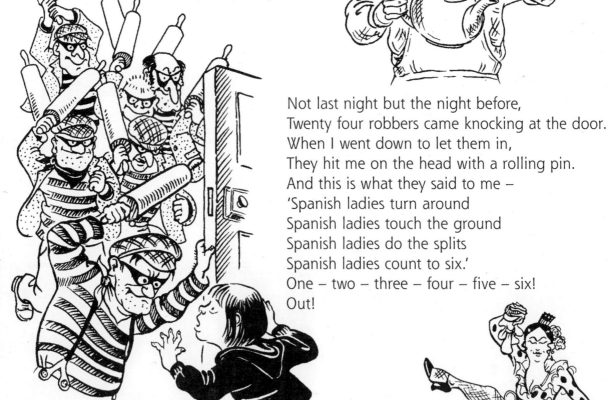

Not last night but the night before,
Twenty four robbers came knocking at the door.
When I went down to let them in,
They hit me on the head with a rolling pin.
And this is what they said to me –
'Spanish ladies turn around
Spanish ladies touch the ground
Spanish ladies do the splits
Spanish ladies count to six.'
One – two – three – four – five – six!
Out!

I'm a famous dancer and I can do the kicks
I'm a famous dancer and I can do the splits
I'm a famous dancer and I can turn around
I'm a famous dancer and I can touch the ground
I'm a famous dancer and I can do the kicks, the splits, turn around
and touch the ground.

Follow-up

IT'S TOO FRIGHTENING FOR ME!: A PLAY

OBJECTIVES

UNIT	SPELLING/VOCABULARY	GRAMMAR/PUNCTUATION	COMPREHENSION/ COMPOSITION
WRITING FICTION A playscript based on *It's Too Frightening For Me!* by Shirley Hughes.	Understand and use vocabulary related to drama conventions.	Understand how to write dialogue in a playscript. Adverbs.	Write a playscript using the story as a basis. Compare organization of playscripts with stories. Improvise dialogue.

ORGANIZATION (2 HOURS)

	INTRODUCTION	WHOLE-CLASS SKILLS WORK	DIFFERENTIATED GROUP ACTIVITIES	CONCLUSION
HOUR 1	Shared reading of pages 72 to 73 of story (author's suggestion to act as a play). Discuss how this could be done. First look for speech in text and in speech bubbles; then look at narrative for other indications of what was said and done. Find examples from text.	Review the use of speech marks to convey dialogue in stories and compare to how speech is conveyed in playscripts. Model, using examples from story.	1–4*: Mixed-ability groups. Divide story into four sections: pages 7–27; 28–41; 42–62; 63–end (this last section is entirely narrative so give special support here). Allocate one to each group. Children sketch out a playscript and decide on parts. Double up on parts if necessary. Encourage improvisation for filling in or amplifying bits not in the story.	Share the work of groups working on first two sections of story. Pick up on effective ways of transferring text to playscript. Give support and solicit suggestions where problems have occurred. Encourage children to bring in any basic props they wish to use in tomorrow's concluding session.
HOUR 2	Groups working on the last two sections of story share their work. Discuss the conventions of showing setting and stage directions in playscripts.	Examine use of adverbs in story text. Look particularly at adverbs expressing how something is said and demonstrate how to incorporate this into playscript.	1–4*: Groups work to refine scripts and polish up presentations.	Groups present their sections in order to 'perform' entire play. These can be read from scripts if necessary. Suggest children might like to work further on the play outside the hour in order to perform for a wider audience.

(SEE 'HAIKU', PAGE 51)

A HAIKU YEARBOOK

OBJECTIVES

UNIT	SPELLING/VOCABULARY	GRAMMAR/PUNCTUATION	COMPREHENSION/ COMPOSITION
WRITING POETRY A Haiku Yearbook.	Identify syllabic pattern. Choose appropriate vocabulary for own writing.	Learn how to bend rules of grammar for poetic purpose. Use punctuation to clarify meaning.	Read and write haiku to develop understanding of verse format and economy of expression. Compare poems on similar themes and in similar format.

ORGANIZATION (1 HOUR)

INTRODUCTION	WHOLE-CLASS SKILLS WORK	DIFFERENTIATED GROUP ACTIVITIES	CONCLUSION
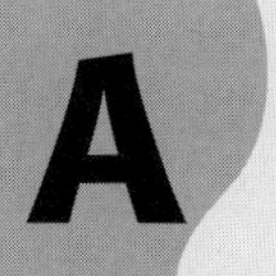 HOUR 1 Re-read poems from photocopiable sheet or different ones from another source. Locate Japan as origin of the form on a map. Review the syllabic form of the haiku poem, reciting one and clapping out syllables.	Model writing a haiku together as a class. Use a season theme. Take suggestions for first line. Count syllables – too many/few? Refine. Continue as above.	Divide class into 12 mixed-ability groups, each writing a haiku on a different month of the year. Support groups as necessary.	Share poems. Evaluate and compare how effective each is in capturing essence of month. Discuss how to 'publish' as a class book.

'ZARG ENTERS': FROM PLAY TO STORY

OBJECTIVES

UNIT	SPELLING/VOCABULARY	GRAMMAR/PUNCTUATION	COMPREHENSION/ COMPOSITION
WRITING FICTION 'Zarg Enters': From Play to Story'.		Revise and consolidate punctuation of dialogue.	Compare organization of playscripts with stories. Write a story based on a playscript.

ORGANIZATION (2 HOURS)

	INTRODUCTION	WHOLE-CLASS SKILLS WORK	DIFFERENTIATED GROUP ACTIVITIES	CONCLUSION
HOUR 1	Retell the play as story. Compare and contrast how setting, characters, dialogue and action are depicted in plays and stories. Use a grid format on board or flip chart to record information .	Use evidence from the play to model a story beginning which describes setting and characters. Demonstrate how to add description (for example physical description) not included in play.	1: Write a story beginning, including description of setting and character descriptions of Mrs Scratchit, Zarg and Bof. 2 & 3*: Write character descriptions of Mrs Scratchit, Zarg and Bof. 4: Choose one main character and write a character description.	Selected children share their writing. Discuss what has come from evidence in the play and what has come from children's own imagination.
HOUR 2	Re-read the first part of the play, up to the asterisks. Identify the main sections which can be developed into paragraphs for telling the plot as a story.	Model how dialogue from the play can be turned into direct speech in story. Revise and consolidate work on punctuation of speech.	1*: Identify and plan middle and end of story, writing according to time available. 2 & 3: Plan story in outline, identifying events to include in beginning, middle and end. 4*: Write out beginning of story.	Discuss how the play has been rewritten as a story with a beginning, middle and end. Discuss children's preferences – better as a play or a story? Why? Suggest finishing off if they wish in their own time.

(SEE 'SCHOOL CARDS', PAGE 86)

A COLLECTION OF SCHOOL STORIES

OBJECTIVES

UNIT	SPELLING/VOCABULARY	GRAMMAR/PUNCTUATION	COMPREHENSION/ COMPOSITION
WRITING FICTION School stories: Publishing a collection of school stories.	Check spelling of uncertain words for redraft of stories.	Redraft stories to agreed format, incorporating correct grammar and punctuation.	Explore examples of collections/anthologies to see their features. Redraft and present final version of a story to an agreed format for a class collection.

ORGANIZATION (1 HOUR)

	INTRODUCTION	WHOLE-CLASS SKILLS WORK	DIFFERENTIATED GROUP ACTIVITIES	CONCLUSION
HOUR 1	Collect a number of story anthologies, including school stories. Explore the features of a collection – cover details such as title, illustration, blurb, internal layout and design (eg the stories are different but are probably presented in the same way with the same illustrator throughout).	Make a list of the various features that need to be agreed for a class collection. Then agree them for your collection – What will the title be? Will the stories be on lined or unlined paper? Will the first letter of each story be a large, coloured one? Will there be illustrations? If so, in black and white, or colour? And so on.	1–4*: Finish off stories according to the agreed format. The teacher supports all.	Publish the stories by binding them into a cover. Give each group a different task – front cover, back cover, contents page and so on.

MORE CRIC CRAC

(SEE 'CRIC CRAC', PAGE 163)

OBJECTIVES

UNIT	SPELLING/VOCABULARY	GRAMMAR/PUNCTUATION	COMPREHENSION/ COMPOSITION
READING FICTION *Cric Crac: A Collection of West Indian Stories* by Grace Hallworth.	Develop vocabulary from text. Use dictionaries and thesauruses. Revise antonyms.	Identify connectives used for sequencing. Identify common punctuation marks and respond appropriately when reading.	Read folk stories from other cultures. Identify morals, common themes, characters. Use paragraphs in writing.

ORGANIZATION (3 HOURS)

	INTRODUCTION	WHOLE-CLASS SKILLS WORK	DIFFERENTIATED GROUP ACTIVITIES	CONCLUSION
HOUR 1	Shared reading of 'Rabbit and Tiger', pages 19–26 (approx 8 minutes). Pause at page 24 to predict: what is the golden ball?	Explore use of connectives as sequencing for words, eg *so, then, but, when.* Identify various punctuation marks in story.	1*: Guided writing of first part of the story (up to where Corbeau sets Tiger free) as a playscript. 2 & 3: Describe the two tricks Konehu played on Tiger. Write one paragraph for each. 4*: Describe orally the two tricks Konehu played on Tiger.	Discuss: This story is both a trickster story and a pourquoi story. Why?
HOUR 2	Shared reading of 'Put mi back where yo' find mi', pages 47–54 (approx 8 minutes). Pause after introduction to discuss terms: *cautionary tale, punch line, anecdote, moral.*	Read relevant sentences to demonstrate ability to respond appropriately to punctuation.	1–4*: Dictionary and/or thesaurus work based on unfamiliar vocabulary from the story. Lists differentiated for each group.	Discuss moral: Is the story telling us not to rescue abandoned baby (literal vs figurative meaning)?
HOUR 3	Shared reading of 'John and the Devil', pages 65–78 (approx 12 minutes).	Identify and use antonyms in sentences, eg *masters/slaves, clever/ stupid, alive/dead, ill/well, opened/closed.*	1: Discuss: who is the real trickster in this story? Give evidence from story. 2 & 3*: Guided writing of a short summary of story under headings: beginning, middle and end. 4: Practise work on opposites.	Summarize concept of oral tradition by discussing: what would happen if books disappeared from the world? How would people share stories they know and create new ones?